GREEN STATES AND SOCIAL MOVEMENTS

D0913827

Green States and Social Movements

Environmentalism in the United States, United Kingdom, Germany, and Norway

JOHN S. DRYZEK

DAVID DOWNES

CHRISTIAN HUNOLD

and

DAVID SCHLOSBERG

with

HANS-KRISTIAN HERNES

OXFORD

UNIVERSITY PRESS

OXFORD
UNIVERSITY PRESS

Great Clarendon Street, Oxford OX2 6DP

Oxford University Press is a department of the University of Oxford.
It furthers the University's objective of excellence in research, scholarship,
and education by publishing worldwide in

Oxford New York

Auckland Bangkok Buenos Aires Cape Town Chennai
Dar es Salaam Delhi Hong Kong Istanbul Karachi Kolkata
Kuala Lumpur Madrid Melbourne Mexico City Mumbai Nairobi
São Paulo Shanghai Taipei Tokyo Toronto

Oxford is a registered trade mark of Oxford University Press
in the UK and in certain other countries

Published in the United States
by Oxford University Press Inc., New York

British Library Cataloguing in Publication Data
Data available

Library of Congress Cataloging in Publication Data
Data available

ISBN 0-19-924902-4 (hbk.)
ISBN 0-19-924903-2 (pbk.)

1 3 5 7 9 10 8 6 4 2

Typeset by Hope Services (Abingdon) Ltd.
Printed in Great Britain
on acid-free paper by
Biddles Ltd.,
Guildford & King's Lynn

To Robyn Eckersley

PREFACE

The political shape of the contemporary world owes much to at least two hundred years of interactions between states and social movements. The late twentieth century saw a proliferation of movements and the kinds of claims they make. Here we examine the significance of the environmental movement in particular, though we hope our study will interest students of social movements more generally. Environmentalism is emblematic of late twentieth-century social movements in its post-materialist commitments, the variety of struggles pursued under its banner, its linkages to other movements, and the kind of policy response it received from states. We look at the history of the movement since the 1960s, showing how and why the movement took shape in very different ways in four very different states: the passively inclusive United States, passively exclusive Germany, actively inclusive Norway, and the actively exclusive (at least for a substantial time) United Kingdom.

Interest groups, parties, mass mobilizations, protest businesses, and oppositional public spheres vary in their weight and significance across the four countries. We look at the movement's effectiveness in these four different contexts. We explain why the United States was an environmental policy pioneer in 1970 but then lost that standing; why Norway could then become a leader but is unlikely to improve upon a solid record; why the United Kingdom has been a laggard throughout; and why the most promising developments can now be found in Germany. The end in view is a green state, on a par with earlier transformations that produced first the liberal capitalist state and then the welfare state. Of course, no green state exists yet.

The green state in our title and the emphasis on states in our analysis does not mean that we are in any sense statists, committed to a centralization of power in the state. Indeed, one feature of the green state may be an eventual dispersal of state functions across a broader array of political actors, and the migration of political authority down to local governance and up to transnational bodies. Though in a fashion quite different from the traditional (and wrong) Marxist prognosis, one feature of the green state might be that it facilitates its own withering away. The focus on the state is for historical reasons: the state *has* mattered hugely in determining the prospects for different kinds of movements, and for better or for worse still does.

Though we are not statists, we are democrats. Indeed, our conception of democracy extends beyond the state and into society as a whole—specifically, public spheres that organize in civil society. The significance of social movements lies, we believe, not just in their potential to advance particular goals such as environmental conservation. They are also central to democracy and democratization. The connection between democracy and environmentalism is not merely contingent. As a recent explosion in the theoretical and empirical literature on democracy and the environment attests, they are mutually reinforcing values. We will examine in some detail how environmental movements have contributed to democratization in our four countries, and how different states have either facilitated or impeded that democratization. Some of our findings on this score are counterintuitive: in particular, our claim that (passively) exclusive states can actually promote democracy more effectively than inclusive states.

In Chapter 1 we lay out the basics of this book in terms of its grounding in the history of states and movements. We justify our focus on the environmental movement, and say just what we mean by some core concepts such as the state, social movements, and civil society. We also explain our classification of different types of state and the strategy of inquiry we will follow. Chapter 2 introduces our four countries in more detail, with special reference to the relationship between the state and the movement, and gives a sketch of the history of each of them in the modern environmental era, showing why the movement took very different form in each country. The oppositional public sphere confronting the state in Germany looks very different from the well-behaved set of interest groups in the United States or the Norwegian organizations tightly integrated into government.

In Chapter 3 we try to establish when the movement inclusion in the state that has occurred has been genuine, and when it has involved co-optive access without real influence. We argue that inclusion can be genuine when the movement's defining interest can be attached to one of the core imperatives of the state; this explains why the United States alone could prove such an environmental success story around 1970. Later in the 1970s energy crisis meant environmentalism was kept away from the state's core in all four countries, though there was substantial variation in how this played out. More recent history reveals environmentalism generally kept away from the core, though there are exceptions (especially in Norway and, later, Germany). Chapter 4 looks at the implications of inclusion in the state for the movement itself. We show that inclusion almost always means moderation and bureaucratization of movement groups, though again we see substantial cross-national variation.

Chapter 5 broadens the focus to democracy within society as a whole, and the contributions that movements can make to it. The counterintuitive conclusions are that inclusive states can actually be bad for democracy in society as a whole (even if they look positive when it comes to democracy within the state), while passively exclusive states such as Germany can promote democracy. States with a prescriptive orientation to civil society, be it on behalf of inclusion or exclusion, stifle movement diversity.

In Chapter 6 we evaluate and compare movement success in influencing public policy within the state when environmentalists act in conventional interest group or political party fashion. We also show that movements can influence public policy when they confront the state from civil society. In addition, movements in civil society can take effect more directly by changing the terms of political discourse and political culture, and engage paragovernmental governance that bypasses the state. In light of these possibilities, we develop some guidelines for movements contemplating whether to act within the state, in oppositional civil society, or in both. We show when and how the popular 'dual strategy' for movement action can work – and when it cannot.

Chapter 7 looks at how two recent developments could completely change the picture we have laid out. Ecological modernization suggests that environmental values can now be attached to the state's core economic imperative: 'Pollution prevention pays,' in the popular slogan. Ulrich Beck's risk society thesis suggests an environmental attachment to the state's core legitimation imperative, as risk issues signify a legitimation crisis. These developments could conceivably add up to a conservation imperative of the state: the green state. No state is yet close to this situation. Norway has entrenched ecological modernization in a moderate 'weak' form. Germany is closest to a 'strong' form of ecological modernization that, in combination with risk-induced legitimation crisis, points the way to a more reflexive and democratic political economy. The United States has the sort of movement that could facilitate such a transformation—but its state has moved in exactly the opposite direction, casting economic and environmental values in old-fashioned conflictual terms. Even the United Kingdom at long last appears to be capable of taking on board some of the key precepts of ecological modernization and democratization.

This study was made possible by a large grant from the Australian Research Council (Number A79802823) to John Dryzek. David Schlosberg's research was supported by a research grant from Northern Arizona University. David Downes worked as a research fellow on the project for two years, also doing most of the field research for the United Kingdom and New Zealand. For reasons that will become apparent, New Zealand had to be dropped as a case for the book (though this research is published separately in Downes, 2000). David Schlosberg, Christian Hunold, and Hans-Kristian Hernes did the field research for the United States, Germany, and Norway, respectively. US interviews were transcribed by Jon Jemming. David Downes helped draft early chapters before departing academia for life in the public service. The subsequent drafting and rewriting was done by Dryzek, Hunold, and Schlosberg, though making use of text on the UK and Norway supplied by Downes and Hernes.

We have presented portions of this research at the 2000 Annual Conference of the Western Political Science Association in San José, California; to the European Consortium for Political Research Joint Workshops in Grenoble, 2001; at the 2001 Annual Conference of the American Political Science Association in San Francisco; to the Department of Political Science and International Studies at the University of Birmingham; to the School of Politics, International Relations, and the Environment at Keele University; at the Environment Workshop of the Social and Political Theory Program at Australian National University in 2001; and at the 2002 World Congress of the International Sociological Association in Brisbane. At these venues and elsewhere, for advice, comments, and criticism we thank John Barry, Peter Christoff, Richard Couto, Andrew Dobson, Robyn Eckersley, Robert Goodin, Carolyn Hendriks, David Marsh, James Meadowcroft, Claus Offe, Val Plumwood, Chris Rootes, Dieter Rucht, and Leslie Thiele. Christian Hunold thanks his brother Joachim for letting him share his cramped apartment in Bonn-Königswinter in June and July 1999. We also thank all those activists, officials, and observers of environmental politics who gave generously of their time to be interviewed by us.

Portions of the text, now dispersed throughout the book, were previously published in two journal articles. The first is David Schlosberg and John S. Dryzek, 'Political Strategies of American Environmentalism: Inclusion and Beyond', *Society and Natural Resources*, 15 (2002). The second is John S. Dryzek, Christian Hunold, and David Schlosberg, with David Downes and Hans-Kristian Hernes, 'Environmental Transformation of the State: The United States, Norway, Germany and United Kingdom', *Political Studies*, 50 (2002): 659–82.

Our colleague and friend Robyn Eckersley has been working on the green state longer than we have and will shortly be publishing a book under the title *The Green State: Rethinking Sovereignty and Democracy*. Robyn is perhaps more of a statist than we are and disagrees with a lot of what we have to say. As partial compensation for taking her title, and in admiration of her work on environmental politics, we dedicate this book to her.

CONTENTS

LIST OF AUTHORS

David Downes was a Research Fellow in the Department of Political Science at the University of Melbourne. He is currently Assistant Manager in the Office of Higher Education in the Victoria Department of Education and Training, Australia. His articles on environmental politics have appeared in the *Australian Journal of Political Science*.

John Dryzek is Professor of Social and Political Theory in the Research School of Social Sciences at Australian National University. His recent books include *Deliberative Democracy and Beyond: Liberals, Critics, Contestations* (Oxford University Press, 2000) and *Post-Communist Democratization: Political Discourses Across Thirteen Countries* (with Leslie Holmes, Cambridge University Press, 2002).

Hans-Kristian Hernes is Associate Professor in the Department of Political Science at the University of Tromsø, where he teaches public policy and political theory. He has published in journals such as *Internasjonal politikk* (Norway) and *Mobilization*, and is currently the editor of *Norsk Statsvitenskapelig Tidsskrift* (Norwegian Political Science Review).

Christian Hunold is Assistant Professor in the Department of History and Politics at Drexel University, where he teaches environmental policy and comparative politics. He is the author of *European Politics Reconsidered* (with B. Guy Peters, Holmes and Meier, 2nd edn. 1999). His articles have appeared in journals such as *Governance, Political Studies, Environmental Politics*, and *German Politics and Society*.

David Schlosberg is Associate Professor of Political Science at Northern Arizona University, where he teaches political theory and environmental politics. He is the author of *Environmental Justice and the New Pluralism* (Oxford University Press, 1999), and editor, with John Dryzek, of *Debating the Earth* (Oxford University Press, 1998). His articles have appeared in journals such as *Environmental Politics, Political Studies*, and *Society and Natural Resources*.

LIST OF ABBREVIATIONS

ALARM-UK	Alliance Against the Road building Menace
BBU	Federal Association of Citizens Initiatives for the Protection of the Environment
BUND	German Association for Environment and Nature Protection
CCA	Concerned Citizens in Action
CCHW	Citizens' Clearing House for Hazardous Wastes
CDU	Christian Democratic Union
CEQ	Council on Environmental Quality
CPRE	Council for the Protection of Rural England
DNR	German League for Nature Conservation and Environmental Protection
EC	European Community
EDF	Environmental Defense Fund (Now Environmental Defense)
EIS	Environmental Impact Statement
EPA	Environmental Protection Agency
FDP	Free Democratic Party
FoE	Friends of the Earth
NAACP	National Association for the Advancement of Colored People
NABU	German Nature Protection Association
NAFTA	North American Free Trade Agreement
NATO	North Atlantic Treaty Organization
NEJAC	National Environmental Justice Advisory Committee
NEPA	National Environmental Policy Act
NGO	Non-Governmental Organization
NMT	Norwegian Mountain Touring Association
NOU	Norges Offentlige Utredninger ('Official Recommendation', Norway)
NRDC	Natural Resources Defense Council
NVE	Norwegian Water Resources and Energy Administration
OECD	Organization for Economic Co-operation and Development
OPEC	Organization of Petroleum Exporting Countries
PACDAC	Public Advisory Committee on Disarmament and Arms Control
PCSD	President's Council on Sustainable Development

POS	Political Opportunity Structure
RSPB	Royal Society for the Protection of Birds
SNEEJ	Southwest Network for Environmental and Economic Justice
SPD	Social Democratic Party
SSSI	Site of Special Scientific Interest
USDA	United States Department of Agriculture
WWF	World Wildlife Fund

1

States, Movements, and Democracy

In this introductory chapter we show how our analysis is rooted in the comparative history of states and social movements, and explain why we choose to look at the environmental movement in particular. We classify states into four different types, with major consequences that we elaborate in the chapters that follow. Social movements take form in a context largely shaped by the state, so our story begins with the state.

A Brief History of the State

The early modern authoritarian state had three core tasks: to keep order internally, compete internationally, and raise the resources to finance these first two tasks (Skocpol, 1979). These can be termed the domestic order, survival, and revenue imperatives.

Revenue was raised via extractive taxation from a fairly static economic base. With the development of capitalism, a growing economy enabled states to increase their revenues without any increase in rates of taxation, while simultaneously promoting social order by increasing the size of the economic pie. Thus a fourth imperative developed from the domestic order and revenue imperatives: the economic one of securing economic growth (what Marxists would call accumulation). This development enabled the entry of the bourgeoisie into the state, for their defining interest in profit maximization was now in harmony with the economic imperative. Thus was born the capitalist state, or, less pejoratively, the liberal state.

The further development of capitalism produced an organized working class that threatened the stability of the political economy. At first this challenge was met by political repression. Eventually the welfare state developed in order to cushion the working class against the dislocations and fluctuations of capitalism. Thus a fifth imperative developed from the domestic order one: what post-Marxists (e.g. Offe, 1984) would call legitimation. This development enabled the entry of the organized working class into the state, for its defining interest could be assimilated to the legitimation imperative. Thus was born the welfare state.

These seismic changes in the character of the state were accompanied by social movements: the social movement of the emergent bourgeoisie against monarchy, theocracy, and aristocracy, the social movement of the working class against the capitalist state. Crucially, each of these movements could then connect its defining interest with an emerging core state imperative. In the history of modern Western states, significant political innovation generally begins with social movements (other than when it is forced by economic or international crisis). We owe the liberal state to the movements of the bourgeoisie against monarchy, church, and aristocracy. We owe the welfare state to the movements of the organized working class against a capitalist-dominated liberal state.

It matters a great deal to a social movement whether or not it can make a connection to a core state imperative. If it can, then there are in principle no limits to the degree to which the movement can penetrate to the state's core once the movement has sought and achieved entry into the state (be it as a political party, interest group, or party faction). If it cannot, then there are systematic limits to what the movement can achieve as a result of its engagement with the state, for, whenever the movement's interest comes up against the core, the movement will lose. Rather than take on the entire array of contemporary social movements in these terms, in this study we focus on environmentalism. Long banished from the core of the state, environmentalism is tied up with some contemporary developments that may, in the end, produce a new kind of state whose emergence is of comparable historical significance to the earlier emergence of the liberal capitalist state and then the welfare state. At present there are no green states. But some states are greener than others in these terms—and we can explain why.

Social Movements

A social movement can be characterized as an association or set of associations organized around a common interest that seeks to influence collective outcomes without obtaining authoritative offices of government. A broad definition is necessary here because, like 'democracy' (about which we will have more to say later), 'social movement' is a concept that is both historically variable and contested. Moreover, that contestation is in many ways intrinsic to the idea of a social movement. As we will see in a moment, 'new social movements' are generally defined in terms of their preoccupation with identity issues: one of which can be 'should we be a political party, an interest group, a loose collection of people sharing and defining a way of life, or a dis-organization?' Our broad definition allows that movement leaders may aspire to a share of state power (just as the social movement of the working class once did), but once that share is secured, it is hard to speak of a 'movement' as such—although sections of the erstwhile movement may choose to reject the share of power on offer, and so still maintain movement credentials. The broad definition allows interest groups (such as the mainstream environmental groups in our four countries) to shelter under the 'movement' umbrella—though, as we shall see in Norway, such groups can end up as arms of the state.

The last four decades of the twentieth century saw a great deal in the way of social movement activity in the developed liberal democracies, unprecedented in its sheer variety. Movements on behalf of (and sometimes against) women, gays, lesbians, non-human animals, peace, the environment, youth, students, racial and ethnic equality, indigenous peoples, hunting, religious fundamentalism, national autonomy and secession, joined more established movements that were mostly based on social classes defined in economic terms. Unlike these earlier movements, we cannot (yet) rename the state in honor of any of the more recent arrivals, though in this study we will explore the movement that is, we believe, the most promising candidate for such a renaming.

What are the prospects for each of these newer movements eventually making the link to an established or emerging state imperative? If a movement cannot make the connection, this does not mean that its entry into the state ends in complete futility. Contemporary states engage in many activities that are not captured by the five essential functions we enumerated, and movements might fruitfully influence these activities. However, the five imperatives define the core of the state. This core is a zone of necessity: it constitutes an area of activity that the state simply must carry out. It features only highly restricted democratic control, because democracy connotes indeterminacy in the content of public policy. The periphery of state activity is more indeterminate, hence potentially more democratic and open to the influence of social movements. Yet movements confined to the periphery of the state are of meagre historical significance, and the fact that there is a substantial area of governmental activity off-limits to them is likely to be a continual source of frustration.

What we seek to do, then, is place contemporary social movements in this deeper state history. In so doing we differ from the popular 'life cycle' account (e.g. Offe, 1990), for which social movements begin as radical protests against the established order, their activists regarded with horror by existing power holders. Gradually movement demands come to be framed in ways acceptable to power holders, and the de-radicalized movement eventually enters the corridors of power. In this light, social movements can be interpreted as incipient interest groups; indeed, the hallmark of success is transformation into such a group (Jordan and Maloney, 1997). Yet this account misses some critical variations; sometimes it is downright wrong. For in the category of relatively open societies we find some very different sorts of state structures, and so some very different things that can happen to social movements. Sometimes a state will put up few barriers to movement influence in policy making. In other times and places the state may try to destroy a movement. Sometimes a movement will be largely ignored by the state, neither accepted nor undermined. At other times and places a movement will be quickly organized into the state— sometimes even organized by the state, hardly giving activists time to draw breath. In short, the stylized history of the state with which we began turns out in the past few decades to be no longer the history of *the* state, but rather the history of different kinds of states (though all share the basic core imperatives). And, as we shall show, that history becomes more interesting as, perhaps for the first time since its inception, the modern state may be in the process of losing its exclusive claim to the governance of society (a development about which we will have more to say in our last chapter). This development results from the interaction of the activities of social movements, state imperatives, and the changing character of collective problems facing states, movements, and the societies in which they move.

States and Movements

The contemporary variations in the character of states that we will analyse have substantial implications for both attainment of the goals sought by a movement and the quality of a society's democracy. On the face of it, a state which either places few barriers in the way of movement influence on public policy or organizes the movement into the state is both good for the degree of democracy prevailing in society, and good for the likelihood of the movement's goals being realized in collective outcomes. Such a state is 'inclusive'. Inclusion can take a number of different forms. The movement might organize as an interest group or groups that engage in lobbying. The group or groups might participate in the development and implementation of public policy through negotiations with government officials. Or the movement might sponsor a faction of an established party, perhaps even forming a party itself with the intention of becoming a serious player in electoral and coalition politics. Inclusion can even take the form of a strengthening of the group's capacity to participate in policy making, or becoming an object of government policy itself.

In fact, we shall demonstrate that this seemingly easy generalization about inclusion being both good for democracy and good for the substantive goals sought by a social movement is wrong: that the conditions for benign inclusion of a movement in the state are both rare and demanding. This contention has substantial implications for movement strategy: if inclusion may be hazardous, movement members should think long and hard about whether their substantive goals might be better served by a more uncompromising oppositional orientation to power structures, together with a focus on civil society and perhaps the economy as alternative sites for political action.

We are, then, interested in a range of questions concerning the relationship between states and social movements, and how these play into the history and future of contemporary societies.

From the point of view of social movements in general, it is important to identify the circumstances under which benign inclusion in the state is possible, in light of the dangers of co-optation and neutralization. We will argue in Chapter 3 that answers to this question have a lot to do with the relationship between a movement's defining interest and the prevailing or emerging configuration of state imperatives. If a movement spurns the state, we need to investigate the ways it might still exercise power over collective outcomes in society (Chapter 6). We also need to look at the degree to which state structure can affect the degree of diversity of the movement, and the relationship between different parts of the movement, which might range from hostility to respect to co-operation to homogenization (Chapter 5).

From the point of view of environmentalism in particular, we need to ascertain whether or not state imperatives are changing in a way that makes a connection between the movement's defining interest and these imperatives possible—and that may even point to an emerging environmental conservation imperative (Chapter 7). The presence or absence of such connections will have major implications when it comes to evaluating movement effectiveness in influencing public policy (Chapters 6 and 7).

From the point of view of democracy, we need to establish whether or not inclusion means hierarchy in the movement (Chapter 4), and if it does, whether that means a net loss when it comes to democracy in society. More generally, we need to ascertain the consequences for democracy of different kinds of states in the orientation they adopt toward social movements, and what happens when a movement migrates from the public sphere to the state (Chapter 5). Some of the findings on this score will be quite counter-intuitive as we focus on the democratic vitality of civil society as well as the state. It will turn out that exclusive states can have some surprising democratic benefits—though some kinds of exclusion can also devastate civil society.

The democratic and the environmental points of view are analytically distinct, but there is a link between them. Environmental political theorists have in recent years devoted substantial attention to the connection between democratic values and environmental ones. While some differences remain about the kind of democracy most conducive to the realization of environmental values, the majority view now points to the positive implications of democracy for the environment (see e.g. Doherty and de Geus, 1996; Goodin, 1996; Lafferty and Meadowcroft, 1996; Mathews, 1996). This consensus is in sharp contrast to the popular 1970s view that environmental crisis demanded authoritarian government (for an extreme statement, see Heilbroner, 1974)

Clearly we believe that state structures matter enormously when it comes to social movements in general, environmentalism in particular, and the degree of democracy in society as well as the state. These structures also vary substantially in both their receptiveness to, and constraints upon, the organization and influence of social movements. Let us now try to be a bit more systematic about exactly how states vary in these respects.

Different States

On one dimension, states can be either *exclusive* or *inclusive* in their structure when it comes to interest representation. An exclusive state restricts effective representation to a small number of political actors, and denies access to others. The actors in question might actually represent large numbers of people—for example, a trade union federation—but in an exclusive state of this sort we would expect ordinary union members to have little voice. At one extreme, a military dictatorship is exclusive, but in this study we are for the most part interested in relatively open societies. Even exclusive governments in such societies normally find it necessary to welcome at least some actors— if only large corporations, or a powerful church.

An inclusive state is more open to a variety of different interests. That it is open does not mean that all actors, interests, and movements begin with a presumption of equal access and power. There may still be systematic inequalities in access and influence, possibly reflecting power structures in society more generally.[1]

On a second dimension, states can be either *passive* or *active* in the kinds of interest representation they allow or seek. A state that is active in this sense concerns itself with the character and range of interests that exist in civil society, and which might, for better or for worse, matter politically. As a result, an active state intervenes in society to try to affect both the content and power of these interests. A passive state, in contrast, is agnostic about the pattern of

---

[1] The inclusive–exclusive distinction bears some similarities to the school of thought that emphasizes 'political opportunity structures' in explaining the form taken by social movements. For a comparison between this school and our own approach, highlighting important differences as well as similarities, see Ch. 4 below.

interests, organizations, and movements that exists in society, and does little or nothing to either advance or impede the standing of particular groups.[2]

Combining these two dimensions yields four categories or ideal types of state, as shown in Table 1.1 (this classification was originally developed in Dryzek, 1996*a*: 64–70).

A *passively inclusive* state accepts and accommodates whatever constellation of interests, groups, and movements that social forces generate. Acceptance can take the form of lobbyists on behalf of interest groups walking the corridors of the legislature, a social movement forming a political party to contest elections, representation of a movement's activists in the organizational structure of an established political party, or responsiveness of a legal system to actions on behalf of a group's interests (for example, by providing a class action option). In today's world, the most prevalent kind of passively inclusive state structure is pluralism. Now, the term 'pluralism' has several meanings, as we will see in subsequent chapters. But for the moment we shall be using the term as it is generally deployed by students of comparative politics, to denote a kind of state that is open to a variety of interest groups. In these terms, the United States has the most pluralistic political system of any country in the world—despite any shortcomings it may have when measured against pluralism as some kind of normative ideal. (There is a massive critical literature written by radical US social scientists that tries to explode claims that their political system is truly pluralist; see e.g. Connolly, 1969. This literature leaves our comparative classification of the United States as a pluralist system unmoved.)

TABLE 1.1 *A Classification of States, with Exemplars*

	Inclusive	Exclusive
Active	Expansive corporatism: Norway	Authoritarian liberalism: UK 1979–90 and beyond
Passive	Pluralism: USA	Legal corporatism: Germany

[2] Kitschelt (1986), Kriesi et al. (1992), and Kriesi (1995) distinguish between strong and weak states as a dimension of classification. This classification is different than ours, for strong/weak is essentially an output measure, in terms of the state's ability to impose its agenda on society. Kriesi's (1995) examples of strong states are France and the Netherlands; his weak states are Germany and Switzerland. In our classification, Germany and France would both qualify as passively exclusive.

An *actively inclusive* state is not content to await and eventually accept whatever constellation of interests that social and economic forces produce. Instead, public officials try to anticipate and organize interests into the state. Proposals for such an actively inclusive state may be found among political theorists who believe the existing pattern of politics in developed societies features less activity and influence than it ought to on the part of the 'right' kind of associations, representing a fuller range of interests (see e.g. Cohen and Rogers, 1992; Walzer, 1994; Young, 1992). But for present purposes real-world examples of actively inclusive states are more interesting than (and quite different from) the proposals of these political theorists. The best cases are Mexico and Norway. Mexico's actively inclusive regime has for decades been especially astute in identifying social sources of discontent and co-opting militants into the regime. Norway is rather more benign than Mexico; but it can be hard to start a social movement in Norway because the state usually gets there first (for example, in funding and guaranteeing privileged policy access to women's groups and environmentalists).

Norway is an example of a corporatist society. Corporatism is usually defined in terms of tripartite concertation under which policy is made by agreement between the executive branch of government and peak business and labour federations (see Schmitter and Lehmbruch, 1979). Business and labour federations agree to discipline their members in return for privileged access to policy making. Parliament is largely irrelevant, and policy content is insensitive to election results. Norway's corporatist arrangements remain intact, more so than in some other countries. Norway is, however, unusual in its expansive interpretation of corporatism to include groups beyond business and labour. More traditional corporatist countries are less expansive: once labour and business have been organized into the corporatist system, all other interests are systematically excluded. This exclusion is passive because the state does nothing to undermine these other movements, interests, and organizations: it simply leaves them alone, and provides them with few real channels of political influence. Thus corporatist countries such as Sweden, the Netherlands, Austria, and Germany are the main examples of *passively exclusive* states. (They are not the only examples: for example, consociational regimes as characterized by Lijphart, 1977, feature exclusive policy making by agreement between elites usually drawn from different ethnic, religious, or sometimes secular blocs.)

Students of protest politics have long noted that corporatist states should and do feature low levels of protest overall (e.g. Schmitter, 1981)—but that is only because they are designed to defuse class-based protest. Nollert (1995) also believes the explanation lies in the superior performance of these regimes when it comes to economic growth and income equality, but again this affects class-based protest only. As we shall see, passively exclusive states do not provide for 'social peace' beyond the realm of tripartite concertation.

An *actively exclusive* state is one that tries to undermine the conditions under which oppositional social movements are likely to form. The best contemporary examples of such states in relatively developed societies can be found among those under the sway of market liberal ideology. (In less developed societies, actively exclusive dictatorships are of course plentiful.) The public choice theory that is central to market liberalism interprets the political behaviour of all actors in self-interested terms, such that organized interests are seen as securing benefits for themselves at substantial cost to taxpayers in general or to the economic efficiency of the economy as a whole. In this light, market liberalism requires smashing the power of all movements, interests, and organizations capable of distorting the operation of the competitive market place. Trade unions come in for special treatment, but active exclusion can be applied more generally. Market liberalism in developed countries has been pursued most assiduously since 1980 in the Anglo-American countries: notably, the United States in the Reagan presidency, Britain in the Thatcher years and beyond, and New Zealand from 1984 to 1994.

This categorization of states has been developed with relatively open societies in mind—the countries normally classified as developed democracies by students of comparative politics. But the scheme can be applied elsewhere. We have already noted that Mexico, hardly a developed open society, has long had an actively inclusive state. When it comes to the Soviet bloc, the active exclusion of true Stalinism can be contrasted with the more passive exclusion characterizing many late Soviet regimes—with implications for social movements and even democracy that can be linked to the kind of analysis we develop here.

Which States? Which Movements?

Our fourfold classification of states as they present themselves to social movements is necessarily a bit of a simplification. In the real world, some states combine features of two or more of these categories, and over time may even shift position in relation to the categories. Nevertheless, the four categories have utility as relatively enduring ideal types. In undertaking comparative empirical analysis it is, then, most instructive to look for the closest approximation to each ideal type. The answer is quite easy when it comes to passive inclusion and active inclusion. We have already noted that the best example of a passively inclusive state is the pluralist polity of the United States, and that the best example of active inclusion is the expansive corporatist system of Norway. Thus it is easy to decide that these should constitute two of our countries.

The answers for passive and active exclusion are less clear. Corporatism is the most prevalent form of passive exclusion in developed democracies, and scholars argue with one another as to which is the most corporatist country. The most popular answer is probably Austria from the 1950s until 2000. Germany is not quite so corporatist; but we choose it over Austria because it has additional features beyond corporatism that render it a better example of passive exclusion. These are, most notably, the *Rechtstaat* tradition that sees the public interest in abstract, legal, and unitary terms, and an associated organic view of state and society that does not recognize conflicts, and so regards any opposition to the work of the administrative state as illegitimate and obstructive (see Chapter 2 for more detail). This selection is fortuitous (but more than mere coincidence) in that Germany has played a pioneering role in developing policy responses to environmental problems, and also possesses what is arguably the most significant green movement of any country. Germany is also the home of two important theses about the political-economic significance of environmental issues, ecological modernization and the risk society, which will play major parts in our study.

The active exclusion associated with market liberalism has been practised most assiduously in the Anglo-American countries, as we have already observed. Market liberalism at the national level was taken to an extreme in New Zealand in the decade following 1984. However, some ambiguities in the way market liberalism was applied in that era, especially in relation to the environmental movement, means that we decided to look instead at Britain during the period after 1979, when Margaret Thatcher was elected prime minister (though we shall also pay some attention to New Zealand). The market liberal era in Britain did not end with Thatcher's own departure in 1990, but continued into the 1990s, if with diminishing momentum.

It should be stressed that though the four states we will examine represent the closest approximations we can find to the ideal types, the real-world case should not be mistaken for the ideal type. Inevitably, the real world turns out to be less clear-cut than the ideal. To illustrate, we find episodes of active exclusion in the 'passively inclusive' United States. The targets have included the Civil Rights movement (at least in the South) and the counter-culture in the 1960s, and environmentalism in the Reagan presidency of the early 1980s and Bush/Cheney administration in 2001. (However, we shall show that the passively inclusive aspect of the United States generally undermines these attempts at active exclusion.) When it comes to the active exclusion associated with market liberalism, we shall see that United Kingdom governments occasionally found it expedient to soften their exclusive posture.

For the cases we have selected, we focus on the environmental movement only, rather than the whole range of social movements. Much more can be said about the connection to core state imperatives for environmentalism than for most social movements of the late twentieth and early twenty-first centuries. Unlike these other movements, there is at least a possibility that the state could be renamed as a consequence of the success of environmentalism. In Chapter 7 we shall explore the implications of the ecological modernization thesis, which in its depiction of an emerging compatibility between environmental and economic values suggests, we argue, that environmental conservation can attach itself to the economic imperative. We will also attend to the risk society thesis, which in its argument that contemporary politics is increasingly organized around the selection, distribution, and amelioration of risks, especially environmental risks, suggests, we argue, that environmental conservation can attach itself to the legitimation imperative.

A focus on environmentalism makes our study tractable because the movement has a well-defined beginning in the 1960s. Thus we have history as grist for our study, but not too much history. While organizations that we can in retrospect style 'environmentalist' existed long before that, there was no consciousness of 'the environment' as such, nor any sense of a movement that united the concerns that came to be grouped under the environmental heading. And in sheer numbers and political influence, these pre-1960s developments look tiny compared to their successors. Environmentalism is in many ways emblematic of late twentieth-century social movements: it exists in all developed countries and beyond, and it began in earnest around the same time in all of them. In terms of grist for cross-national analysis, its only rival would be the women's movement. We would welcome a parallel cross-national study of this movement in the terms we follow, but we will leave that for others.

Environmentalism and feminism cover the best examples of what are often termed 'new social movements' (see e.g. Cohen, 1985; Offe, 1985; Dalton and Kuechler, 1990). These new movements have a number of features that distinguish them from 'old' social movements, especially class-based ones. The first is their self-limiting radicalism. That is, the movement generally does not wish to capture, overthrow, or even share state power (though Green parties eventually compromised on this last point), even as its members may look to radical paradigms beyond industrial society. The second is that identity concerns are always close to the top of the movement's agenda: that is, there is a preoccupation with questions of 'who are we, how are we constructed, and what do we want?', rather than just 'how do we get it?' The third is an organizational style and structure that is often fluid, participatory, discursive, and impermanent (see Diani 1992, 1995; Melucci, 1989); though again, more mainstream and long-established environmental groups do not always measure up. Fourth, the tactics can be unconventional, involving protests, community organizing, and media events, rather than just lobbying or negotiating through parties and pressure groups. Finally, new social movements

are not explicitly class-based, though their members are drawn disproportionately from the new middle class of knowledge-workers. Clearly, not all
environmental groups are 'new movements' in these terms, especially when it
comes to self-limitation; but a substantial section of the movement in most
countries does share these features.

A final justification for looking at the environmental movement is that it
constitutes a hard case when it comes to establishing the influence of state
structures on the character taken by social movements. As Kriesi (1995: 193)
suggests, because the environmental movement deals with a 'highly differen-
tiated and complex problem structure' it is 'less dependent on aspects of the
POS [political opportunity structure]' than are more narrowly focused movements such as the anti-nuclear and peace movement. That is, the sheer variety of the movement's concerns means that it can range across different
aspects of the state's orientation to society, whereas a narrowly focused
movement will face only one aspect of the state (such as a secretive and milit-
arized nuclear bureaucracy).

Key Concepts: State, Civil Society, Democracy

While we have already said much about different kind of states, we need to be
a bit more explicit on what we actually mean by 'the state'—especially in view
of the fact that this is something of a conceptual minefield. What we mean by
the state also has implications for what we mean by another key yet often
murky and contested concept, civil society, which forms part of the terrain in
which social movements operate. Let us now try to be clear on what we mean
by the state and by civil society, which will in turn help to clarify what democracy and—as it turns out, more usefully—democratization can mean.

The simplest definition of 'the state' is that it is composed of the set of individuals and organizations legally authorized to make binding decisions for a
society within a particular territory. Referring to 'the state' in the active voice
implies that the operative organizations and officials (but not *all* state organizations and officials) in some sense constitute a coherent set, with a common
collective interest that is something more than the sum of the interests of its
components. In contrast to simple Marxist theory, this common collective
interest need not be reducible to the interests of the dominant class in society;
rather, the state can be 'autonomous' (Skocpol, 1985).

We will treat these common collective interests of state actors in terms of
state imperatives: that is, the functions that governmental structures have to
carry out to ensure their own longevity and stability. As we argued at the
beginning of this chapter, there are five such imperatives: the domestic order,
survival, revenue, economic, and legitimation imperatives; though more

might eventually join this list. Such imperatives will always be in the *interests* of public officials, and override any competing *preferences* these actors may have. To illustrate, consider the many cases where left-of-centre parties are elected to government, and seek to pursue the sorts of income redistribution, reductions in defence expenditure, and commitments to ethical and open foreign policy that they generally favour when in opposition. Once in power, the party may find that the imperative of survival in a dangerous international context means it has to maintain defence capability and retreat on its ethical principles. Proposals for increased taxation needed to finance income redistribution may cause capital flight, such that the economic imperative of maintaining the confidence of capital and financial markets overrides the party's preference for income redistribution (Pierson, 2001).

Now, if all public officials gave priority to these imperatives at all times, the state would have very clear boundaries, with those actors who were part of it pursuing a common agenda forced upon them, those outside the state more at liberty to pursue a variety of agendas. But a glance at real-world governments shows that they have internal conflicts and unclear boundaries. Central budgetary departments have many conflicts with spending departments. An agriculture department may promote farming practices that cause heavy water pollution, appalling pollution control agencies. Boundaries are permeable inasmuch as farmers' organizations may line up with the agriculture department on this issue while fishing and environmental organizations join with the pollution control agency (perhaps in the form of quasi-governmental advisory groups).

These sorts of considerations long led the vast majority of US political scientists to denounce 'the state' as an unobservable, mystical concept that had no place in political *science*. The state's exile from the discipline's vocabulary lasted from the 1930s to the 1980s, while the purportedly more observable and scientific concept of 'the political system' held sway (Easton, 1953). The concept of the state did however make a return to both political science and non-Marxist sociology in the 1980s (Evans, Rueschemeyer, and Skocpol, 1985 applaud this return; Almond, 1988, denounces it).

Those favouring the vocabulary of 'the political system' might well ask how defenders of 'the state' can hold their position in light of the internal conflicts and porous boundaries that we observe in real-world governments. We believe the best answer here is to distinguish between the *core* and the *periphery* of the state. Inside the core set of functions, the actions of individual members of government are indeed co-ordinated such that they are consistent with the imperatives. We can then speak of 'the state' in the active voice. Our distinction here between the core functions of the state and the rest of government resonates with Charles Lindblom's (1982: 335) contrast between 'imprisoned' and 'unimprisoned' zones of policy making. For Lindblom, 'imprisoned' policy is that which must be carried out, irrespective of the desires of public officials, in order to maintain investor confidence (though his notion here can be extended to non-economic state imperatives quite straight-forwardly). 'Unimprisoned' policy is more open-ended and conflictual, with compromise outcomes influenced by bargaining across competing interests. However, it is important to note that there is some flexibility even within the imprisoned zone or core of the state. This flexibility can arise when there is functional indeterminacy (i.e., imperatives do not dictate a single correct answer), cross-pressures between competing imperatives, and changes in the relative weight of imperatives over time (Dryzek, 1996a: 40–4).

The very need for the state is defined in terms of its core functions; these are the essential areas of state activity. The policy areas that these core functions would cover include, most obviously, major matters of foreign policy, defence, and national security; the welfare state; policing and criminal justice; and economic policy. Of course, governments are also active in many areas beyond this core. It is however important *not* to define the state's core and periphery in terms of two mutually exclusive and unchanging sets of policy issue areas. Core functions can become relevant in any policy area once the stakes become high. If, say, environmentalist defence of the British country-side is a matter only of securing public access to areas of natural beauty then no aspect of the state's core is at issue. But if that defence takes the form of massive opposition to road-building projects that the government considers vital to the economic infrastructure of the country, then both economic and legitimation imperatives enter the picture. Just about any policy area could conceivably connect to the core if the amount of government money it demands becomes large enough. Correspondingly, just about any kind of issue could conceivably impinge upon the legitimation imperative if public opinion on it is sufficiently intense. For example, in New Zealand the issue of not allowing ships with nuclear weapons on board into New Zealand waters has been a key symbol of national identity since the mid-1980s, and no government could survive if it renounced this policy.

The concept of 'the state' is often paired with 'civil society' (for a detailed discussion of the importance of civil society in political theory, see Cohen and Arato, 1992). To put it crudely, civil society is all social life beyond the state that is not purely economic in character. But from the point of view of the relationship between states and social movements, it is only the politicized aspects of civil society that are of interest. Martin Jänicke (1996) defines civil society in these terms as public action in response to failure in either the state or the economy. Public action of this sort often involves social movements, exerting pressure on states in various ways. Jänicke also observes the exist-ence of civil society's 'paragovernmental' activities that bypass government and aim at economic actors. One of the best examples of such activity occurred in 1995 with the effect of Greenpeace action on the Shell corporation in the context of the Brent Spar issue, which we will discuss at length when it comes to British environmental politics, where Shell was forced to take the action favoured by Greenpeace but opposed by the British government.

The politicized aspects of civil society constitute what are often called 'public spheres' of political activity. Such spheres are concerned with public affairs, but are separate from, and often confront, the state, while not seeking any formal share in state power of the kind sought by interest groups and electorally-oriented political parties (Isaac, 1993). This last feature is consistent with the definition of new social movements as 'self-limiting'. The basic shape taken by public spheres is oriented to the state, and so influenced by the state's patterns of inclusion and exclusion. At a fundamental level, what we now recognize as social movements began only in the context provided by the modern nation-state, which, unlike its medieval and monarchical predecessors, was open to policy change in response to social pressure (Tilly, Tilly, and Tilly, 1975). The early bourgeois public sphere celebrated by Habermas (1989) took shape in the coffeehouses and newspapers of European cities as the emerging bougeoisie created a parallel political realm of their own precisely because they were excluded from the state. Particular social movements that constitute public spheres may come and go in response to state actions; for example, a short-lived but very lively public sphere was constituted by opponents of the poll tax in Britain in the late 1980s. Other widely-discussed examples of public spheres include the 'free spaces' that have been constituted in US political history when women, blacks, workers, farmers, and others found themselves politicized but without easy access to state power (Evans and Boyte, 1986), and the democratic opposition in Eastern Europe prior to and during 1989 (Arato 1993), which of course confronted rigidly exclusive Soviet-style states.

Because public spheres often feature relatively egalitarian and discursive politics in their internal workings, they often meet with applause from democratic theorists (especially radical democrats). However, here we are concerned with civil society and public spheres as empirical rather than normative categories. Thus we should be alive to the existence of groups operating in politicized civil society that are undemocratic in their internal workings—Greenpeace is often accused of this failing—and/or conservative in their objectives. Examples of the latter would include the 'countryside movement' mobilized against the Blair Labour Government in Britain in the late 1990s in defence of blood sports such as fox hunting; anti-abortion groups such as Operation Rescue in the United States; and right-wing militias and paramilitary groups in the United States and Australia. Operation Rescue is in fact quite democratic in its internal workings.

Offe (1985: 853) would exclude right-wing groups from the category of new social movements by defining the latter in terms of their commitment to a 'selective radicalization of modern values'. However, Offe's distinction only makes sense in the context of a progressive account of society's modernization. While we sympathize with this account (and will address it quite explicitly when we discuss ecological modernization and reflexive modernization in later chapters), committing ourselves to it analytically and in advance would be a mistake. Rather, we should be cued in to what social movements and associated groups actually do, empirically, rather than accept or dismiss them in terms of their stated aims. For example, even white supremacist groups sometimes help provide meaning to the lives of troubled young adults, facilitating their eventual entry into more truly 'civil' society. Even right-wing militias, which we might be tempted to rule out on the grounds that their only orientation to the state is to seek its destruction, might sometimes have the effect of reducing violence by giving a social structure to paranoid individuals who might bomb and kill if left to themselves (Rosenblum, 1998: 9, 16).

We are concerned with public spheres and civil society as arenas of political activity that are in some sense distant from state power. We should, however, emphasize that this does not mean that these arenas are powerless and irrelevant when it comes to influencing collective outcomes—including public policy outcomes. In Chapter 6 we will elaborate the kinds of influence that politicized civil society can exert.

Because our conception of politics covers meaningful and influential action in civil society as well as the state, this means that our conception of democracy extends beyond the state too. 'Democracy', like 'social movement', is an example (perhaps the very best example) of what Gallie (1968) long ago called an 'essentially contested concept'. It is *essentially* contested because dispute about the precise meaning of democracy is intrinsic to the idea of democracy; it is hard to imagine a democratic society without such dispute.[3] What this essential contestation means is that it is hard to make comparisons across countries (or other units) in terms of how democratic they are, except in very rough terms. So in 2001, it is not hard to conclude that Norway is a more democratic country than North Korea; but no such summary judgement is meaningful when it comes to Norway against Germany or the United States. In Chapter 5 we will demonstrate that it is still possible to make meaningful comparisons across our four countries in terms of how particular configurations of state structures and movement activity affect democracy. But the comparison can only be done in dynamic, historical terms: that is, in relation to how state-movement configurations promote or impede democracy.

---

[3] This dispute does however take place within boundaries. Dryzek (1996*a*: 4) defines the democratic concourse as a communicative arena 'defined as pertaining to the collective construction, distribution, application, and limitation of political. authority'.

A Note on Method

The method we follow involves comparative and historical case study analysis. The main justification for comparative analysis is simply that it turns constants into variables. The comparative analysis will be historical in the sense that it is based on a history of the environmental movement and its relationship to the state in each country, oriented by the theoretical issues at stake. Comparative historical analysis can, as Skocpol (1979: 36) puts it, enable us to 'develop, test, and refine causal, explanatory hypotheses' using a small number of cases. As Skocpol also notes, we need to apply both the 'method of agreement', wherein similar conditions seem to produce similar outcomes, and the 'method of difference' where the pertinent outcome differs across cases that are similar in most respects but do have some key differences.

In case selection, we need variation in both circumstances and outcomes. King, Keohane, and Verba (1994: 137–8) suggest that researchers should try to select cases on the basis of the 'key causal explanatory variable', and this is exactly what we have done in selecting cases based on our fourfold classification of states developed in the previous section.

When it comes to outcomes, the main error to avoid is what King, Keohane, and Verba (1994: 129–37) call 'selection on the dependent variable'. In other words, one should not pick only cases with similar outcomes (such as success of the movement). Given that we did not select cases on this basis, we should it seems have little reason to worry. Yet if we were unlucky there might still turn out to be little variation in outcomes (though this in itself would be an instructive finding, if a negative one!). However, a quick glance at the outcomes in which we are interested, notably the shape taken by the environmental movement, the vitality of the movement as a source of innovations and ideas, the degree of influence of the movement as reflected in environmental policy outcomes, and the degree of democratization occurring in society as a whole, reveals substantial variation across our cases. In choosing to look at the comparative historical experience of the environmental movement in four countries—the United States, Germany, the United Kingdom, and Norway—we find considerable variation in movement accomplishment over time and space. In terms of environmental outcomes, the cross-national evidence would suggest that Germany and Norway are among the very best performers in the 1980s and the 1990s (see especially the systematic comparative work of Martin Jänicke and his associates; Jänicke and Weidner, 1997a is the most comprehensive statement, though unfortunately it does not have a chapter on Norway). The United States was a leader in the late 1960s and 1970s that has turned into a laggard. With the possible exception of the pre-history of environmental concern in the 1950s, the United Kingdom has always been a laggard.

We also find variation across the five cases in the form taken by the environmental movement. In the United States, we find a vast array of interest groups and direct action groups, ranging from the sedate and conservative (The Nature Conservancy) to the rebellious and colourful (Earth First!). The United States possesses a green party that was weak and inconsequential until its showing in Ralph Nader's 2000 presidential campaign. The United Kingdom resembles the United States, though its range of environmental groups is not quite as broad, and its green party briefly in 1989–90 looked set to escape irrelevance and weakness, though it soon thought better of it. In Norway, we find the environmental arena dominated by a much smaller number of groups than the United States, all pursuing highly co-operative relationships with government. In Germany we find some long-established sedate pressure groups. More significant, though, is a political party, *Die Grünen*, with a long-running dispute between factions believing in action through parliament (the *Realos*) and action in the street (the *Fundis*), whose long march through the institutions culminated in 1998 with entry into the governing federal coalition. As well as examining variation across countries in the experience of movements, we can look at variation across time (As King, Keohane, and Verba, 1994: 221 point out, this is effectively a way of overcoming the small-n problem in comparative research by expanding the number of observation points.). The analysis will therefore look at the history of the environmental movement in each country from the late 1960s (which witnessed the initial upsurge of environmentalism) to 2000. In this history states can change their level of performance (witness Germany's transformation from laggard to leader), and their patterns of interest representation (witness Norway's movement beyond tripartite corporatism to include a wider range of groups, such as women and environmentalists; and Britain's turn to active exclusion in 1979). Movements can change too. So the green movement in Germany turned into an 'anti-party party' in the late 1970s, which by the early 1990s and the victory of the *Realos* had changed into a party much more like the established 'grey' parties. The standard account of such changes in the basic orientation of movements (for example, Offe, 1990) sees such changes as part of an ineluctable life cycle, culminating in entry into the state. We hypothesize, in contrast, that such changes have much more to do with the modes of inclusion and exclusion available to or forced upon a movement.

The research will combine examination of published sources on environmentalism (and political history more generally) in each of the four countries with interviews with key movement participants and public officials in each country. Such interviews are necessary because published sources are often silent on the kinds of questions that become interesting in light of our theoretical framework. In addition, the quantity of literature varies across the four countries. The literature on the US movement is massive. That on the British movement is not quite so extensive. That on the German movement is substantial, with a reasonable quantity in English translation. That on Norway is small.

With these methodological preliminaries out of the way, let us now begin our comparative analysis of the four countries in terms of how the histories of their environmental movements relate to the character of their states.

2

Patterns of Movement Inclusion and Exclusion in the Four Countries

In some countries environmental groups, especially those that looked like conventional interest groups, were involved in influencing policy making from the start of the environmental era that arrived around 1970. In other countries environmentalism was more like a new social movement, prominent in oppositional civil society but largely excluded from institutional political processes. As we saw in Chapter 1, life-cycle theorists believe that the normal trajectory of any social movement begins in oppositional civil society with radical confrontation and ends in accommodation with government. In this chapter we will sketch the history of the environmental movement and its relationship to the state in our four countries, Norway, the United States, Germany, and the United Kingdom. We will show that in no case does the trajectory of the environmental movement quite fit a neat life cycle progression, and that its shape and fortunes are heavily influenced by the state's orientation to societal interests.

To begin questioning this alleged life-cycle progression, we can simply note that our four countries all possess moderate environmental organizations that predate the new social movement activism which emerged in the 1970s. These established groups have always featured little inclination towards grassroots democratic processes, or the oppositional relationship to the state and radical tactics of new social movements. They have pursued particular instrumental goals (such as the preservation of wilderness or countryside areas, or particular legislative reforms), and are centrally organized, with most members passive supporters removed from decision making processes.

This type of organization is apparent in all four of our cases, irrespective of the relative openness of their political systems (although institutional openness does determine their comparative prevalence). The movement in the United States has long been dominated by moderate mainstream organizations that utilize the plurality of institutional lobbying channels. Notable organizations are the National Wildlife Federation, Environmental Defense Fund, Sierra Club, Friends of the Earth, Wilderness Society, and the Natural

Resources Defense Council. Environmental concern in Norway has long been represented by centralized, policy-oriented organizations such as the Norwegian Society for the Conservation of Nature, and recreational organizations like the Norwegian Mountain Touring Association.

Britain's movement has traditionally been dominated by conservation organizations such as Royal Society for the Protection of Birds (RSPB), the National Trust, the World Wildlife Fund (WWF), the Council for the Protection of Rural England (CPRE), and The Ramblers Association. These organizations all pursue conventional lobbying strategies and are comfortable with bureaucratic and informal opportunities to access government officials. The Green Alliance formed in 1978 could be added to this list, as it aims more explicitly to foster links between the movement and governmental decision makers.[1] In Germany, scholarly emphasis on a progressive and controversial Green Party has tended to overshadow a number of conventional, long-standing environmental organizations. Prominent among these are the German Nature Protection Association (NABU), the World Wildlife Fund Deutschland; and the umbrella organization German League for Nature Conservation and Environmental Protection (DNR). Participation in government processes has never posed ideological or organizational quandaries to these mainstream organizations, although as we shall explain in Chapter 4, they have had to respond to the challenges of professionalization when presented with enhanced possibilities for inclusion in the state.

The fact that moderate organizations of long standing can be found in all four of our countries should not however obscure the major cross-national differences in the form taken by the movement—including, notably but not exclusively, the relative weight of conventional interest groups, political parties, new social movements, and direct action. The form taken by a country's environmental movement and its relationship to the state—be it confrontational, co-operative, or some point in between—is framed (though not completely *determined*) by the structural characteristics of the state. However, this framing itself is only the starting point for historical analysis, because the shape taken by the movement and its associated strategic choices can themselves ultimately affect the character of the state, as will become clear in subsequent chapters.

In terms of the four categories of state-movement relations set out in Chapter 1, we look at the United States and Germany as exemplars of passive forms of inclusion and exclusion respectively, while Norway illustrates active

---

[1] In contrast to the grassroots-style organizations that began to emerge at this time, the Green Alliance maintained a relatively select, professionalized membership. In the words of one of its founders, the Green Alliance was formed as 'a sort of club that would facilitate the osmotic processes of absorbing environmental awareness into the body politic' (Grove-White, interview, 1999).

inclusion, and the United Kingdom in the Thatcher era and beyond represents active exclusion. This chapter will introduce the post-1970 history of environmental politics in each of these countries with special reference to trajectories of inclusion and exclusion. We will reserve discussions of movement impact, the content of public policy, and the implications for democracy for subsequent chapters. Throughout, bear in mind that inclusion in the core of the state (as defined in terms of domestic order, external security, economic, legitimation and revenue imperatives) does not necessarily follow from apparent access to governmental processes. We will show in Chapter 3 that for each country there are key episodes that reveal the presence or absence of inclusion in this core as defined.

Active Inclusion: Norway's Expansive Corporatism

Norway is normally classified as among the strongest of corporatist systems. Corporatism exists in the form of concertation across the standard triumvirate of labour, government, and business in managing the political economy as a whole, also within economic sectors. But for our purposes, Norway is interesting because among developed countries (and facing competition only from Mexico among all countries), Norway is the most institutionally integrative of all kinds of organized interests, not just business and labour. This feature has been present for several decades, though we will trace its history only as it concerns the environment. Norway is also among the most social democratic of countries, its politics having long been dominated by the Labour Party (with only brief interludes of governments led by other parties in 1965–71, 1981–6, 1989–90, and 1997–9). Yet its corporatism has been strong enough that such parliamentary balances of power are not crucial; as Stein Rokkan (1966) famously put it, 'votes count, but resources decide'. Thus Norwegian political history reveals a great deal of stability throughout the era of interest to us.

Norwegian environmentalism has deep roots among those interested in protecting the country's natural environment, especially with outdoor recreation in mind. The Norwegian Mountain Touring Association (NMT) was founded in 1868, and remains today a 'breeches aristocracy' active in environmental protection. In 1914, scientific professionals founded the National Association for Nature Preservation (Landsforeningen for naturfredning i Norge). In 1963 its name was changed to the Norwegian Society for the Conservation of Nature (Norges Naturvernforbund) and it became more recognizably a mass-membership campaigning group—though from this new beginning on, it also continued to co-operate with government. This Society, also known as Friends of the Earth Norway, became the largest and most influential environmental group for the next several decades (though by 1999 it was on the verge of bankruptcy, despite government financial support; Seippel, 1999: 56).

The Brundtland Report that launched the era of sustainable development on the global stage in 1987 had a substantial impact on Norway, given that Brundtland herself was a Norwegian prime minister from 1986. A movement for sustainable development was endorsed by the state, though it involved ways of living as community members and consumers rather than public policy. This was, notably, the focus of the Environmental Home Guard (Miljøheimevernet), formed in 1991 with support from the Conservation Society, organized as an umbrella group to which communities and other groups can affiliate, and largely funded by the government. The Home Guard has no members as such, just 'participants' who promise to behave in environmentally-friendly ways. The period around 1989–90 was a high point in membership and support for organizations such as the Conservation Society and The Future Is In Our hands (Framtiden i våre hender)—a group founded in 1974 but whose philosophy resembled sustainable development's integration of environmental and economic concerns.

The consistent picture that characterizes these decades is one of environmental groups working in close consultative relationships with the state. In a comparative light, the main distinguishing feature of environmentalism in Norway is the degree to which it has been financed by government, as early as 1934 when the Ministry of Church and Education gave support to the Conservation Society (Bernsten, 1994: 94). The environmental sector is not unique; voluntary groups in general are recognized as producers of services, as arenas for democratic action, as important for the fulfillment of interests. It is in this sense that Norway is 'an organisational society' (Selle and Stromsnes, 1998a: 5). There is a political consensus that the 'third sector' should therefore receive financial support from government (NOU, 1988, no.17; St. Meld. Nr 27 (1996–7)). By 2000, 19 groups were receiving operating and project grants administered by the Ministry of the Environment (though the grants actually predate the establishment of the Ministry in 1972). The total level of funding had expanded consistently over the years.

Do these transfers compromise the independence of groups? Certainly the mainstream groups have come to depend very heavily on government finance. Group leaders themselves see at most only marginal policy adjustments being at issue, and can point to a few cases where funded groups have initiated legal actions against the government. But clearly the distribution of support strengthens the hand of nationwide groups prepared to co-operate with government, and disadvantages groups critical of government policy, which are not funded (for example, animal welfare groups). Project grants are distributed in accordance with government's priorities (for example, sustainable consumption in the early to mid-1990s), and the grant of course specifies what must be done with the money. Even operating grants are distributed on the grounds that a group is implementing public policy.

Along with state finance and such 'implementation' functions, organizations 'act as interlocutors between their members and government, and participate actively in decision making and policy formation' (Smillie and Filewod, 1993: 217), especially via the system of committees. Norway has been described as 'the country of a thousand committees' (Klausen and Opedal, 1998). Committees are set up by cabinet, and used to generate proposals for parliament. They can be permanent or short-lived. The committees are central to sectoral corporatism, especially in fields such as industry, trade, energy, agriculture, and fisheries. Welfare state ministries such as education, science, culture, health, and welfare have also made good use of committees. By contrast, as of 1989 only 2.8 per cent of the permanent committees were in the environmental area (Nordby, 1994: 86). However, environmental groups were also represented on committees outside the Environment Ministry's jurisdiction (such as fisheries).

What can sometimes happen on committees is that a coherent government is able to dominate fragmented interest groups (Nordby, 1996: 287 f.). Group leaders end up as hostages, often pressured to take positions that their members would oppose. Participation in committees is further problematic inasmuch as representation is secured by having some relevant expertise, not possession of an alternative viewpoint. And the fact that committees generally work behind closed doors means that ordinary members of groups have little influence. In this light, it is perhaps not surprising that Norway's environmental organizations have a significantly lower member support base than those in neighbouring countries. Norway's largest environmental organization—the Norwegian Society for the Conservation of Nature—has just 28,000 members, whereas its equivalents in Sweden (which has about double the population) and Denmark (with about the same population) exceed 200,000 members (Selle and Stromsnes, 1998a: 7). Any capacity to mobilize bottom-up support is further hindered by public perception that Norway is leading most other European nations in its response to environmental concerns (Sverdrup, 1997: 74). (Selle and Stromsnes, 1998a: 5, suggest that another reason for low membership is that the environmental movement encounters competition from other sectoral groups sympathetic to environmental concerns.) This perception was corroborated in 2001 with the release of a ranking of countries according to their score on an 'environmental sustainability index' by the World Economic Forum (online at http://www.ciesin.org/indicators/ESI). Norway was ranked second among the world's countries (after Finland).

For better or for worse, then, Norwegian environmental groups generally operate in close co-operation with government in a system that values consensus. Sverdrup (1997: 76) observes: 'A rapid institutionalisation of environmental policy both at the political and administrative level seems to have taken place . . . Environmental considerations have to a large extent been coopted into already existing legislative and political-institutional systems.' Given the lack of importance of parliament, organizations tended to engage in 'administrative lobbyism' (Rommetvedt et al., 1998: 10), mostly directed towards central administrative agencies (Klausen and Opedal, 1998). On the one hand there is a large voluntary sector in Norway in terms of the sheer number of organizations that exist and effectively engage government. But on the other hand, civil society interpreted as the grassroots of organizations is weak. Seippel (1999: 67) finds that two-thirds of the members of Norwegian environmental groups are 'passive', though it is not easy to ascertain the cross-national significance of this figure. If civil society is interpreted as the leadership of organizations, it is hard to distinguish from government. Civil society is therefore more often a reference point for quasi-governmental organizations than a site for counter-cultural activities or a seedbed for further democratization of the state.

Yet there has been one area of environmental politics that appears to be an exception to the consultative and co-operative rule. This concerns dams, hydropower, and free-flowing rivers, and in many ways is Norway's parallel to the issue of nuclear energy as it arose in Germany and galvanized a social movement. Norway has never pursued the nuclear power option, a strategy made easy by widespread public opposition (though not joined by the Nature Conservation Society), the availability of hydroelectric power, and the fact that no political party has been at all committed to nuclear energy (Flam, 1994b: 315–16). A government committee did recommend in favour of nuclear power in 1978, but by then the issue had been left behind. The 'hydropower complex' on the other hand is central to the Norwegian political economy, and proved immune to environmentalist influence through the normal consultative and committee channels. Norway's only real experience of environmental protest has occurred in connection with large dam proposals.

The first such protest occurred in the early 1970s with the ultimately unsuccessful campaign against the Mardøla Dam, in which philosophers Arne Næss and Sigmund Kvaløy and student activists were prominent. The Conservationist Society worked against the dam through conventional channels, and its leadership (though not its membership) disapproved of the kinds of civil disobedience and direct action aimed against a decision already endorsed by parliament. 'Mardøla' became a symbol for a different way of thinking about environment and development in a way that challenged traditions of political consensus and the dominance of the hydropower complex (Gundersen, 1996: 55 ff.; Midttun, 1988).

This challenge was renewed in the late 1970s in the campaign against the hydroelectric Alta Dam, though this case is also illustrative of the range of conventional avenues open to the environmental movement. Public opposition to the dam proposal initially took the form of a public petition (14,000 signatures) submitted to parliament, and protest marches were held in Oslo (2,000 people) and Alta (500 people) (Andersen and Midttun, 1994: 254). After several years' delay parliament approved the dam's development in 1978. Protest continued with the settlement of an activist camp in Alta in 1979 to obstruct construction before protesters were forcibly removed by police. Concurrently, the Norwegian Society for the Conservation of Nature pursued legal avenues against the Ministry of Petroleum and Energy to prevent the development (Andersen and Midttun, 1994). The Court ruled in favour of the Ministry, a position reaffirmed by the Supreme Court in 1981. According to Andersen and Midttun (1994: 254), the conflict not only mobilized the local community, but 'also led to civil support for irregular political means to an extent that is not customary in Norwegian politics'.[2] A White Paper, released in 1980, concluded that there were no substantive reasons for preventing the project. Following further parliamentary discussion, the dam was approved.

Frode Gundersen (1996) suggests that the Alta case and concurrent failure of environmentalists to prevent offshore oil drilling occurring in the northern part of the North Sea signalled a decline of environmentalist influence in the 1980s. However, part of this may have been a shift in focus from nature preservation to pollution, emphasized especially by Nature and Youth, the youth organization of the Conservationist Society. A few activists broke away from Nature and Youth in 1986 to form the Bellona Foundation, whose tactics resemble those of Greenpeace (for example, staging media events such as climbing smokestacks). Bellona has gone from strength to strength, especially concerning toxic and nuclear waste issues (beyond Norway's borders), despite not being a membership organization; its revenues come mostly from individual donations, magazine sales and advertising, and other donations from business. Because it is organized as a private foundation, looking more like a business than a membership group, it receives no operating grants from government—and this sets it apart from other groups (though Bellona does receive some project funding from government).

Another slight weakening of Norway's expansive corporatism occurred in the 1990s with the increasing tendency of the Storting to do more than

---

[2] In a survey of the local community Andersen and Midttun (1994: 255) found that almost 30 per cent of respondents signed petitions on the issue, while almost 18 per cent were involved in demonstrations and 5 per cent in civil disobedience. Almost half of respondents did not object to civil disobedience as a form of protest.

rubber-stamp agreements made elsewhere. This has provided an additional point of leverage for the environmental movement (Klausen and Rommetvedt, 1996). 'For organizations which have not succeeded in promoting their viewpoints through the corporative channel, the procedure in the Storting represents a new opportunity to influence the outcomes of the decisions' (Rommetvedt, Farsund, and Melberg, 1998: 6). A group like Greenpeace, with a very small Norwegian membership and no presence in corporatist counsels, can therefore attempt to lobby members of the Storting. However, access of this sort does not always translate into real influence.

One other anomalous feature of Norwegian environmental politics deserves mention: the inability of the Green Party (formed in 1988) to make much impression or to win any seats despite a comparatively minimal electoral barrier to parliamentary representation (in 1990 there were seven political parties represented in the Storting). Aardal (1990: 150) attributes this to the prior existence of two parties sympathetic to the environmental agenda: the Liberal Party and the Socialist Left Party, which have effectively denied green parties a niche in which to secure a support base.

Nowhere in this sweep of Norwegian history can we find much that looks like a new social movement, the anti-dam protests notwithstanding. Organizations have always been encouraged to form established, hierarchical structures to engage in corporatist negotiations with government agencies. Even the more direct action-oriented organizations which emerged in the mid- to late 1980s have relied on small, professionalized structures rather than mass membership, which further illustrates the difficulty in mobilizing membership in the context of an amenable state. Closest in tactics to new social movement groups have been the Bellona Foundation and Greenpeace (weaker than its sister organizations in our other countries). These groups have no tradition of grassroots participation and rely on members who are supportive mainly in financial terms. In more recent years they have combined dramatic, media worthy events and consultative work with government and industry. The Bellona Foundation, for example, accepts government project work and also receives much of its money from trade and industry (Selle and Strømsnes, 1998*b*).

Passive Inclusion: The United States' Pluralism

Pluralism is the most common form of 'passively inclusive' interest representation, as whatever constellation of interest groups emerges from society at any given time can attempt to influence government. The United States is the best example of a state with a pluralist form of interest representation (see e.g.

Lehmbruch, 1984).[3] While most conventional pluralist authors focus on the abilities of interest groups to organize and to put pressure on legislative bodies, forms of passive inclusion exist in all three parts of the US system: the legislative, the executive/administrative, and the judicial. Certainly, the massive lobbying complex in the US demonstrates passive inclusion in the legislative arena.[4] In addition, the Administrative Procedures Act of 1946 was a landmark of progressive legislation for open government; it specifies a minimum for public input and government response to that input. The Act requires that advance notice be given of proposed rules and procedures, and that there be an opportunity for public comment before new rules can be adopted. There is no requirement for agencies actively to seek this input, only to give the opportunity for participation. Again, this fits with our classification of the US as a passive inclusive state. Finally, the judicial system in the US (passively) gives citizens another opportunity to participate in the development of public policy. There are numerous examples of interest groups and social movements bringing cases or class action suits into the court system in an attempt to change existing law (for example, the NAACP's representation of Linda Brown in the landmark 1954 Brown vs. Board of Education case that overturned the 'separate but equal' doctrine in race relations). In addition, many laws and statutes allow for citizen challenges to administrative rules and regulations. If, for instance, an agency adopts a rule in a manner that excludes citizen input, citizens have standing to sue the agency. Increasingly, public interest groups have used this avenue to challenge agencies on consumer safety, health, and a range of other issues. So while there is certainly worthy debate about just how open and inclusive the US version of liberal pluralism is, and the economic barriers decried by critics of pluralism certainly still exist, there are many open avenues for citizens and groups at least to *attempt* to insert themselves into the political process.

In keeping with this pluralist model, the United States' environmental movement was long organized into a wide range of interest groups (Brulle, 2000). Some of these can trace their origins to the nineteenth century. The

---

[3] This is not the same as saying that American government lives up to the pluralist ideal as articulated by political scientists defending the system in the 1950s and 1960s. There have been numerous critiques of this characterization of the US system, sometimes by pluralist authors themselves (e.g. Lindblom, 1977); most of these centre on the exclusion of individuals and groups without high levels economic resources and the political influence that comes with those resources (e.g. Wolff et al., 1965; Domhoff, 1967).

[4] See e.g. Berry, 1977; Zeigler and Baer, 1969. By the middle of 1999, there were 12,113 active lobbyists in Washington, DC; and reported expenditures on official federal lobbying alone (i.e. excluding unofficial lobbying and efforts outside the federal realm) came to $1.45 billion in 1999 (Centre for Responsive Politics). Public opinion (via polling) is similarly influential upon legislators (see e.g. Lippmann's 1922 classic, or, more recently, Mendelsohn and Crespi, 1970; Yeric and Todd, 1996).

Sierra Club, founded in 1892, began to take on a more campaigning character in the 1950s under the directorship of David Brower. Brower eventually went too far in this direction for the taste of many members, was deposed, went on to found Friends of the Earth, and, after a repeat falling-out with the rest of its leadership, the Earth Island Institute. By the 1970s a well-defined set of large, 'mainstream' groups was established, which would dominate the subsequent three decades of organized environmentalism. These groups are the Audubon Society, National Wildlife Federation, Environmental Defense Fund, Sierra Club, Friends of the Earth, Wilderness Society, and Natural Resources Defense Council. A host of state and local organizations supplements these major players. While these mainstream environmental organizations have maintained a mass membership on which they rely for much of their funding, their leadership has operated easily and comfortably in the corridors of power in Washington DC and elsewhere. So effective has been the institutional integration of movement groups that some academics (mistakenly) interpret any other forms of direct action or protest 'as temporary aberrations from the prevailing American pattern of assimilative protest' (Kitschelt, 1986: 72, referring to protests following the nuclear accident at Three Mile Island).

Yet the mainstream groups have never encompassed the whole movement. From the mid-1970s there was also a more radical green movement. Often disorganized, this movement provided a meeting place for philosophical discussions about deep ecology, social ecology, ecofeminism, bioregionalism, green spirituality, animal liberation, and alternative lifestyles (Brulle, 2000: 195–207); but it rarely had any interest in, and so impact, on public policy, leaving that field free for the mainstream groups. The greens' exclusion was self-imposed, and so makes no difference to our categorization of the United States as an inclusive state. Most of its members have been quite uninterested in the world of politics, especially as it involves the state. Among the greens the question of whether they should be in any sense a political organization, let alone a party, has itself been a matter of great dispute. In 2000, however, the US Greens made their first impression on the national stage. The presidential ticket of Ralph Nader and Winona Laduke gained 2.6 per cent of the vote nationally, exceeding 5 per cent in eleven states and highlighting many issues ignored by the major candidates and the mass media. Critics accused them of denying the presidency to Al Gore and handing it to George W. Bush, but that outcome owed much to a partisan US Supreme Court, the electoral college (Gore won the popular vote), and numerous electoral irregularities. Nader himself blamed Gore's uninspired middle-of-the road campaign for Bush's victory.

More recently, a second alternative to the mainstream groups has arisen with the environmental justice movement. This movement had local beginnings in

1978 with the discovery of toxic wastes under houses in Love Canal, New York, and in 1982 with the opening of a toxic waste dump in primarily African-American Warren County, North Carolina. By 1990 it was a national force. The environmental justice movement focused upon the inequitable distribution of environmental risks across race and class lines (see e.g. Bullard, 1993), an aspect often ignored by the mainstream groups. Such risks related to air and water pollution, toxic waste dumps and incinerators, pesticide application, and other hazards. Unlike the green fringe, environmental justice activists concerned themselves with concrete issues and struggles, with a strong orientation to state power and policy.

As Kitschelt (1986: 66) noted in a comparative study of anti-nuclear movements, the United States' political system remains relatively open because of the 'comparatively strong position of the Congress, the lack of tightly integrated political parties, [and] the relative openness of a deeply fragmented administration'. Interest groups have opportunities to lobby members of Congress, the Executive, or pursue redress through a strong, independent judiciary. The mainstream environmental movement in the United States utilizes these multiple opportunities for inclusion.

Andrews (1999: 240), in his history of US environmental policy, argues that 'one of the most distinctive features of modern US environmental protection policy . . . is the unprecedentedly broad right of access to the regulatory process, which extends not only to affected businesses but to citizens advocating environmental protection'. Daniel Beard of the Audubon Society observes that in the last three decades of the twentieth century there developed 'a culture in the United States where government agencies . . . don't make decisions without considering public input' (interview, 1999). Rosenbaum (1989: 215) notes that more than 75 per cent of all public participation programs in the US originated in federal statutes since 1970, and the vast majority of those are in environmental legislation. The National Environmental Policy Act of 1969 (NEPA) has been particularly influential. For every federal project with a possible substantial environmental impact the Act requires the development of environmental impact statements (EIS) and avenues for public involvement in the review process. The public can provide comment after the submission of the EIS, and can appeal the eventual administrative decision (though only in regard to the adequacy of the EIS, not the quality of the decision). This type of passive openness to input has been written into nearly every environmental statute in the US

It may be a culture for US government agencies to *consider* public input, but that does not mean that agencies are required to *abide* by it. Still, there is evidence that this 'culture' of public input has had an effect. For example, in the toxics arena numerous laws, including the Toxic Substances Control Act,

Resource Conservation and Recovery Act, and Superfund, require public notice and hearings on cleanup plans and the licensing of dumping sites. There is evidence that the constant public involvement in the process has slowed the licensing of new facilities (Rosenbaum, 1989: 232). A notable recent example is the US Department of Agriculture's response to massive public concern about the agency's branch charged with writing the rules for defining organic foods under the Organic Foods Production Act, The National Organic Program (see Shulman, 2000). Having received over 280,000 public comments, USDA removed allowances for sewage sludge, genetically modified foods, and irradiated foods in the proposed organic category, and published a revised rule for another round of public comments in 2000. USDA Secretary Dan Glickman announced the final national standards for the production, handling, and processing of organic agricultural products in December 2000.

Public consultation on policy issues is more extensive through Federal Advisory Committees, which seek viewpoints on policy issues through open public meetings that include public submissions. There are nearly one thousand such Committees, though after 1993 President Clinton sought to reduce their number.[5] The EPA alone manages twenty-seven of these out of its Office of Cooperative Environmental Management. Clarence Hardy, past Director of the Office, argues that EPA tries to 'get all of the interests that should be represented in' each advisory council, with all twenty-seven having representation from the environmental community (interview, 1999).

The influence of the environmental movement upon Congress or the Executive is through lobbying rather than direct representation. Unlike in many European countries where green parties have secured an institutional foothold in parliament (O'Neill, 1997), in the United States direct political representation for the green movement is effectively made impossible by the first-past-the-post electoral system. This system ensures domination by the Democrat and Republican parties. Beyond the self-imposed problems we described earlier, any more effective national green party therefore faces enormous obstacles (Slaton, 1992). Not surprisingly, the movement has instead sought influence via its interest groups. As Dan Beard, Chief Operating Officer at the National Audubon Society, asserts, while once 'environmental lobbyists . . . were generally viewed as activists who were out of touch with reality . . . [Now] we are viewed as genuine or legitimate public interest groups who must be considered when undertaking decision making processes . . . We're a legitimate constituency that has to be dealt with' (interview, 1999). Yet the doors to political access are often only 'partly open,' as

---

[5] Executive Order 12838 mandates a reduction in advisory committees and limits the creation of new ones to those required by statute.

one lobbyist noted. It is just that another set of lobbyists—those for industry—have the doors more widely opened for them.[6]

With the development of environmental law in the US in the 1960s and
1970s the courts provided a further avenue of redress for the environment
movement and other interest groups. In the 1960s the civil rights movement
was successful in liberalizing the notion of standing—where previously
plaintiffs had to prove personal harm, the federal courts expanded the
notion to any 'legally protected interest' (Andrews, 1999: 220). In the environmental arena, this newly expanded notion of standing was used to challenge a hydropower license in the landmark 1967 Storm King case, and in
the same year an alliance of scientists and lawyers sued to stop DDT spray-
ing by local governments in New York. These court cases often showed
agencies fighting not for the public interest, but for the very industries and
interests they were supposed to be regulating. The environmental regulatory
apparatus, in contrast, was developed after 1970 to be open to public
participation and legal challenges. A very conscious understanding by
Congress of the tendency towards agency capture led to citizen-suit provisions in most of the environmental laws subsequently passed. These provisions allow any person to bring an enforcement lawsuit against an agency if
the agency does not diligently prosecute violations of the law. Consequently,
there has been a rapid expansion of both legal cases and legal expertise on
the part of environmental groups. Eighty per cent of the EPA's major rule
makings since the agency's inception in 1970 have had lawsuits filed challenging them[7] (Lavelle, 1991: 30). NEPA has spawned the largest number of
suits, concerning either agency action or inaction on issues. There are
numerous public interest environmental law firms. At the national level, the
Environmental Defense Fund (EDF, now Environmental Defense) evolved
out of the DDT cases in 1967, followed by the Natural Resources Defense
Council (NRDC) in 1970—which alone filed thirty-five of the first forty
Clean Air Act-related lawsuits—and the Sierra Club Legal Defense Fund
(now Earthjustice) in 1971.

In the United States the existence of institutionalized channels for access
has long encouraged hierarchical, centralized, and professionalized organizations rather than new social movement-style groups. When looked at from
Europe, where environmentalism is as much about identity and fundamental
values as it is about strategy, the American groups look very instrumental,

---

[6] In some cases 'passive' inclusion means that industrial lobbyists actually write legislation
which is introduced by members of Congress, often without congressional staff reviewing it
before heading to a vote.

[7] It is important to note here that the majority of these cases have been by filed by industry
rather than the environmental community.

being oriented towards achieving specific policy goals.[8] During the 1970s, groups sought to act simultaneously as social movements and interest groups, being both adversarial through protests and lawsuits, and engaging fully with the state as part of the growing complex of environmental management. As Gottlieb (1993: 316) describes the situation, 'Environmentalists were activists *and* lobbyists, system opponents *and* system managers.' But by the end of the 1970s, and into the 1980s, professionalism and interest group politics began to crowd out movement tactics. There was also little sign at the national level of grassroots democratic practices. More radical ecological groups were disengaged from institutional politics (until the emergence of the environmental justice movement in the late 1980s), assuming the form of wilderness groups, lifestyle groups, or a disaffected Green Party. The national environmental organizations developed hierarchical representative structures so that their negotiators could secure agreements with the Administration, congressional committees, and government agencies. Policy makers and legislators for their part encouraged this trend—they needed to know with whom they could make deals, and be assured that these deals would be kept.

The environmental movement has encountered very different responses from different presidential administrations. Yet given the relatively decentralized nature of government (owing to federalism, separation of powers, etc.), the attitude of administrations has not been as crucial as in more highly centralized states (such as New Zealand and Britain) as alternative avenues of political access remain open to the movement. The attitude of presidential administrations does nevertheless have an impact on the degree and location of influence exerted by the environmental movement and thus to some degree on its strategies, so let us take a brief look at this history.

While not commanding the resources and political influence of (say) industrial or agricultural lobby groups, during the Nixon years the movement made considerable institutional inroads into government. Declaring the 1970s the 'decade of the environment', on New Years Day 1970 President Nixon signed the NEPA into law on national television. Aside from setting environmental impact assessment into motion, NEPA created the advisory President's Council on Environmental Quality (CEQ). In his subsequent State of the Union address, Nixon called on the US to 'make peace with nature', and later signed an executive order directing all federal facilities to reduce their own pollution. To Congress he delivered a strong environmental message, setting out a thirty-seven point programme for environmental protection. In July 1970 he sent a governmental reorganization plan to Congress

---

[8] Indeed, social movement theory in the US initially followed the more pragmatic resource mobilization approach to interest group development (Hannigan, 1985; McCarthy and Zald, 1977) rather than the ideological new social movement theory applied by European scholars.

which included a new Environmental Protection Agency. Subsequent legislative initiatives included the Clean Air Act (1970), the Water Quality Improvement Act (1970), the Federal Water Pollution Control Act (1972), the Federal Environmental Pesticides Control Act (1972), the Coastal Zone Management Act and a Marine Protection, Research, and Sanctuaries Act (1972), the Endangered Species Act (1973), and the Safe Drinking Water Act (1974).

Surprisingly, this heyday of environmental legislation in the United States was fostered by a conservative President beholden to industrial interests. Nixon was observed to be 'reluctant' about his environmental policies, and William Ruckelshaus, first head of the EPA, had the impression that Nixon saw the environmental issue as 'faddish' (Switzer, 1998: 49). But for the Nixon administration dealing with environmental issues and the environmental movement was much easier than dealing with other controversial social and political issues, and other movements of the time. For example, Nixon signed NEPA in response to polls that showed strong public support for federal protection of environmental health (Dowie, 1995: 32). After the first Earth Day (22 April 1970), polls showed the environment as the second most important problem facing the nation, and the issue remained in the top ten every year in the Nixon presidency (Switzer, 1998: 11). So Nixon saw the environment as a political opportunity to lead on an issue of widespread concern.[9]

The presidency of Jimmy Carter began in 1977 with several environmental initiatives, notably proposals for a 'hit list' of federally subsidized water projects, drawn up by environmentalists, and the promotion of renewable energy and energy conservation. Both policies were eventually defeated by industry's intense lobbying and public relations campaigns.

The Reagan administration in the early 1980s was hostile towards the environmental movement, attempting a strategy of active exclusion. Attempts were made to demonize and exclude environmentalists from government. The regulatory basis of environmental administration was wound back, in keeping with market liberalism and individualist values. Yet in a system structurally geared towards the passive inclusion of interests, Reagan's efforts to subdue the environmental lobby were undermined on two fronts. First, there was a pluralist correction mechanism as the main effect of Reagan's attack on environmentalism was a surge in the membership, funding, and so influence of environmental groups. This shift in public opinion towards environmentalism saw the Reagan administration by 1984 presenting a more environmentally-friendly face, which continued into the Bush the Elder administration after 1988. Second, as a

---

[9] While many middle- and working-class citizens were ambivalent or critical of the antiwar, black power, New Left, and counter-culture movements of the times, as the polls showed, they did express concern about the environment.

pluralist state, the United States is not sufficiently unified or centralized to sustain the relatively authoritarian measures required for effective active exclusion. While Reagan zealously pursued market liberal ideological reforms, the Executive branch was unable to deny movement groups recourse to the judiciary and Congress.

Promising a 'kinder and gentler' America, George Bush the Elder cast himself as a conservationist in the Teddy Roosevelt tradition and promised to be an 'environmental president' (Vig, 2000: 104). Like Nixon, Bush used public support for environmental values to his advantage by pushing for and signing a revised Clean Air Act into law in 1990. By the end of his administration, however, he threatened a US boycott of the 1992 UN Conference on Environment and Development until he had obtained assurances that the climate change convention to be signed there would not contain binding targets for CO_2 cuts, and he refused to sign the biodiversity treaty outright (Vig, 2000: 105). Bush's growing hostility towards international environmental agreements was accompanied by renewed attempts to weaken domestic environmental laws that business viewed as too costly ('regulatory relief'). What inclusion environmentalists had achieved in the Bush administration's first two years—in the EPA and the Council on Environmental Quality, for example—withered away quickly in the resurgence of 'jobs-versus-the-environment' thinking during the economic recession of the early 1990s.

The inclusion of the environmental movement peaked after the election to the White House in 1992 of Bill Clinton and Al Gore, who had exploited the Bush campaign's strident anti-environment rhetoric to their advantage. This wave of inclusion began with appointments of environmentalist leaders to government office—Gus Speth, a founder of the NRDC, was called upon to head the Natural Resources cluster of Clinton's transition team. In the initial days of the new administration, about two dozen environmentalists were hired directly from the national environmental groups, and other pro-environment Democrats were appointed throughout the administration (Dowie, 1995: 178). The mainstream environmental movement celebrated these appointments as recognition that environmentalism was officially part of, and would have influence throughout, the new administration. But just as in the Carter administration, these great hopes ended in much frustration, as the first two years of the Clinton administration turned out to be some of the least environmentally productive in decades.

Passive Exclusion: Germany's Corporatism and Legalism

The structure of Germany's national voluntary associations mirrors the decentralized, federal structure of the German state. National offices tend to be relatively small and focus on co-ordinating the actions of dozens of regional and often hundreds of local branches. Although venue-hopping is a key feature of the strategy of pressure groups in federal systems (Tarrow, 1994), the importance of the federal government as a focus for interest group activity, including that of environmental Non-governmental Organizations (NGOs), has increased over the last thirty years (Sebaldt, 1997). German environmental NGOs are characterized by a tremendous diversity of organizational forms and aims. Organizations concerned about environmental issues include recreational groups, environmental protection associations, foundations, consumer groups, regional organizations, environmental professionals, single-issue groups, and professional organizations such as Greenpeace. There are also approximately eighty ecological research institutes, which have done much to disseminate ecological expertise. Although many environmental organizations view themselves as political pressure groups, relations with the public administration are typically adversarial. Particularly at the federal level, most environmental advocacy organizations have tended to assume a stance of radical opposition towards state actors, for reasons we will explain shortly; hence lobbying of public officials has not actually played a major role in the activities of most environmental NGOs. In contrast, participation in environmental protection projects such as establishing nature reserves has been an important part of their work.

Germany's environmental movement developed from a much more confrontational relationship to the state than was the case in either Norway or the United States. The emergence of the modern environmental movement in Germany in the late 1960s (established and conservative environmental groups had been around much longer) occurred in the wake of the student movement and in close connection with the escalating anti-nuclear and peace movements. Fuelled by a bitter generational conflict over how to acknowledge the legacy of National Socialism and the Holocaust, '1968' marked a profound cultural and political turning point in German post-war history. Environmental concerns stood out among a broad range of previously non-politicized areas of life.

Specifically, opposition to the country's increasing reliance on nuclear power became the new environmental movement's focal point. Large protest marches at sites for proposed or existing nuclear power plants around the country testified to the anti-nuclear movement's growing organizing abilities.[10] Conventional lobbying channels yielded little response as neither parliament nor the executive was willing to engage in a nuclear debate and

---

[10] There were occasional violent clashes between protesters and police, although environmental activists willing to engage in violence directed against property or police were always a small minority, and acts of violence committed during otherwise peaceful demonstrations were sometimes provoked by the police's inept or purposely confrontational crowd control methods. Allegations of violence by mainstream politicians and mass media tended to exaggerate the

none of the major political parties was prepared to adopt an anti-nuclear position (Kitschelt, 1986: 70). The movement was excluded by the techno-cratic government described by Wagner (1994: 266) as an 'opposed totality which could not be won over, but only fought against'. In these circumstances a combination of extra-parliamentary strategies was employed, exemplified by the concurrent legal challenge and occupation of a nuclear reactor site at Whyl in 1974–5. The anti-nuclear movement successfully mobilized large demonstrations which on some occasions exceeded 100,000 people (Wagner, 1994: 279), and there were violent clashes with police at sites such as Brokdorf and Grohnde (Papadakis, 1984; Zirakzadeh, 1997).

The political exclusion of the anti-nuclear movement helped fashion a strong oppositional counter-culture which went beyond specific policy goals to include issues of identity and alternative forms of action and behaviour. For this reason, Wagner (1994: 289) argues, 'the Greens, as one offshoot of the movement . . . dispose of a broad programme for societal change beyond environmentalism . . . [which] emphasises extended democracy, a differenti-ated commitment to welfare state expansion and moderate pacifism'. The German environmental movement's grassroots, citizen-based foundations can be traced to the emergence in the early 1970s of citizens' initiative groups to prompt action on local environmental issues. Between 1973 and 1976 these groups affiliated to form the Federal Association of Citizen's Initiatives for the Protection of the Environment (BBU) (Langguth, 1986: 7).[11] By 1980 the Federal Office of Environmental protection estimated that 5 million people were active in the citizens' initiatives movement (Langguth, 1986: 8).

The formation of the German Green Party (Die Grünen) in 1980 heralded a transition in the movement's approach, though there had been earlier electoral attempts via 'Alternative Lists'. In the 1983 elections Die Grünen surpassed the 5 per cent threshold to secure twenty-seven seats in the Bundestag (Poguntke, 1993). Some members of the grassroots citizen's groups felt the combination of civil protest and legal-administrative strategies was inadequate to bring about significant change to the political system. To reform institutional structures and legislation, they believed the movement should seek direct representation in parliament (Hager, 1995: 175). This view was resisted by many Citizens' Initiative group activists who had engaged in extra-parliamentary activity because of the limitations of the parliamentary system. They felt that party

actual level of violence, extent of damage, and number of casualties associated with anti-nuclear protests. Despite some instances of violent protest, the vast majority of protests were peaceful (Balistier, 1996).

[11] The BBU was founded in 1972 by sixteen citizen action groups primarily opposed to atomic power station developments (Zirakzadeh, 1997), most notably the construction of the Whyl power station. By 1977 there were over 1,000 affiliated groups totalling over 300,000 members (Langguth, 1986: 7).

organizational forms would encourage hierarchy, undermining the experimental, participatory approaches of the Citizens' Initiative groups (Hager, 1995).

The initial push for representation in the Bundestag was underlined by a belief that not only would this provide greater political power, but also that formal political channels would provide the movement with a complementary strategy to campaigning in civil society. One of the Green Party's founders, Petra Kelly (1984: 18) asserted: 'we feel obliged to take, public, non-violent action and to engage in civil disobedience outside and inside parliament, throwing a spotlight on the inhumanity of the system.' As a 'half party and half local action group', the Green Party would bring a new radicalism to the assembly and question its principles (Kelly, 1984: 17, 21). The non-conventionality of the Green Party's Bundestag representatives was illustrated symbolically in their rejection of suits in favour of jeans and sweaters (Zirakzadeh, 1997: 86). In this sense the Green Party was to be an 'anti-party party' which would seek to promote the cause of presently unrepresented interests (Kelly, 1984). As it was, the entry of the Green Party into parliament transformed the environment movement. Hulsberg (1988: 68–9) explains:

as a movement in a strict sense of the term, it outlived itself. It touched a raw nerve in society and, as a result, became drawn into the structures of society. Part of it, in other words, became the Green Party. What remained, the real movement, took on a new dimension in the peace movement.

While the Green Party initially emphasized the continuation of movement organizational values, entry into parliament brought forward differences between pragmatic and ideological elements, which were later delineated as *Realos* and *Fundis*. The battle between these two wings preoccupied the Greens in the late 1980s, and was eventually resolved by the victory of the *Realos* in the early 1990s. Following the departure of prominent *Fundis*, the Green Party pursued a more moderate reformist agenda (Joppke and Markovits, 1994).

Though stronger than that of most European legislatures, the *Bundestag's* influence on public policy is far weaker than that of the US Congress (Peters and Hunold, 1999). The country's federalist system does limit the federal executive's power, but the very logic of corporatism suggests that interest groups will tend to bypass parliamentary representation in favour of direct access to public officials in the executive. What impact opposition Green MPs did have on public policy was therefore largely the result of pushing the Christian Democrats (CDU), Social Democrats (SPD), and Free Democrats (FDP) to take environmental issues seriously. In 1998 the Green Party formed a governing coalition with the SPD, thus for the first time sharing in direct control over federal government policy.

This account of the long march of the 1968 generation of activism into a federal governing coalition might seem to suggest that Germany merely illustrates the standard life cycle of a social movement. But if we put Germany in comparative institutional perspective, we can see why this is not the case, and why Germany illustrates 'passive exclusion' so well.

Like the United States, the German state is decentralized in the sense that power is dispersed between the federal and state governments; the Executive's power is further checked by an autonomous judiciary. But unlike the United States, integration of interest groups into decision making has always been limited and selective. Moreover, there is less scope for action through the courts. While environmental groups in Germany can seek redress through the legal system, German activists have had to get by without some of the legal instruments long taken for granted by their US counterparts. For example, there has been no strongly established right to freedom of information, and class action suits have not been part of the federal legal system (Zahrnt, 6 March 1999). Still, a remaining advantage of the legal strategy is that even when the ruling goes against the group, it creates a delay which buys time for the movement's anti-nuclear values to spread throughout the wider society and to change public opinion in the process. This is arguably what occurred with one of the anti-nuclear movement's early successes in blocking construction of a nuclear reactor at Whyl near Freiburg. Having occupied the construction site, movement groups also appealed to administrative courts at the local, regional, and federal level to review the construction license. Although the environmentalists eventually lost their case, the government was unwilling to start construction by the time the Federal Administrative Court finally found in favour of the Government of Baden-Württemberg in 1985 (Reimer, 19 February 2000). A limitation to such legal strategies is that environmentalists cannot file a suit unless they can find a local resident whose property may be adversely affected by noxious emissions to do it for them. No property rights, no legal standing, no case. While there are usually plenty of disgruntled property owners in disputes concerning the siting of hazardous industrial facilities, the lack of class action suits hampers efforts to devise legal strategies for representing the public's interest in a clean environment.

Germany's dominant policy style has often been described as legal corporatist, with extensive co-operation between government and various private associations granted public standing by law (Lehmbruch and Schmitter, 1982; Offe, 1981). German officials frequently consult with selected interest groups, and semipublic organizations carry out many governmental functions. Basic social services such as health care are delivered by private entities empowered by the state. Peter Katzenstein's (1987) portrait of the Federal Republic as a 'semi-sovereign state' captures the central state's dependence on private associations, as well as sub-national levels of government and administration, for informational support and policy implementation.

Some might think the prospects for participatory policymaking under corporatism would actually be quite good (see Mansbridge, 1992). Corporatism legitimates the idea that societal interests ought to participate in formulating and implementing public policy, and it awards substantial influence and decision-making power to some groups. But German corporatism (unlike Norway) has strong *étatiste* elements (Joppke, 1993). Public officials are also committed to seeking scientifically justifiable decisions that will withstand legal scrutiny. Thus scientists critical of nuclear energy have been integrated more readily into policy making circles than have anti-nuclear political activists. While scientists concerned about the risks of nuclear energy have little difficulty in joining the search for engineering solutions to technical problems, the broader political concerns of eco-radicals for whom nuclear energy policy symbolizes the repressive nature of the German domestic security state are difficult or impossible to include in the search for a 'rationalist consensus' (Pulzer, 1992).[12] Most activists were unwilling to participate in the search for a rationalist consensus on nuclear energy, and the state was unwilling to change course in light of their objections.

Germany's corporatist approach to interest intermediation elevates peak interest organizations—usually capital and labour—to the exclusion of non-economic groups. This approach to decision making often bypasses parliament, downplaying that institution's role in policy making. The responses to challengers outside of formal institutional openings 'have, in line with Germany's historic legacy, often been of a confrontational, unresponsive, and repressive nature' (van der Heijden, Koopmans and Giugni, 1992: 23–4).

Commonly, the government administration has restricted information to societal groups. Merely being affected by or concerned about an environmentally sensitive project was not considered sufficient grounds for access to government files—citizens needed a legally valid claim based on property rights to obtain such data. In 1994 the CDU/FDP Government passed the Environmental Information Act in response to the European Union's 1990 transparency directive. This change in law, however, has not been very successful in changing agency culture or processes regarding information. We will return to this issue in Chapter 7. For the most part though the German environmental movement has had to contend with a public bureaucracy hostile to freedom-of-information requests. The paternalistic behaviour of civil servants noted by environmental advocacy organizations is rooted in the country's legalistic state tradition (Dyson 1980; Loughlin and Peters 1994); hence the term legal corporatism. In the Germanic state tradition the law is more than a regulatory tool—it represents a more or less tangible manifestation of the state

---

[12] 'Rationalist consensus' is Dyson's (1982) term for the legalistic, science-based style of reasoning in public affairs favoured by the country's politicians and bureaucrats.

and is the central expression of state authority. This feature of the *Rechtsstaat* tradition has dramatic consequences for public administration and the relationship between the state and its citizens. The value attached to the law as an incarnation of the will of the state limits opportunities for citizen participation insofar as the public bureaucracy, in order to preserve the state's authority, will tend to favour narrowly legalistic interpretations of provisions for public participation. The public interest is viewed in terms of abstract legal norms rather than societal interests—regardless of what citizens may demand or need in any particular case. Critics have noted the irony of agencies using data protection laws, hailed by civil libertarians to be among the more progressive features of German administrative law, to justify denials of environmental freedom-of-information requests (Bennet, 1992: 104).

This tendency is compounded by the Germanic tradition's conception of state and society being part of an organic whole. This metaphor encourages political actors to think of society as a well-regulated system and to underestimate the existence of conflict among competing interests. The participatory revolution (Kaase, 1984) launched by the new social movements in the 1970s can be seen as a reaction against organic views of state and society. Public officials today can no longer hope to avoid public scrutiny by appeals, without argument, to economic growth or bureaucratic expertise (Hager, 1995). Although the organic conception of state and society may not be the predominant conception held by Germans today, the values and practices associated with this idea have persisted, keeping administrators from embracing a more participatory style of decision making as a means to deal with political conflict. Many administrators thus continue to think of citizens opposed to the government's economic development agenda as cranks, prone to disrupt the work of government for no good reason.

Once we recognize not just the presence of corporatism, but also the influence of the Prussian administrative tradition, a legalistic conception of the public interest divorced from public opinion, the importance of scientific justification for policy decisions, an organic view of the state and society, and administrative secrecy, we can see why Germany is a passively exclusive state *par excellence*—more so, indeed, than states such as Sweden and Austria that are normally classified as more strongly corporatist. The environmental movement in Germany therefore encounters passive exclusion in which opportunities for formal political inclusion are limited and unconventional challenges to governmental authority have been strongly resisted.[13] The passively exclusive

---

[13] This interpretation differs from Kriesi's (1996: 161) characterization of Germany's political system as '*formalistic inclusion*', although we concur with Kriesi that outside of these formal opportunities for inclusion, the state is relatively closed to informal challenges and will make few, if any, concessions.

structural arrangements in Germany did however provide more fertile ground than our other three countries for the emergence of new social movement groups. Early political exclusion saw the foundations of the modern environmental movement emerge as grassroots, participatory and oppositional citizen's initiatives groups. By 1972 these had formed the Federal Association of Citizens' Initiatives for Environmental Protection (BBU), an organization closely identified with the environmental movement's radical wing as well as the peace movement. *Die Grünen*, which from the early 1980s provided the central political core of the movement, advocated (initially at least) participatory and anti-institutional values. The BUND[14] (established in 1975) remains the largest environmental organization in Germany, and was instrumental in the anti-nuclear protests in the 1980s, and those at Wackersdorf in particular. From 1990 the BUND has served as the German branch of the Friends of the Earth, comprising over 2,500 local environmental groups which it seeks to include in its decision making. Thus the BUND is a very different kind of organization from the Norwegian branch of Friends of the Earth (the Norwegian Society for the Conservation of Nature). Greenpeace (established 1980), as in other countries, pursues radical, media-attracting strategies but departs from new social movement values in organizational terms, being hierarchical and restricting participation in decision making to just thirty members who hold meetings closed to the public (Bluhdorn, 1995; Klein, 1996). Greenpeace has nevertheless held on to its oppositional character, refusing to register as an official NGO, a requirement of access to state fora.[15] More akin to the early new social movement groups is Robin Wood, a smaller organization that splintered from Greenpeace in 1982. Robin Wood pursues dramatic actions that draw extensive media attention, although in contrast to Greenpeace it reaffirms grassroots participatory values through a decentralized structure that provides relative autonomy to regional groups (Hager, 1995).

Active Exclusion: Authoritarian Liberalism in Britain

Active exclusion is relatively rare as a durable form of the liberal democratic state, but in recent times has been evident in the dramatic imposition of market liberalism in countries such as Britain and New Zealand. In Britain under Margaret Thatcher in 1979–90 market liberalism entailed overt exclusion of environmental movement groups and an attack on social democratic institutions and the associational basis of civil society. These attacks continued into

---

[14] Bund fur Umwelt- und Naturschutz Deutschland
[15] This was not solely for ideological reasons—Greenpeace lacked the internal democratic structures the state required for registration as a non-governmental organization.

the 1990s, notably with the passage of the Criminal Justice Act in 1994, even as environmental issues made their way back onto the government's agenda.[16]

Active forms of exclusion rely on a strong state, and among liberal democratic states few are stronger than the majoritarian governments in the Westminster system installed under first-past-the-post elections. These allow a Government with a clear majority to push through a reformist agenda despite strong opposition. While in the United States, the existence of numerous checks and balances within the political system restrained Reagan's market liberal reformist zeal, in Britain the transition towards a market liberal state was enforced rapidly with minimal consultation. The approach of the Thatcher Government in Britain we characterize as 'authoritarian liberalism', entailing the imposition of a free market agenda, a corresponding suppression of dissent in civil society, and an 'individuation' of social and economic life that undermines the conditions for public association and action. More so than with the other case studies, the focus in the British case is upon a period of time in which the state's approach to interest groups deviated from prior structural conditions and established practices. The 'authoritarian' aspect diminished with the departure of Thatcher herself, but neither market liberalism nor active exclusion vanished with her.

In terms of the four categories of state orientations to movements and groups developed in Chapter 1, Britain until 1979 featured some inclusion, though not on the face of it very profound, in that channels were limited and did not extend very far into government. Exclusions were a matter of practice rather than conscious policy, but nonetheless present. Britain's most visible environmental groups pre-dated the upsurge of environmental concern in the late 1960s. For many of these groups engagement with the state did not entail the angst associated with new social movements (as seen, for example, in Germany). Organizations such as the Royal Society for the Protection of Birds (founded 1889), the Council for the Protection of Rural England (1926), the Royal Society for Nature Conservation (1916) and the World Wildlife Fund UK (1961) clearly preceded the wave of social movement activism which swept through Europe in the 1970s. Their relationship to the state was co-operative rather than oppositional—a number even receiving royal patronage[17]—yet their influence on public policy remained minimal.

Public involvement in the political decision making process is not encouraged under the Westminster system of government, which assumes citizen

---

[16] In New Zealand certain sectional interests were excluded by the market liberal reform process, although at the same time the 1984–90 Labour Government embraced other groups, of which the environmental movement was one—and this is why we have chosen Britain rather than New Zealand as our case.

[17] For example The Royal Society for Protection of Birds, The Royal Society for Nature Conservation, and the World Wildlife Fund (Doherty and Rawcliffe, 1995: 238).

passivity outside of elections. Under the principle of executive mandate, policy making is deemed to be a ministerial responsibility. Traditionally, the Executive has been inaccessible to public interest groups, and government information has been restricted rather than open. Contentious political decisions are often decided beyond public scrutiny within the confidentiality of cabinet.[18] During the 1960s and 1970s interest group involvement in decision making also tended to revolve around exclusive liberal corporatist agreements with peak industry and union groups (Holliday, 1993), with few possibilities for other sorts of groups to influence policy. Parliament, which through convention subjects government decision making to broader debate, in reality exerts little pressure upon governments that command a clear majority.

For interest groups outside of liberal-corporatist arrangements, opportunities for political access did eventually arise, though they were filtered through the bureaucratic system. In the 1970s a number of new institutional channels opened to the environmental movement. Most significant of these was the Department of the Environment, established in 1970. The Environment Department was an amalgamation of environmental, housing and local government portfolios—of which the environment was arguably the least important area[19]—but it did provide movement groups with an avenue of access to central government, however limited and uncertain. Movement groups were only occasionally invited for infrequent and perfunctory consultations with generally unreceptive development-oriented departments (Lowe and Goyder, 1983: 64–5). Unlike the situation in the United States, access was extended by custom rather than as a regulatory or legislative requirement.

Matters were little better beyond the administrative departments of government. Some environmental groups channelled energies towards quasi-autonomous government agencies like the Nature Conservancy Council and the Countryside Commission, which developed close relationships with conservation groups but lacked real political influence. Government advisory committees provided another institutional source of access. More important governmental actors such as the Standing Royal Commission on Environmental Pollution (established in 1971), a scientific body that provided independent assessments to the Government, remained off-limits to movement groups.

---

[18] From the 1970s increasing use was made of smaller, specialized cabinet committees to address complex policy issues. The terms of reference and membership of these cabinet committees were kept secret from the public on the grounds that to identify them would undermine collective responsibility (Hillyard and Percy-Smith, 1988: 54). The use of cabinet committees reached its zenith during the term of the Thatcher Government.

[19] Weale (1992: 15) notes that even 20 years later reforms to local government finance took precedence over the environmental aspects of the Department's portfolio.

These institutional access points, however unpromising when viewed in a comparative light, encouraged a moderate, accommodative response to environmental group lobbying. Lowe and Goyder (1983: 63) estimated that by the early 1980s 40 per cent of the environmental groups they surveyed had either formal or informal representation on official advisory committees. As access to the government bureaucracy was 'entirely by discretion and custom', environmental groups were expected to adhere 'to an unwritten code of moderate and responsible behaviour' (Lowe and Flynn, 1989: 270). Van Zwanenberg (1997: 194) points out that since 'participation in the civil domain is hampered by the absence of alternative routes of dissent . . . virtually the only way the environmental groups have been able to engage *formally* with the policy process is by being accepted as members of the various policy communities'. The charitable status of almost all these groups affected their structure and culture, requiring accountability through appointed office holders and discouraging overtly political or confrontational behaviour (McCormick, 1993: 278).

O'Riordan (1985: 117) describes the Environment Department and advisory committees as 'the two bulwarks of environmental administration . . . [which] act as buffers between the policy-making and decision-taking machinery and the watchdog interest groups . . . They also protect government from the necessity to be open because they have become intermediaries of accountability'. He further explains:

Whereas in many other countries this [growing environmental concern] led to the emergence of new and politically active environmental pressure groups, innovations in environmental law, and much greater active political participation, in Britain all these reactions were muted . . . The British response is to accommodate, to 'fudge and judge', but only to make marginal concession to established ways of doing things. (Ibid.)

The effect of these limited and ambiguous procedural openings was to downgrade and depoliticize environmental issues to the extent that they remained 'outside the mainstream of national politics for nearly two decades' (Grove-White, 1991: 15).

In the 1970s the British Government's response to environmental policy making was 'informal, accommodative and technocratic' in contrast to the 'formal, confrontational and legalistic' approaches adopted in some European countries, Germany being a prominent example (Lowe and Flynn, 1989: 257).[20] British environmental groups found little solace through legislative appeal, since the British judiciary has no formal separation of powers

---

[20] See also Lowe and Goyder (1983: 62). They argue that 'the general receptivity of the British political system to group activity, pervasive cultural pressures and fear of disrupting established relationships operate strongly to discourage militant and unorthodox approaches'.

from the legislature. Environmental court challenges in Britain were relatively rare, and in any case unlikely to prove successful—as was illustrated by the failure to prevent the M42 motorway construction in the Midlands in the 1970s (Tyme, 1978).

Radical environmental activism was therefore rarely a feature on the British political scene. During the 1970s there were brief episodes of direct action against highway construction and heavy road transport, as well as in a site occupation and demonstration to prevent the Torness nuclear power development (Rudig, 1994). In most cases though the combination of public inquiries, consultative bureaucratic agencies, and a moderate police response the government effectively managed environmental conflict. This may help to explain why the issue of nuclear power never galvanized a social movement of the sort seen in other European countries (the opposition of groups such as Friends of the Earth to nuclear energy notwithstanding).

Britain has been labelled 'exceptionalist' because of its lack of new social movement development in comparison to many other European nations (Rootes, 1992). Before the exclusionary Thatcher era, the state often took a moderate and accommodating stance in relation to environmental movement groups. Rootes (1995: 82) highlights a long-standing reluctance within the environment movement to pursue either activist tactics or participatory values, arguing that when activism has been used it has served 'tactical necessity rather than . . . [a] principled commitment to grass-roots democratic participation'. Chris Rose, formerly of Greenpeace, reflects on the limits of a tactical repertoire in Britain in comparison to Germany:

[Greenpeace's] big problem in this society is the fact that the use of direct action throws up many connundra and questions and difficulties to people as to whether or not they think this is a legitimate thing to do, that that becomes the issue sometimes instead of what it is they're trying to campaign about . . . if you went to Germany, say, direct action, street theatre and street politics is seen as a completely legitimate form of political expression . . . whereas here it seems totally alien in this culture . . . (Interview, 1999).

The inspiration for environmental activism in Britain during the 1970s came from organizations originating in North America. Greenpeace (since 1977), much as in Germany, adopted more radical tactics centring upon media-based activist campaigns and displayed a comparatively greater reluctance than other national environmental organizations to engage in governmental processes. As in Germany, Greenpeace UK from the mid-1980s favoured a hierarchical decision making structure rather than a participatory one, relying on 'supporters' rather than an active membership.[21] Friends of the Earth,

[21] In contrast Greenpeace London displayed more participatory, 'libertarian' values (Wall, 1999: 121).

which was established in Britain in 1971, was initially faithful to new social movement participatory values. It encouraged active involvement from the grassroots branch membership, and maintained a decentralized structure with a high degree of local autonomy (Byrne, 1997: 132–3). Its mission statement explicitly declares a commitment 'to increase public participation and democratic decision-making,' a commitment reflected in the organization's own consensual and non-hierarchical decision making processes (Byrne, 1997:133). The British Green Party advocates both post-material values and participatory organizational practices. Operating in an electoral system hostile to minor parties, the Green Party has been notably less pragmatic and instrumental than mainstream environmental organizations (we include here Greenpeace and FoE). To the mainstream groups it has been viewed as less relevant a player in environmental politics, though its successes in the late 1990s with the election of two members to the European Parliament and a representative to the Scottish Assembly enhanced its political influence.

This consistent failure to generate a high degree of social movement mobilization, especially in relation to the nuclear issue, remains something of a puzzle if we are correct in our claims about the exclusive aspects of the British state in the 1970s. Another potential source of social movement dissent, the peace movement, was defused by the Campaign for Nuclear Disarmament, founded in the 1950s, developing a close affiliation with the Labour Party. (This affiliation was retained in the 1970s, rather than any alignment with the weaker radical environmental fringe as represented for example by the Ecology Party—see Rootes, 1992: 184.)

In the 1970s most opportunities for interest group participation were found in informal consultative networks rather than, say, the formal institutional structures that facilitate pluralist inclusion in the United States or the committee system in Norway. Britain's mainstream environmental groups responded to these opportunities by cultivating relationships with government. Yet the closest that groups ever got to the levers of central government power was through their limited and uncertain access to the Department of Environment. It should be remembered that the environmental portfolio was marginal to the operations of this Department (despite its name). Thus access to the Department should not be mistaken for real access to the core activities of the state (as defined in terms of the five core imperatives listed in Chapter 1). From the perspective of the environmental movement (indeed, all movements), Britain until the 1970s was for the most part a passively exclusive state—though the picture is complicated somewhat by at least the appearance of passive inclusion, always on terms dictated by government. When it came to issues such as the construction of the motorway network, defence and national security, and nuclear energy, the movement had zero influence.

The political circumstances for the environment movement and other groups in civil society altered considerably following the election of the Thatcher Conservative Government in 1979. Non-producer sectional interests were delegitimated as participants in the policy making process. While the privileged access of corporate and professional groups (such as the British Medical Association, National Farmers' Union, and Confederation of British Industry) was retained (Holliday, 1993; Jordan and Richardson, 1987), trade unions were expelled from government and subjected to legislative attack. Thatcher's distinctive political style has been described as 'authoritarian populism'.[22] It was populist in that it capitalized upon public dissatisfaction with elements of a failing social democratic programme,[23] while the authoritarian impulse derived from the strong, centralized state control which was thought necessary to overcome opposition to the economic reform agenda (Gamble, 1988: 183). Given that the state's exclusion and oppression of movement groups occurred in conjunction with market liberal ideological reform, we describe the Thatcher Government's approach as 'authoritarian liberalism'.

Political access, already limited along lines we have discussed, became still more difficult for the environment movement. The Conservatives' efforts to promote business enterprise and to wind back state intervention reduced government involvement in the environmental policy area. As Robinson (1992: 177) explains, there was a clash between the environment movement's call for intervention and the Conservative agenda:

internationalism, so desperately needed to tackle the 'big' environmental issues, fell foul of nationalism; public spending, needed to tackle some environmental problems, gave way to a propensity to accumulate wealth privately . . . [and] the essential mechanisms of regulation and control were overtaken by a commitment to free market economics.

Leaked cabinet papers in the first year of the Thatcher government revealed intentions to 'reduce over-sensitivity to environmental considerations' (*Sunday Times*, 18 November 1979, cited in Lowe and Flynn, 1989: 261). Prior to 1988, Thatcher had met with leading environmental NGOs and environmental agency representatives on only one occasion. Thatcher had indicated her personal disdain for the environmental movement when she dismissed environmental issues as 'humdrum' in comparison with the excitement of fighting the Falklands War in 1982 (Robinson, 1992: 177). Along with the movement's demonstrated lack of capacity to destabilize the political economy, this

---

[22] See e.g. Hall and Jacques (1983); Jessop et al. (1988); and Gamble (1988).
[23] Wolfe (1991: 246) explains that in the wake of strikes throughout 1979 and 'a mix of excessive group representation and state concessions, the social democratic formula failed to foster public authority or prescribe effective economic management'.

dismissal perhaps explains why the movement did not immediately present itself as a target worthy of attack by her government. Yet by 1986 the movement had clearly raised Thatcher's ire, as she derided environmental organizations as part of an 'enemy within' (Porritt, 1997: 62). Consistent with this hardening of attitude, the market ideologue and anti-environmentalist Nicholas Ridley was appointed Secretary of the Environment in 1986. During the early 1980s the comparatively sympathetic William Waldegrave and Michael Heseltine had held the Environment portfolio—though Heseltine had engaged in active exclusion in taking the axe to the quangos (quasi-governmental organizations such as the Clean Air Council) that provided major routes of access to government for environmentalists (Flynn and Lowe, 1992: 13). In fact, throughout the years of Conservative government from 1979 to 1997 the Environment portfolio was with the exception of Ridley held by an individual willing to make an environmental case—perhaps most of all John Gummer, who assumed the portfolio in 1993. The problem was, however, that this individual—be it Waldegrave, Heseltine, Chris Patten, or Gummer—could never be any match for the hard-line market liberal discourse that dominated cabinet.

Ministerial sympathy notwithstanding, its shift away from regulation meant that the government in the 1980s disbanded many of the institutional points of access for environmental groups. Regulatory agencies were undermined through budget reductions, and advisory bodies such as the Clean Air Council and Noise Advisory Council were dismantled (Lowe and Flynn, 1989: 261, 264). Local government—often the primary point of contact for environmental and other community groups—was eroded by central budget cuts and a reassertion of central government power (Riddell, 1989: 177–8). Local government was further overridden following the creation of Urban Development Corporations and British Urban Development (Lowe and Flynn, 1989). The Greater London Council and six metropolitan county authorities were dissolved through legislation pressed quickly through parliament, to be replaced by non-elected joint boards which were more secretive and less accountable to citizens (Hillyard and Percy-Smith, 1988: 76). Development approval processes were streamlined to bypass traditional environmental consultative arrangements seen as unnecessary 'red tape'. A government White Paper entitled *Lifting the Burden*, for example, advocated the removal of onerous regulation and the need to 'accept a presumption in favour of development' in planning (cited in Blowers, 1987: 281). Developers benefited from the removal of regional and county planning authorities which had been more receptive to conservationists (Blowers, 1987: 284).[24]

---

[24] There was also a reduction of grants to voluntary groups during the transition of power from local government, as the Department of the Environment failed to make up for shortfalls in funding (Hillyard and Percy-Smith, 1988: 77).

Enterprise Zones, Simplified Planning Zones, and Special Development Orders were all introduced to encourage development.

In contrast with its 'hands off' ideology for the economy, the Thatcher Government was prescriptive and centralist in its approach to civil society. It sought to dismantle social democratic institutions through the imposition of market liberal philosophy and individualistic, material values. Thus, for example, the Greater London Council, which had provided a focus for opposition to Thatcherism and fostered environmental groups, was abolished.[25] Thatcher's authoritarian style left little room for challenge from those opposed to her government's market liberal agenda. There was little tolerance of political dissent: public debate and criticism of 'conviction' politics were dismissed, information about government activity was curtailed, and social democracy undermined by attacks on the welfare state and the legal status of trade union activity. Controversial policy decisions were more commonly made within secretive cabinet committees, which pre-empted (and foreclosed) debate even within cabinet (Hillyard and Percy-Smith, 1988: 54). Civil servants who divulged confidential government information were prosecuted. The security services were deployed to harass activists. For example, members of Friends of the Earth involved in making the case against nuclear power at the 1985 Sizewell B Public Inquiry were bugged by MI5, the counter-intelligence service (Lamb, 1996: 106). Reforms to the Official Secrets Act in 1989 claimed to enhance government openness, but there remained no public interest defence as justification for the release of documents. Parliamentary opposition in the form of the Labour Party was weak and divided. In fact the Labour Party arguably performed a very useful role for Thatcherism in this period by absorbing social movements into its ineffectual politics. As Rootes (1992: 185) points out, during its long term in opposition 'the Labour Party has loomed so large and has been so permeable that no radical oppositional movement could develop without being embroiled in its affairs'.[26]

Thatcherism redefined the relationship between people and state, recasting citizens as consumers and privileging individual over collective action. 'Active citizenship' meant individual responsibilities and obligations rather than rights and entitlements (Fyfe, 1995). The 1986 Public Order Act diminished freedom of political action by making protest organizers responsible for the actions of participants. As Fyfe (1995: 186) points out, there is no statutory right to assembly in Britain, so protest is only legal when no other law is broken. The Public Order Act broadened the definition of a breach of public

[25] The GLC provided grants to bodies such as the London Wildlife Trust and London Ecology Unit (Philip Lowe interview).

[26] This was more the case with the anti-nuclear movement than its environmental counterpart, as Labour was reluctant to embrace environmental ideas which appeared to threaten the materialist 'old politics' of the socialist left.

order as 'serious disruption to the life of the community', driving home the point that the rights of individuals to conduct (economic) affairs were more important than collective political expression in public spaces (Fyfe, 1995).

Under the Act, trade unions were denied the right to picket and groups had to provide police with a week's notice of a march, thus making spontaneous protests illegal (Gamble, 1988: 134–5; Hillyard and Percy-Smith, 1988: 260–1). Police used these powers for political purposes, such as establishing road blocks to prevent protesters from reaching peace demonstration sites outside Molesworth and Greenham Common air bases (Hillyard and Percy-Smith, 1988: 264). In 1983 Greenpeace had been fined £36,000 for breaking an injunction sought by British Nuclear Fuels Ltd. to prevent the organization interfering with a discharge pipeline from Sellafield nuclear facility into the Irish Sea. In 1987 Greenpeace activists were tried and convicted for placing a symbolic block in the end of the pipe.

While the conditions of association in civil society continued to decline, institutional access for moderate environmental groups improved markedly following Margaret Thatcher's famous speech to the Royal Society in September 1988. For the first time she acknowledged that action on global pollution was necessary and proclaimed for Britain a leading role in the global response. Thereafter the environment movement's relationship with the government improved significantly. The appointment of Chris Patten as Secretary of State for the Environment in place of Nicholas Ridley in July 1989 elevated the status of the environmental portfolio.

Patten was instrumental in developing a White Paper on the Environment, *This Common Inheritance* (1990) which in turn led to much greater funding of the environmental portfolio which, as a senior officer in the Environment Department reflected, had 'up until then . . . been small, a bit of a backwater . . . [and] run on a shoestring' (interview, 1999). However, Patten was unable to secure reform commitments for the White Paper from Treasury or the Ministries of Transport, Agriculture, and Energy (Flynn and Lowe, 1992: 33). Thus the *Financial* Times could criticize it as 'a compendium of muted decisions and hesitant intent' (26 September, 1990; cited in Flynn and Lowe, 1992: 33). Tom Burke, a former Director of the Green Alliance and Friends of the Earth, was chosen as Patten's Special Adviser, becoming the environmental movement's first advocate inside government. He advised a succession of Secretaries for the Environment until the end of Conservative government in 1997. Patten himself spoke in 1989 of the need to strengthen dialogue with 'constructive and well-meaning environmental groups' (speech to the Conservative Party Conference, quoted in Flynn and Lowe, 1992: 31), a sign that exclusion was due for reversal.

In the early 1990s it was, then, plausible to speak of 'The Greening of the Tories' (Flynn and Lowe, 1992). The marginalized 'wet' wing of the party had evidenced concern with the environment as an issue in the 1980s, but they had been thoroughly overridden by the market liberal 'dry' hegemony. Under the government of John Major, who took office in 1990, many of the new-found opportunities for political inclusion for movement groups revolved around the creation of sustainable development policies prior to the 1992 Rio Earth Summit. For the first time environmental representatives were recognized as legitimate participants in the environmental policy making community. Senior members of CPRE, FoE, RSPB, and WWF were actively involved in the government roundtable on sustainable development prior to the Earth Summit,[27] and NGOs were even taken to Rio as observers with the British delegation. In 1994 environmental NGOs, business, local government associations, and other interest groups were brought together in the UK Roundtable on Sustainable Development (Voisey and O'Riordan, 1997). A year later a Parliamentary Environmental Audit Committee was set up to promote sustainable development across government departments.

The increasing political access provided to movement groups corresponded with greater access to government information. Since the early 1990s the European Commission has required the British Government to report on its compliance with EC Directives and make information on environmental decisions publicly available (Lowe and Ward, 1998: 89). Beginning in the 1980s, the increasing importance of the European Community helped change British environmental politics. Groups were no longer reliant on 'discretionary access' to government (Lowe and Ward, 1998: 89). And if shut out of the domestic policy process, they could redirect activity to Europe, notable examples being the RSPB's lobbying for the Birds Directive and the CLEAR campaign's influence on the Lead in Petrol Directive (Long, 1998: 110).

These developments notwithstanding, the British state as it confronted the environmental movement retained substantial aspects of active exclusion in the early 1990s. The legal system remained capable of enforcing active exclusion. In the high-profile case of protests against a proposal to cut a motorway through Twyford Down near Winchester in 1992, Friends of the Earth withdrew their participation based on legal advice that they risked having their assets seized. Around the same time Greenpeace backed down on its plan to hold a protest concert on the Sellafield nuclear site after a legal injunction which again might have led to the group's assets being seized (Connelly and Smith, 2000: 82). At Twyford Down, activists without assets stepped into the gap. So environmental protest carried on, but in somewhat different form than before, and the state's actively exclusive aspect had a massive impact on

---

[27] WWF and FoE, the two major environmental organizations in Scotland, also became members of the Secretary of State for Scotland's Advisory Group on Sustainable Development (Rawcliffe, 1998: 88–9).

what sorts of groups could engage the fray. But activists without assets were then targeted by the Criminal Justice and Public Order Act of 1994, which criminalized kinds of protest that were until then either perfectly legal or at most subject only to civil action. The Act created the offences of 'aggravated trespass' and 'trespassory assembly', and specified increased police powers to control those intending, let alone engaging in, such actions. Police were allowed to prevent potential protesters from travelling within five miles of a demonstration site, putting the burden of proof on the individual to show his or her intentions (Smith, 1995: 23).

Though clearly an attack on the conditions of association and action in civil society, the Criminal Justice Act actually had the effect of inspiring a movement against it, joined by travellers, ravers, anti-hunting activists, and squatters, as well as environmentalists (Connelly and Smith, 2000: 85). That this counter-attack could happen perhaps indicated the limits of active exclusion in the 1990s. The decade saw a resurgence of environmental protest in Britain in the form of civil disobedience on the part of new direct action groups such as the British version of Earth First! (founded 1991), the Dongas Tribe, Reclaim the Streets, Road Alert!, All London Against the Roads Menace (later ALARM-UK), and disorganized activists (see Rootes, 1999). The early 1990s saw something like a 'dual state' that welcomed the most moderate environment groups into dialogue while taking the actively exclusionary hammer to any sort of action that stepped outside these carefully prescribed limits.

The Blair Labour Government elected in 1997 appointed Deputy Prime Minister John Prescott as Secretary for the Environment, a symbolic upgrade of the portfolio. Yet environmental concerns were not a priority for the government, though it undertook a number of initiatives designed to make government more transparent to the citizenry (even as it clung to older traditions of secrecy in other respects). For example, many government documents were now released on the internet. An Advisory Group on Openness in the Public Sector was set up, and in 1998 a 'People's Panel' of 5,000 randomly selected citizens was established, to be consulted regarding their views on contemporary issues and the provision of public services. A Sustainable Development Education Panel was also established in early 1998, including representatives from RSPB, WWF, and Forum for the Future. With the devolution of power to Scotland and Wales environmental groups became involved in regional sustainable development initiatives, and the Green Party secured representation in the new Scottish Assembly. The most prominent green initiative considered by the Blair government, a scaling back of road building and car use in favour of an emphasis on public transport, made limited headway given the Labour leadership's fear of alienating the car drivers of middle England seen as vital to Labour's electoral success (Paterson, 2000).

This picture of increasing access for the environmental movement in the 1990s should be qualified by noting continued exclusions, as highlighted by the road-building area, where groups such as CPRE and FOE made little headway. Beginning in 1992, this exclusion stimulated new activists groups such as ALARM-UK, Critical Mass, Reclaim the Streets, and Earth First!. These groups captured media attention, notably in terms of unconventional tactics such as tunnelling on construction sites, which put protesters' safety at risk, and iconic images of David and Goliath struggles. The tunneller 'Swampy' became a media star. Anti-roads groups joined a broader direct action movement, including opponents of the 1994 Criminal Justice Act, in wide-ranging critique of capitalism and globalization, highlighted in the 'Carnival Against Capital' on 18 June 1999. The direct action groups avoid formal organization, partly as a matter of ideology, but also to avoid an identifiable decision making body that would be vulnerable to prosecution and asset seizure. Word of mouth and the internet are used to mobilize actions by groups such as Reclaim the Streets.

In the 1980s and 1990s Green Party politics on the face of it was less important in the UK than in several other European countries. This difference is a direct consequence of Britain's first-past-the-post electoral system, which makes it virtually impossible for minority parties to secure parliamentary representation (unless their strength is regionally concentrated, as for the Scottish and Welsh nationalists). The Greens have never won a seat at Westminster; their poor electoral prospects have meant that the mainstream environmental groups found it easy to shun the Greens—and their radicalism (Rootes, 1992: 186). The British Greens actually hold the world record for percentage of votes in a nationwide election achieved by a green party; in the 1989 election to the European parliament, they secured 15 per cent of the vote. But the first-past-the-post system translated this 15 per cent into no seats. Under a new electoral system in 1999 the Greens secured two of the British seats in the European parliament with 6.3 per cent of the vote. However, their lack of parliamentary representation notwithstanding, the British Green Party and its precursor, the Ecology Party, did provide the main platform for a very visible and radical critique of established policies and practices, of a sort not engaged by the mainstream environmentalist groups.

In sum, Britain's trajectory involves passive exclusion until 1979, and active exclusion from 1979 to 1988. In 1988 active exclusion began to give way to passive inclusion; though elements of active exclusion lingered when it came to the more radical aspects of environmentalism and protest more generally, as exemplified by the Criminal Justice Act. These transformations in the character of the state are made possible by the extraordinary degree of centralization of power in the Westminster system; they are barely imaginable in, for example, the US political system.

Conclusion

To sum up:

- Norway has a highly institutionalized and conventional environmental movement, whose relation to the state has been very stable.
- The United States features a mainstream movement of interest groups oriented to the policy process, with interesting anomalies presented by the green fringe and environmental justice movement. Again, the relation of the movement to the state has been stable, though from the 1980s on sections of the movement pursued more radical strategies.
- In Germany environmentalism long took the form of a new social movement excluded from the state, though in the late 1990s inclusion in the state for a moderate form of the movement arrived on the agenda.
- Britain reveals the greatest change over time in the character of the state, its movement facing first passive exclusion, then active exclusion, then limited passive inclusion with residues of active exclusion along with renewed social movement activism.

The variety we have demonstrated across our four countries shows that the environmental movement and its relation to the state can take strikingly different forms. This form is also subject to change over time. Of course, this begs a number of questions. What are the advantages and disadvantages of each form when it comes to environmental interests? What about advantages and disadvantages from the point of view of democracy? Are the variations we see across place and time structurally determined, or do the strategic choices of state actors and movement groups make a difference? If strategic choice is important, how should it be guided? Is the relative balance of freedom and necessity changing over time? Does any such change reflect the relationship between movement aspirations and state imperatives? How confident can we be in generalizing about these sorts of issues?

In all these variations, sometimes inclusion may be beneficial, sometimes hazardous from the point of view of both movement interests and the democratic vitality of the polity. It is to this issue we now turn.

3

Co-optive or Effective Inclusion? Movement Aims and State Imperatives

In Chapter 1 we argued that the fate of social movements—their continued existence, their capacity to influence public policy, their likelihood of transformation into more conventional forms such as interest groups or even components of the state, and the pay-off of such transformations—depends crucially on the degree to which the defining interest of the movement can be linked to an established or emerging state imperative. Inclusion in the state can be advantageous in some instances and more destructive in others, from the point of view of both the movement's interests and the democratic vitality of the polity. In this chapter we will examine the issue from the point of view of movement interests, leaving democracy to Chapter 5. We will explain why the United States became an environmental policy pioneer in 1970, why it then lost that status amid energy crisis, and how energy crisis and associated economic and security concerns then excluded environmentalists from the core in all our countries. We will analyse the opportunities and difficulties that environmentalism has had in the ensuing decades in making connections to the state's core.

We have defined the core of the state in terms of organization and activity to meet a set of imperatives: notably, to keep order internally, compete internationally, raise revenues, secure economic growth by preventing disinvestment and capital flight, and legitimating the political economy. In Chapter 7 we will explore the prospects for an emerging conservation imperative, which obviously portends a more direct linkage for environmentalists. But such an imperative has not yet emerged, and for the purposes of our historical analysis can be kept in the background for the moment.

Some environmental issues bear little relation to core imperatives. Such issues might include protection of wilderness or habitat in areas with little or no extractive economic value; litter control; access to countryside; urban aesthetics; or pollution issues where the economic stakes are not high. It is quite conceivable that groups may have both access and influence on such issues while remaining without influence when it comes to the state's core. If a movement cannot connect its interest with a state imperative then that core is always going to remain off-limits. Given the importance of the core, we maintain that social movements of any historical significance can only be included in the state in benign fashion when the defining interest of the movement can be connected to an established or emerging state imperative. Inclusion in the state without this connection means co-optation.

In this chapter we will examine the history of our four countries (already introduced in general terms in Chapter 2) with a view to determining when inclusion has been effective, and when it has been co-optive. We should be alive to changes over time, for variation in the content and relative weight of imperatives, as well as changes in the content of environmental interests and their expression in movements, can influence the fortunes of groups engaging with the state. Identifying the imperatives that come into play at particular times allows us to look beyond specific governments and their issue alliances with movement groups to identify deeper connections and conflicts between the movement and the state's core. The benign inclusion of movement groups should reveal some intersection of movement goals with a state imperative, or at the very least, there should be no conflict between them.

Obviously, we only need to ask whether inclusion has been effective or co-optive where inclusion in the state has in fact occurred. For passively exclusive Germany and actively exclusive Britain in the 1979–88 period, we see inclusion only at the margins, and so the answer is pretty clear in advance—though to drive home this point, we will look briefly at this sort of marginal inclusion in the two countries. Where inclusion has occurred, we need to look for key episodes that reveal whether or not environmental interests have been allowed to enter the core. As we will see, there are many occasions when environmentalists have been badly bruised as a result of hitting the core and coming away empty-handed.

How the United States Became the Environmental Pioneer

Perhaps surprisingly, the prehistory of environmentalism contains an effective link between movement concerns and state imperatives. In the United States, concern with what we now call the environment is normally traced to two competing ideologies that emerged at the very beginning of the twentieth century, respectively, the wilderness preservationism of John Muir and the Conservation Movement associated with Gifford Pinchot (see e.g. Taylor, 1992; Andrews, 1999: 136–53.). 'Conservation' was explicitly justified in economic terms: the idea was to stop the wasteful and rapacious use of precious natural resources such as water, minerals, grazing land, and forests, and instead manage them scientifically in the service of maximum sustainable yield and so long-term economic well-being. There was a clear assimilation here to the state's economic imperative—so it is no surprise that Pinchot himself could occupy a key policy making position as head of the US Forest Service. Pinchot himself learnt his conservation ecology in Germany. With time, however, the Forest Service retreated from Pinchot's managerial ideals and conservation ethos to become the lapdog of timber corporations more concerned with quick profits to themselves than with long-term national economic prosperity.

When modern environmentalism arrived in the late 1960s it did so in a manner that directly challenged the core economic imperative of all states. Aside from the inchoate idealism and anti-materialism of the first Earth Day in 1970, the discourse of the movement was predominantly one of limits and survival. This discourse crystallized in the efforts of the Club of Rome, which sponsored the *Limits to Growth* study carried out by a team at Massachusetts Institute of Technology and published in 1972 (Meadows, Meadows, Randers, and Behren, 1972)—which soon sold over four million copies worldwide. The basic message of the book was that exponential human economic and population growth would eventually hit limits imposed by either the fixed quantity of the world's resources or the carrying capacity of the ecosphere. It is hard to imagine a more direct challenge to the state's economic imperative: indeed, the challenge appears very precisely in terms of the intersection of two lines on a graph, where rising economic activity hits the horizontal line of the limit. Given this challenge, it is perhaps understandable that in the end the limits discourse did not have the profound impact sought by its exponents on the policies of states—let alone on the identified need for co-ordinated global action. Not all environmentalists of this era may have sought implementation of the draconian social, economic, and political prescriptions of the survivalists. But the very success of the discourse of limits and survival in portraying the environment as a global problem did, paradoxically, keep environmentalists away from the core of the state, even when they were in fact pursuing more limited ends, or focusing only upon local or regional issues with no clear and direct connection to global resource scarcity and impending ecological collapse.

Yet if the early 1970s did not see any progress at all on the survivalists' global agenda, it did see a massive burst of environmental policy innovation. The United States was the trailblazer in setting up a federal Environmental Protection Agency to oversee pollution control, in passing a National Environmental Policy Act to force all government agencies to consider the environmental effects of their plans via the new device of environmental impact assessment, and in a host of legislative initiatives such as the Clean Air Act and Water Pollution Control Act. This comprehensive embrace of (moderate) environmentalism on the part of the federal government suggested that environmentalists were, at least for a while, welcomed into the core of the state. How could this happen, in the face of the evident conflict between early 1970s environmentalism's defining interest and the economic imperative of the state?

The answer is that environmentalism could be linked to the state's legitimation imperative. In the United States around 1970 the legitimacy of the state was under much greater threat than in Norway (which experienced no legitimation crisis at all) or Britain (where political unrest was confined largely to a few university campuses). The United States in the late 1960s saw a massive movement against the Vietnam War, a radicalization of sections of the civil rights movement for racial equality, which along with movements for women's liberation and radical movements aligned with an anti-system 'counter-culture'. To contain this destabilization, the Nixon administration sought to 'make peace' with the environmental movement, which appeared to be the least radical and threatening aspect of the counter-culture. Nixon and his associates had no personal commitments to environmental values.

By embracing this one movement the Nixon administration, enthusiastically supported by Congress, sought to regain legitimacy for the political economy without acceding to any more radical counter-cultural demands. Certainly, the environmental movement was not in itself a viable threat to the legitimacy of the state, but the vast outpouring of discontent manifest in the numerous movements of the time *was* widely perceived as a threat to the state and to democracy (Crozier, Huntington, and Watanuki, 1975). It is not that the imperatives of the state and those of the environmental movement were identical, but that the threat to legitimation from one direction—especially the anti-war and New Left movements—could be defused by inclusion from a different direction—environmentalism. By identifying his administration with the environmental cause, 'Nixon explicitly sought to distinguish between the antisystem New Left and counter-cultural activists and the consensus-seeking effort to fix the system' (Gottlieb, 1993: 109). In his State of the Union address in 1970, Nixon argued that the environment was an issue of 'common cause' which would allow the nation to move 'beyond factions.' Not only was Nixon trying to gain legitimacy in the face of pressure from anti-war and other activists, he hoped to pull the environment movement beyond the grasp of the New Left. In this the Nixon administration succeeded brilliantly.

The indirect connection between environmentalism and legitimacy imperatives in the United States was sufficient to bring about a raft of environmental legislation. This flurry of activity abated as soon as the legitimation threat waned. President Nixon's reluctant embrace of the environmental movement does however indicate how even a brief intersection between the environmental movement's agenda and state legitimacy imperatives can bring about significant and lasting policy change. The United States was the clear global leader in environmental policy in this era, and many other countries copied its policy initiatives, such as a national regulatory agency for pollution control, impact assessment, a council of environmental advisers (modelled on the US Council on Environmental Quality), and professional resource management bureaucracies. However, in almost every case the copy did not have the power of the original—precisely because nobody else faced the urgent legitimation threat that the United States had experienced.

The legitimacy of the German state was also under threat from an extra-parliamentary opposition, with 1968 the defining point for 'New Left' mobilization. But in Germany, there was no vocal environmental movement associated with the counter-culture until 1974–5 though a number of environmental policies, such as industrial point-source emissions regulations, preceded the movement's arrival. In the 1969 national election that brought a Social Democrat–Free Democrat coalition to power, SDP leader Willy Brandt did promise 'bluer skies over the Ruhr' and 'to venture more democracy', which appeased at least some members of the New Left.

Inclusion developed somewhat differently in this era in Norway. The early 1970s were in some ways a golden era of Norwegian environmentalism (Gundersen, 1996). The secretariat for the European Nature Conservation Year in 1970 was located in Norges Naturvernforbund, the Nature Conservation Society, and became an integral part of the Society. Beginning in 1971 the Society received increased government financial support. A comprehensive Nature Conservation Act was passed in 1970. The Society also played an important role in the formation of the Ministry of Environment in 1972. The coverage of environmental policy was extended to pollution issues with the creation in 1974 of the Norwegian Pollution Control Authority (Reitan 1997: 292), although the major confrontations over industrial, pollution came only a decade later. Revolving doors between voluntary groups and environmental administration began to operate (Gundersen, 1996: 58). Many environmentalists (but not the Conservation Society) participated in the successful 'no' campaign in the 1972 referendum on Norway's entry into the European Community, which helped to highlight conflicts between economic growth and environmental values (Berntsen, 1994: 157).

Energy, Environment and Economy in the 1970s

Any effective inclusion that did occur around 1970 in Norway and the United States was vitiated by the arrival of energy crisis in late 1973, with an echo in 1979. For Germany and the United Kingdom, energy crisis meant that the doors of the core of the state were locked still more firmly against environmentalism. Obviously energy supply is essential to economic growth. If that supply is disrupted, the economic imperative means that other concerns, including environmental ones, must yield as states seek reliable, cost-effective power sources to fuel production. In Germany, Britain, and the United States nuclear power was heralded as a cheap and unlimited energy source that would reduce economic pressures and alleviate OPEC's stranglehold on world oil supply. This commitment put these states on a collision course with environmentalists who vigorously opposed nuclear power because of its threat to human health, its reinforcement of economic centralization, and its fuel cycle's complicity with the manufacture of nuclear weapons. Oil, synthetic fuels, nuclear power, and hydro-power differed in their relative importance across our four countries in the 1970s, but in each case energy allied to economy came into conflict with environment. Let us see how the conflict played itself out in the four cases.

In the United States, the environmental impact assessment process mandated by the NEPA had stalled approval of the proposed Trans-Alaska Pipeline, which would bring oil from the vast fields newly discovered on the North Slope. In the context of the crisis of energy supply caused by the OPEC oil embargo of October 1973, Congress simply voted to exempt the pipeline form the NEPA process. In 1976, Jimmy Carter was elected to the Presidency with the backing of the environmental movement, promising a new approach to energy policy. The focus was to be on conservation and the development of renewable sources. However, once in office the Carter administration retreated from both conservation and renewable energy, devoting huge sums to the development of synthetic fuels (which subsequently proved a failure) and nuclear energy. Carter's change of course cannot be attributed solely to the force of the state's economic imperative: the political power exerted by industry also played a part. In his 1983 memoir, Carter lamented that 'the influence of the special interest lobbies is almost unbelievable, particularly from the automobile and oil industries' (1982: 99). But one reason these particular lobbies are so influential is that they can play the economic card: the industries they represent are crucial to the operation of the economy.

Germany responded to energy crisis in part by declaring an 'environmental moratorium' and through a programme to expand nuclear power. The nuclear issue in Germany also involved missiles under NATO command, though the latter aspect did not peak until the 1980s with the deployment of new cruise missiles on German soil. But be it nuclear power tied to the economic imperative or nuclear missiles linked to the security imperative, policy making on these issues was completely closed to oppositional voices. This era was of course the heyday of new social movements in Germany, foremost among which was the anti-nuclear movement, which in turn formed the nucleus of the emerging green movement. There was a clear clash between movement aims and state imperatives, resolved by complete separation between the two sides. The German environmental movement was excluded from the corporatist decision making structure, constituting, as Wagner (1994: 266) described it, 'an opposed totality'. It was a case not just of an area of the state proving resistant to environmentalist concerns, but the state as a whole refusing any point of entry, even into its periphery. In the United States exclusion was not as overt: movement groups were presented with opportunities for political inclusion, but of course risked co-option.

Britain too pursued an emphasis on nuclear power, but the government's response to the anti-nuclear lobby was more moderate than in many other European nations.[1] In the wake of the Three Mile Island controversy in the United States, the Thatcher Government was sensitive to public concerns over nuclear power and keen to avoid conflict with the movement. Leaked cabinet minutes revealed that the Government considered it 'might make more rapid progress towards its objective by a low profile approach, which avoided putting the Government in a position of confrontation with . . . protesters' (cited in O'Riordan, Kemp, and Purdue, 1988: 3). The result was symbolic inclusion in planning inquiries that served to reduce confrontation and to legitimize nuclear decisions. The first such inquiries had already taken place before Thatcher came to power, notably concerning expansion of the Windscale nuclear facilities in 1977. These processes were in many cases a *fait accompli* for developers.

At Windscale, objectors were required to bear the 'burden of proof' in their challenge against a government that was 'both promoter and judge' of nuclear development proposals (Wynne, 1982: 72). The Inquiry's terms of reference were restricted to the details of that particular development and therefore excluded the broader efficacy of Britain's nuclear policy (OECD, 1979: 66). The views of groups opposed to nuclear power development were consequently discounted in the Inquiry Chairman's report, which concluded in favour of the development. Because submissions were required to be technical and legalistic in nature, the lay public was effectively shut off from the debate.[2] Saward (1992: 89) surmised: 'the role of objecting value and expert groups was a more or less symbolic or token one . . . objectors were co-opted into advisory and informational roles at the inquiry but the origins, structure and processes of the inquiry militated against their views receiving a full and

---

[1] Anti-nuclear campaigning in Britain revolved around two related but operationally distinct concerns—the peace and disarmament activists, most notably represented in the Campaign for Nuclear Disarmament, and resistance to nuclear power development, which was co-ordinated by several mainstream environmental organizations, most notably Friends of the Earth, CPRE, and the Town and Country Planning Association.

[2] An OECD report on the Inquiry later concluded that its technical nature dissuaded active public involvement and 'served to depoliticise and decrease public debate' (OECD, 1979: 68).

considered hearing.' To Grove-White (1991: 18), the Inquiry ensured that 'these controversies were "contained" and prevented from becoming unmanageably upsetting in government's terms'.

At the 1983 Sizewell B Inquiry the Government had already made its commitment to nuclear power development clear through its financial investment in the proposal process, and the Central Electricity Generation Board had even ordered parts for Sizewell B before the Inquiry had concluded (O'Riordan, Kemp, and Purdue, 1988: 383). The nuclear development debate became further entwined with economic imperatives when the Thatcher Government entered into an ideologically driven conflict with coal mining unions in the early 1980s. Nuclear power was to provide alternative sources of power to coal, rendering the economy less vulnerable to coal miners' strikes.[3] Stung by its experience in the Windscale Inquiry, Friends of the Earth limited its participation to safety issues when it came to the Sizewell B Inquiry. Clearly the inquiries were acts of co-option designed to include objectors in the state but keep them away from the state's core.

Nuclear power did eventually fall from favour in Britain, but not due to the efforts of the anti-nuclear movement. Instead, the cost of nuclear power was eventually highlighted through the Conservatives' privatization programme. The reluctance of the corporate world to acquire nuclear power plants emphasized their true cost, and it is this that has led to the demise of Britain's nuclear development programme.

In Norway during the 1970s the Norwegian Water Resources and Energy Administration (NVE) had explored the development of nuclear facilities and undertook a public information campaign. Following public protest, the NVE withdrew from the public debate, and in 1975 parliament postponed plans for nuclear development . A government report in 1978 in favour of the nuclear option proved inconsequential (Andersen and Midttun, 1994: 246). Although Labour Party Prime Minister Trygve Bratteli was personally for nuclear energy (Bernsten, 1994: 246), no political parties were explicitly supportive of the nuclear agenda. Nuclear power development was not crucial to meet economic imperatives due to the abundance of hydro-electric power. Yet in Norway too there was conflict between the movement and the state's economic imperative, manifesting instead over hydro-electric power generation and the Alta Dam controversy in particular. In the Alta dispute the Norwegian Society for the Conservation of Nature was actually supported by the Ministry of the Environment in opposition to the development. There was also an intensity of public protest unusual by Norway's standards. But the Norwegian government approved the Alta development in 1978 and

---

[3] This position was outlined in leaked cabinet papers in October 1979 (O'Riordan, Kemp, and Purdue, 1988: 3).

reaffirmed its decision in 1980 (Andersen and Midttun, 1994: 256). Ultimately it was state economic imperatives that prevailed on the energy issue, with both environmental groups and the Ministry for the Environment excluded from core state decision making.

More Revealing Episodes

The energy issue as it arrived in the 1970s is instructive in that it brought into vivid relief the existence of an economic and security core that environmentalists included in the state could not enter. Let us now take a look at other episodes in the 1970s and beyond in each country that reveal the existence and boundaries of this core, and the relationship of environmentalism to it. These episodes in turn will help us to determine the relative weight of co-optive and genuine inclusion in each country over time.

The United States

In Chapter 2 we described the passively inclusive character of the United States political system and the numerous points of access for environmentalists and others that this system provides in all three branches of government. We also noted that the reality of access often falls short of the appearance. Requirements for government agencies to consider public input do not necessarily translate into acting upon that input. The system is often systematically skewed in favour of business. But can we be a bit more systematic about when inclusion is effective and when it is co-optive, especially as we approach the core of the state?

Inclusion was clearly effective around 1970 when environmentalism could be brought into alignment with the legitimation imperative, as we have already discussed. We saw too that matters changed very quickly with the arrival of energy crises in the 1970s, and eventually we see the Carter administration rapidly reversing direction on energy-related issues. There were other disappointments in store for environmentalists in the Carter years. On coming into office the President announced a 'hit list' of wasteful and environmentally destructive federally subsidized water projects, a list that had originally been developed by environmental organizations. On the face of it these pork barrel projects made no economic sense, and so scrapping them would have been consistent with the economic imperative. The political power exerted by the water lobby, and especially the arid states that would benefit from the projects, meant that Carter had to back down. The fact that the legitimation imperative was no longer in play for environmentalism meant that this back-down could not be resisted.

Environmentalists had far lower expectations of the Reagan and Bush the Elder administrations than they did of Carter, and received no pleasant surprises. Expectations were raised once again with the arrival of the Clinton administration in 1993. Environmentalists were appointed to government in the central agencies of Interior, Agriculture, and the EPA; they were also included in a variety of other areas of the administration, such as the State Department, Office of Management and Budget, and the National Security Council. Sympathetic appointees included Bruce Babbitt (former head of the League of Conservation Voters) as Secretary of the Interior and Carol Browner at EPA. Audubon lobbyist Brock Evans is famously quoted as saying 'I can't tell you how wonderful it is to walk down the hall in the White House or a government agency and be greeted by your first name' (quoted in Dowie, 1995: 179). Later in the Clinton years, before the 1996 election, the administration asked the major groups what it could do for the environment. Officials in these groups suggested saving the Headwaters Forest in Oregon, stopping the New World Mine on the border of Yellowstone National Park, cancelling a long-term contract with a logging company in Tongass National Forest in Alaska, and protecting a large swath of southern Utah. And so it was done, often with Clinton and Gore basking in the splendour of their achievements on the evening news, with beautiful backdrops now protected.

Yet these sorts of appointments and site-specific wilderness preservation belie a deeper problem in an administration that often featured access without influence. In 1992 Clinton campaigned on proposals to raise fuel economy standards in cars, and to elevate the EPA to cabinet level; he quickly backed down on both. He proposed a tax on energy use; Democratic friends of the oil and gas industry persuaded him to drop the idea. Babbitt at Interior proposed to protect rangelands by raising grazing fees on government lands closer to their true market value, and to reform antiquated and costly mining laws. But he was defeated on both grazing and mining. Babbitt also created a new National Biological Service; it was eviscerated within two years. Other setbacks included an Everglades 'protection' plan that allowed sugar growers to continue destructive pesticide use, support of bovine growth hormones in milk production, the first move towards a replacement of the Delaney Clause (specifying zero tolerance for carcinogens) with risk assessment, and the start-up of a hazardous waste incinerator which Clinton had campaigned against. All of these occurred in the first two years of the Clinton administration, while the Democrats still controlled Congress. As Andrews notes, 'Clinton's commitment quickly proved to be shallower and more symbolic than it had initially seemed' (1999: 363). When one lobbyist for a major environmental organization was asked if he saw examples of inclusion with no real effect, he simply responded 'constantly'. One director of a major environmental organization, one of the most enthusiastic co-operators, saw this lack of follow-through: 'I feel definitely that our voice is heard . . . but clearly politics plays a big role in Washington life and what people tell you they would like to do, they often don't do' (interview, 1999).

One clear example of co-option came with the environmental justice movement's success in getting the Environmental Protection Agency to establish a National Environmental Justice Advisory Committee (NEJAC). Luke Cole, who served for four years on the committee, calls the NEJAC 'a kind of federally sanctioned, formal mechanism for offering advice to EPA, which they generally don't pay attention to'. Cole reflects that

it is not in my emotional or psychological interest to have to acknowledge that four years of my life has basically been a waste of time . . . but I often feel, what are we doing here? This agency has no interest in changing its policies and even when it does have an interest in changing policies, it has no political will to do so . . . I guess the bottom line is getting together in a room and talking about what the agency should do is all very well and good, but there is no power in it . . . And unless there is some power to actually change agency policy, I don't think it's going to change. (Interview 1999)

When environmental justice proposals and positions ran into a conflict with economic imperatives, the result was always that the imperatives prevailed— even within the EPA, let alone beyond it.

A similar story arises in connection with the President's Council on Sustainable Development (PCSD) established in 1993. Six years of work of the PCSD culminated in a 'National Town Meeting for a Sustainable America' and a final report to President Clinton in May 1999. The commission recommended over 140 actions that would, it claimed, 'improve our economy, protect our environment, and improve our quality of life' (PCSD, 1999). The recommendations addressed issues such as suburban sprawl, climate change, urban renewal, and corporate environmental responsibility, but they remained only suggestions. One of the members of the commission was disappointed that 'very few of the overall policy recommendations that would have taken presidential and/or congressional action have been moved ahead' (interview 1999). Six years of deliberation were ignored when it came to policy adoption. The recommendations, though developed in concert with business interests, were simply perceived as a threat to the economic growth imperative of the administration and the state—illustrating, in addition, the degree to which a discourse of ecological modernization was resisted in the United States.

Environmentalists fared little better when it came to policy making on the North American Free Trade Agreement (NAFTA) in the early 1990s, which obviously affected the core economic imperative. The initial proposal for the Agreement had no environmental provisions. The movement then split on the merits of NAFTA. The Clinton administration and some of the major groups, led by the NRDC, worked out environmental 'side agreements'. These groups then tried to persuade other major groups to support NAFTA.[4] Moreover, they directed attacks on environmentalist opponents of the Agreement. John Adams once claimed that he and the NRDC 'broke the back of the environmental opposition to NAFTA' (quoted in Dowie, 1995: 188). Whether or not the NAFTA bargain was a good one for environmentalists is a complex question, though the side agreements saw little in the way of implementation. Adams himself later had second thoughts: 'NRDC supported NAFTA, but there were a lot of people who ... were upset about that and I understand their position. To this day I'm not certain who was right even though I certainly am sure that we never got the promised environmental benefits from the NAFTA [side] agreements' (interview, 1999).

The security imperative has always defined an area of the state immune to environmentalist influence. For example, in the 1980s, proposals to install a vast 'racetrack' to move mobile MX missiles around the arid West promised environmental destruction on a scale unprecedented in this region. While the proposal eventually died when its financial cost became hard to justify amid a waning Cold War, this project was off-limits to environmentalist objection. Environmentalists have also been continually frustrated by their inability to influence policy that might ameliorate environmental abuses associated with military nuclear installations.

Another issue where the security imperative has blocked environmental demands concerns right-to-know legislation in the United States. Under the 1990 Clean Air Act, industrial plants were required to provide the EPA with data on the amount and type of chemicals stored on site, worst-case accident scenarios, and emergency response plans for such accidents. The EPA had planned to make this information available to the public via the internet. The movement pointed out that its ability to publicize such information, such as the existing EPA toxic release inventory, has led to cuts in industrial emissions. However, the chemical industry raised national security concerns that were then echoed by the FBI and Congressional opponents of right-to-know. The industry claimed that 'release of this worst-case-scenario data in an uncontrolled manner would provide targeting tools and new ideas for criminals and terrorists' (Hulse, 1999). Based on this argument, in 1999 Congress passed a law suspending release of this information. Environmentalists argued that 'national security' is invoked to avoid bad publicity for industry, not to thwart terrorists.

The security imperative also takes effect in indirect fashion when it comes to environmental issues with an international dimension. The United States

---

[4] The original supporters included the National Wildlife Federation, the Nature Conservancy, and the NRDC; these groups successfully lobbied Conservation International, the EDF, Audubon, and the World Wildlife Fund to form the Environmental Coalition for NAFTA.

has always been a reluctant participant in international environment agreements, with the Senate in particular often unwilling to ratify international treaties. In the Reagan years of the 1980s, and again with the George W. Bush presidency beginning in 2001, the White House too took a hostile line. The Reagan administration attitude was highlighted by US withdrawal from the Law of the Sea agreement, the George W. Bush administration by its rejection of enforcement protocols on biological weapons, abdication of a voluntary nuclear test ban, and most famously its renunciation of the Kyoto agreements on greenhouse gases (though the public justification of the latter was in terms of the economic imperative). This hostility can be explained in part by the way key policy makers in the United States interpret the security imperative, which makes them reluctant to enter into multilateral agreements for fear of compromising US sovereignty.

On the face of it, the history of inclusion in United States environmental policy since the halcyon days of effectiveness in the early 1970s reveals a complex story, with both gains and losses on particular issues, and periods of advance and retreat in response to the changing partisan configuration of the presidency and Congress. There is no denying environmentalist successes, especially when it comes to protecting particular slices of wilderness, or obstructing particular noxious activities such as an incinerator or a toxic waste site. Even when it comes to issues such as NAFTA, with high economic stakes, some environmentalist influence in policy making is evident. So is there a core to the state resistant to environmentalist influence, guaranteeing that as an issue impinges on the core, inclusion cannot be genuine?

We can be sure that such a core exists in relation to two kinds of issues. The first covers dramatic short-term economic crisis, as occasioned by the energy shocks of the 1970s. The second covers the external security imperative; environmentalists are systematically excluded from this part of the state. Our historical survey suggests that the core does extend beyond these two issues, for example to guarantee frustration of the environmental justice agenda as it threatens systemic change (as opposed to successful site-specific actions). But precisely where the outer boundary of this core lies is much less clear in the United States than in our other three countries—reflecting perhaps the sheer complexity and inconsistency of the US political system.

The United Kingdom

Britain until 1988 is clearly not as inclusive as the United States. Prior to 1979, there were some limited opportunities for consultation for moderate groups, but it is hard to see these in terms of anything other than letting environmentalists have their say, with little influence on major decisions. From 1979 to 1988 the more systematic exclusion of environmentalists was occasionally accompanied by the illusion of access, but there was ultimately no influence on the content of policy allowed, let alone access to the core of the state. Aside from the blatantly co-optive nuclear inquiries we have mentioned, the case of acid rain illustrates the illusion of access. Acid rain was one of the most symbolically important environmental issues of the 1980s. In the early 1980s, organizations concerned about acid rain such as Green Alliance, Friends of the Earth, and the Council for the Preservation of Rural England had relatively good access to the Environment Minister William Waldegrave and his Chief Scientist Martin Holdgate. Yet this access did not translate into making any impression on government more generally, or on the content of public policy (Hajer, 1995: 166). The acid rain issue was framed within an exclusionary scientific discourse in which many environmental movement claims were dismissed as 'unsound science' in the absence of absolute proof about chains of causality from acidic emissions to ecological damage. Hajer (1995: 142) argues that in the governmental response to acid rain during the early 1980s 'the dominant role for science was legitimized as a way of keeping pollution control out of the sphere of corporatism and pressure-group activity' (though we would note that Britain actually featured very little corporatism in the relevant time period).

A similar story can be found in regard to countryside conservation, traditionally the area of greatest concern to British environmental organizations, some of which had developed consultative relationships with government ministries and agencies. Blowers (1987: 279) described Thatcher's conservation policy as 'a mixture of ideology and pragmatism'. When there was no direct conflict with state imperatives and Thatcher's 'conviction' politics, conservation groups did have some success. Conservation areas and national parks were set aside and enhanced (Lowe and Flynn, 1989: 263), while the CPRE in particular was successful in lobbying for the protection of green belts and hedgerows. Yet when countryside issues appeared to conflict with economic concerns the countryside lobby was invariably overruled. When protection of Sites of Special Scientific Interest was opposed by the agricultural lobby, the protection was weakened or lost (McCormick, 1991).[5]

In the 1980s the more conventional conservation organizations were placed on the back foot as traditional consultative channels withered. Following the 1981 Wildlife and Countryside Act that weakened protection of SSSIs, movement opposition was continued through a Wildlife and Countryside

---

[5] The environmental movement was keen to prevent the loss of Sites of Special Scientific Interest (SSSI) and formed the broad network Wildlife Link. Environmental groups had some success in influencing the debate in the House of Lords, though this had little effect on legislation (Ward and Samways, 1992: 125).

Campaign.[6] Peaceful local community protests were organized against threats to particular Sites of Special Scientific Interest. The campaign was marked by occasional successes, but perhaps more importantly from a national perspective, it attracted significant media attention which ensured the issue was highly politicized (Lamb, 1996: 110–16).

After 1988, the British state looked to become more inclusive to environmentalists. But was there more to this development than mere appearance? In the wake of the 1987 Brundtland Report and leading up to the 1992 Earth Summit and beyond, there was a flurry of governmental activity on sustainable development, which brought environmental groups such as RSPB, CPRE, WWF, and FoE into round-tables and dialogue with government departments (Greenpeace maintained its distance). On the face of it, sustainable development ought to provide a point of intersection between environmental interests and economic growth, for the whole idea assumes that growth and conservation can be reconciled. Yet this dialogue had little policy impact; it certainly produced nothing like the reorientation of the whole of government around sustainability concerns that the discourse seemed to imply.[7] Robin Grove-White acknowledges that in the wake of the 1992 Rio Summit 'there are no end of stakeholder fora', although 'the danger with these is always that they become ways of just having your teeth drawn' (interview, 1999).

Perhaps the prospects here were limited in advance by the astonishing claim by the government in 1988 that its policies were already consistent with the idea of sustainable development (Department of the Environment, 1988). The result was largely symbolic; talk of sustainable development never had any impact on economic or energy policies (though the nuclear energy issue was dormant in the 1990s). Certainly issues of national security remained off-limits, though there were few controversies in the 1990s that clarified this.

One important episode occurred in 1995 with the case of the Brent Spar, a redundant oil storage platform in the British sector of the North Sea. Originally the Shell Corporation wanted to dump the platform in deep water in the North Atlantic. A campaign led by Greenpeace, involving a Europe-wide boycott of Shell as well as occupation of the platform, eventually led to Shell backing down and disposing the platform on land in Norway. The

[6] This campaign was led by two environmentalists who were to exert an increasingly influential role within the movement—Friends of the Earth's Charles Secrett (later Director) and Chris Rose (formerly of the British Association for Nature Conservation, then Friends of the Earth and Greenpeace).

[7] Disappointing results from dialogue on sustainable development are not unique to Britain. Australia's National Strategy for Ecologically Sustainable Development, launched with great fanfare by the Prime Minister in the early 1990s and with extensive environmental organization involvement, culminated in a vague outcome and no mechanism for policy compliance (Downes, 1998).

Major government had been prepared to use force to dislodge the protesters from the platform, and was angry when Shell conceded. Perhaps part of the explanation for this anger is that Greenpeace was contesting key aspects of the state's prerogatives in upholding core imperatives, relating to both the sanctity of private property (itself instrumental to the economic imperative) and internal order. Yet this episode is not quite conclusive because it does not illustrate a group whose access to government ended at a sign that said 'state's core imperatives'—Greenpeace never sought access to government through conventional channels in this case. However, it is pretty clear what would have happened if they had pursued this route: they would have gotten nowhere.

Perhaps a better example of a resistant core of the state arises in connection with road building, where the inability of environmental movement groups to move the state's economic imperative was long apparent. During the 1970s predominantly local groups, but also national environmental organizations like FoE and CPRE, made submission to inquiries to oppose road development plans. A chief difficulty for the anti-roads lobby was that the state refused to set out a national roads policy. The Department of Transport and its Minister had a great degree of latitude, pre-empting parliamentary discussion on the road development issue (Tyme, 1978). Environmental groups were therefore unable to penetrate the state. In their frustration with the narrow parameters of the transport inquiries, groups engaged in disruptive protests of local inquiries, in some cases leading to their indefinite adjournment (Wall, 1999: 31). In the 1980s the roads issue re-emerged under a Conservative Thatcher Government strongly committed to a road development programme to help modernize the British economy. The connection between road development and state economic imperatives was reinforced with Thatcher's ideological struggle against the trade unions, as coal transportation was redirected from the unionized rail network to roads (Wall, 1999: 133). The link with economic imperatives was nowhere better illustrated than in the Government's 1989 White Paper *Roads for Prosperity*. Plans were developed to accommodate a doubling of road traffic within the next 35 years, while public transport and the rail system received cuts in government subsidy and bus services were privatized (Ward and Samways, 1992: 122).

Even with the softening of Tory environmental attitudes in the early 1990s, environmental groups were denied any influence at all on roads issues, be it in the form of lobbying, consultation, or legal action. As Robinson (2000: 199–200) argues, 'the legacy of exclusion from the formal policy process led the direct action movement to search out alternative policy areas (such as the media and construction sites) in order to influence the policy agenda and overcome the institutional bias of the road lobby'. The case of Twyford Down in 1992 was a turning point, as it showed that state actors themselves were prepared to subvert due process in order to get a motorway built. Matters ought to have changed with the election of a Labour government in 1997 whose rhetoric at least promised reduced emphasis on the car. But whether for fear of the votes of the car owners of middle England or fear of the economic consequences of eroding what Margaret Thatcher once called 'the great car economy', Labour delivered little.

In short: the environmental history of the United Kingdom both before and after the Thatcher era is one where inclusion in the state produces very few pay-offs. At most it produces marginal gains, at worst it involves blatant co-optation, be it in public inquiries with preordained conclusions or consultative processes that produce no effect on policy. As a liberal state in a capitalist economy, the United Kingdom is subject to the same set of imperatives as the United States (though given its lack of superpower status, the security imperative plays out slightly differently). Yet the zone of policy making off-limits to real environmentalist influence on the part of those included is much larger in the United Kingdom. Some of this zone is surely contingent on governmental traditions that require scientific proof of a hazard before acting, as well as traditions of secrecy that extend (for example) to secret negotiations between government and industry on required levels of pollution control. So the size of the zone is not completely determined by state imperatives; but the core of that zone is certainly secured by these imperatives.

Germany

Given that exclusion from government has been the norm in Germany, there is less to say about whether inclusion has been co-optive or effective, because there has traditionally been less in the way of inclusion of the environmental movement to begin with than in our other three countries. The acid test of exclusion from the core of the state as we have defined it (in terms of organization to secure five key imperatives) becomes less in need of confirmation, as it follows necessarily from exclusion from government. Of course, matters change in the 1990s, and we will examine these developments in due course (especially in Chapter 7). But there were a few attempts prior to the 1990s to ameliorate the exclusive aspects of the German state when it comes to environmental affairs, so let us examine these.

In corporatist systems, access to the public bureaucracy is more important for interest groups than access to parliament (Sebaldt, 1997). Section 29 of the Environmental Protection Act of 1976 extends to certain environmental NGOs the right to participate in administrative planning processes. Some twenty years later, public officials responsible for environmental policy routinely co-operated with demonstrably competent environmental groups. As actually practised, however, environmental organization participation in public administration has severe shortcomings (Hengsbach et al., 1996; Weiger, 1987). First, environmental groups are not consulted in the early stages of planning and so cannot influence preliminary decisions. A German League for Nature Conservation and Environmental Protection (DNR) official complains that agencies do not notify them of proposals until critical decisions have been made. By the time groups are notified, the basic parameters of the proposal have been set in stone so that little can be done to change them (Inden-Heinrich, interview, 1999). According to a 1987 study of environmental group objections to planning proposals in North Rhine-Westphalia, the public bureaucracy completely ignored 41 per cent of objections, mostly ignored 46 per cent, and modified or dropped proposals in response to only 7 percent (cited in Cornelsen, 1991: 58). When groups do manage to delay planning decisions late in the game, they are often accused of obstructionism.

Martin Jänicke (1996*b*) identifies four stages in the history of modern German environmental policy. Following initial efforts by the state to subject industry to environmental regulation (1969–74), an increasingly vocal environmental movement pressured a recalcitrant state to keep its promises (1974–82). During the next stage, the state and industry pursued co-operative solutions to environmental problems under the watchful eye of the environmental movement and the media (1982–7). Prompted in part by the Chernobyl nuclear disaster, the state, industry, and environmental advocacy organizations then increasingly entered tripartite co-operative ventures, and passive exclusion was lessened. In addition, an emergent sector of 'green' firms and eco-consultancies nudged industry as a whole towards the goal of ecological modernization (1987–94), which we will discuss in Chapter 7. Jänicke's historical survey shows that environmental issues—though not always solutions—have had a secure place on Germany's political agenda since the 1980s (see also Brand, 1999).

The Ministry for Environment, Nature Conservation, and Nuclear Safety created in 1986 (Pehle, 1998; Weinzierl, 1993) offered environmentalists new opportunities for inclusion in the public bureaucracy, but only within this Ministry. Corporatist policy networks in other ministries have remained off limits to environmentalists, who had no reason to think such exclusionary practices were going to change quickly given the political culture's low tolerance for conflict and the pervasive friend-or-foe rhetoric of political elites (Kitschelt, 1989: 34). Cabinet departments friendly to business interests, such as economics and agriculture, are unresponsive to environmentalist demands, suggesting that key areas of the state are off-limits to even the semblance of genuine environmentalist participation (see the study of the role of environmental groups in German politics and society published by the Experts' Council on Environmental Issues; Hengsbach et al., 1996). Outside technical areas of environmental policy, 'environmental corporatism' remains an exercise in endless rounds of 'consensus talks' and 'round-tables' that lack the power to make decisions (Brendle, interview, 1999).

A major problem for environmental groups is that inclusion in official environmental policy consultations, whether in the legislature or the bureaucracy, often brought little or no tangible result. Activists blame their lack of influence on the structural superiority of business described above as well as on their own relative lack of resources. Government officials usually favour the views of business interests, even though particular officials may well show a sincere interest in what group representatives bring to the table. The challenge, then, is not so much that groups with access to public officials will be tempted to resort to self-censorship, but to ensure that their positions will not be ignored.

DNR, BUND, NABU, and WWF all view lobbying government officials as part of their mission. They all realize, however, that some of the means of participation available to them lack any real power. At the federal level, group participation occurs in legislative hearings and, at the ministerial level, in the Ministry of Environment and, to a lesser extent, the Ministry of Research. Environmentalists interviewed for this project distinguish between NGO participation in environmental policy on the one hand and lack of such participation in other policy fields. Environmental groups have meaningful opportunities for influence in environmental policy because public officials who are active in this policy field accept the legitimacy of environmental concerns. Patterns of passive exclusion still tend to prevail in policy areas dominated by powerful economic interests (Hermann, interview, 1999).

The Ministry for Environment, Nature Conservation, and Nuclear Safety is one of the less powerful cabinet ministries (Dirschauer, interview, 1999). Officials from more influential ministries—finance, economics, transport—tend to think of the environment ministry as a place where environmentalists may safely gather without disturbing the serious business of running the country's economy and maintaining its industrial and transport infrastructure. Gaining access to these 'classic' government departments that cover much of the core of the state (as defined in terms of the basic set of five imperatives) has been notoriously difficult for environmental groups, and here patterns of passive exclusion remain in place. On this view, the environment minister's ability to influence public policy differs from that of groups in degree not in kind. The establishment of this ministry has therefore been something of a double-edged sword for environmentalists. On the one hand, environmental groups have welcomed its creation insofar as its existence signals official recognition of the legitimacy of environmental concerns. On the other hand, they are frustrated by its lack of power within the cabinet and by the dearth of initiatives aimed at encouraging ecologically motivated co-operation among all relevant cabinet departments. In this sense, the Environment Ministry acts as a classic co-optive device; and we find little better in the other formal channels for environmentalist influence that we have examined. This picture is consistent with a state firmly under the sway of economic and security imperatives, though the latter soon faded after the fall of the Berlin Wall in 1989.

Now, all this changed somewhat with the Green entry into government in 1998, especially given that the Cold War was long gone. And the rise of ecological modernization in Germany changes the configuration of state imperatives in a way that poses fewer necessary barriers to movement engagement with the state; but we will reserve discussion of that until Chapter 7.

Norway

If we are correct in characterizing Norway as an actively inclusive state, then environmentalists ought to have found it easier to gain real access and influence in the core of the state (defined in terms of the five imperatives) than in our other three countries. While true enough, this comparatively high access remains a matter of degree. In Chapter 2 we described two cases, Mardøla and Alta, culminating in 1970 and 1980 respectively, which demonstrate the power of the 'hydro-power complex' at the core of the Norwegian state. The environmental movement had in 1980 failed to stop the Alta Dam in the face of what seemed like good odds: the need for the energy supplied by the dam was questionable, and its economic benefit disputable when set against the destruction of valuable natural assets. Moreover, Alta for the first time led to mobilization on behalf of the interests of the indigenous Sami people (Thuen, 1995: 23 f.).[8] But this failure was not just one of social movement protest; it was also a failure of more conventional action. What it suggests is that there were areas of the state that were immune to environmentalist influence as a result of the economic imperative prevailing.

Frode Gundersen's (1996) negative evaluation of Norwegian environmentalism in the 1980s is based partly on the Alta outcome, partly on the simultaneous failure of environmental groups to prevent offshore drilling north of a symbolically important line at 62° N; again, the economic imperative prevailed. Whether this feature of the Norwegian state holds after the 1980s is more debatable; since Alta, hydro-electric issues have almost disappeared as an arena for political conflict. There have been few large-scale proposals, and smaller issues concerning (say) building power plants have been dealt with in the bureaucracy, where the conflict between nature and economic progress has been cast in more technical terms.

---

[8] The Sami people gained more from the dispute than did environmentalists. The Alta dispute forced the Labour cabinet to establish a public commission to investigate the rights of the Sami people, which led to a new paragraph in the constitution and a Sami parliament.

We can point to no acid tests since the Alta Dam case that reveal a lack of genuine inclusion. The hydro-power issue, which might have demonstrated such a lack, was depoliticized as no more large projects were proposed; and in the late 1990s some smaller proposals were dropped after environmentalist opposition. In comparison to the United States, Germany, and the United Kingdom, this inclusion in the state is facilitated to the extent that nuclear and defence issues have never been encountered by the environmental movement, such that the external security imperative does not come into play, nor does the economic imperative as connected to nuclear energy.

However, though while Norway since 1980 reveals none of the sorts of episodes that have bruised included environmentalists in our other three states, the real story here may be, as for Sherlock Holmes, the strange story of the dog in the night—the strange story being of course that the dog didn't bark. Norwegian environmentalists have perhaps barked too little, and so, like Sherlock Holmes, we must investigate the reasons. To an outside observer, there appear to be issues where environmentalists should have barked—Norway's involvement in commercial whaling being the most obvious of these. So let us take a closer look at the terms on which environmentalists have been included in Norway.

The major groups are, as we pointed out in Chapter 2, heavily reliant on government funding. We will address the implications of the system of grants for the stances taken by groups, their internal dynamics, and the civil society they help constitute at greater length in Chapters 4 and 5. For the moment, it is more important to look at the other side of inclusion: participation in the committee system that is at the heart of Norway's expansive corporatism.

Committees involve interest group representatives, politicians, and administrators; they can be permanent or temporary. Permanent committees have often been used as the governing body of an institution, such as the Management Board for fisheries. Temporary committees are given a particular task and are charged with producing a public report, the basis for the preparation of proposals to parliament. Interest group membership on temporary committees can range from 50 to 70 per cent (Nordby, 1994: 85). The number of temporary committees is an indicator of the government's reforming zeal (Nordby, 1994: 81 ff.). This number peaked at 229 in 1976, but by 1994 had declined to 62.

The largest number of committees could once be found in the traditional corporatist fields of industry, trade, energy, agriculture, and fisheries. However, since 1945 the share of this group has declined in relation to the welfare state ministries of education, science, culture, health, and welfare. Very few committees have been created under the Ministry of the Environment since its establishment in 1972. In 1979 Environment accounted for 1.8 per cent of Norway's permanent committees, in 1989 for 2.8 per cent

(Nordby, 1994: 86). In 1997–8, Environment had only four of the permanent and temporary councils. Only the Office of the Prime Minister had fewer committees, while the Ministry of Fisheries had nineteen and seventeen committees in these two years. This comparison suggests that the Ministry of the Environment has not adopted the traditional Norwegian practice of using committees as a means to govern. However, the Environment Ministry is very accessible to environmental group leaders; many officials within the Ministry themselves come from the groups, and there is substantial contact between the administrative staffs of groups and Ministry. The Minister for the Environment in the 1997–2000 Conservative–Liberal Bondevik cabinet came from the Nature Conservation Society, and the State Secretary for the Environment in the subsequent Social-Democratic Stoltenberg cabinet had a long career in the Norwegian Association for Hunters and Anglers.

Moreover, environmental groups have been included on committees in other policy sectors. For example, in 1988 the Norwegian Society for the Conservation of Nature sought a seat on the Norwegian Management Board for fisheries, arguing that the Brundtland report meant that NGOs promoting conservation and sustainability should participate in resource decisions. Despite resistance from a sectoral corporatist structure geared to the short-term interests of the industry, the Fisheries Minister accepted environmental criteria and designated a member of the Directorate for the Management of Natural Resources as a 'green' member of the Board. A crisis in the cod fishery in 1989 highlighted problems in the existing regime, and the Nature Conservation Society was then allowed to send an observer to board meetings (over the objections of fishers). However, this representative is excluded when important questions such as negotiation between Russia and Norway for total allowable catch in joint fisheries is determined (Hernes and Mikalsen, 1999).

On another highly significant issue, a (temporary) Green Tax Committee was set up in 1989, charged with making recommendations on a greener tax system, including a carbon tax on fossil fuel burning. This committee featured deep divisions that were not reconciled in its 1992 report. The representative of the Ministry of Finance tried to delay the report so that a government decision on gas-fuelled power plants could be made before it became public that the committee was recommending that the carbon tax also be applied to natural gas. The minority of the committee that represented industry and the trade unions opposed a carbon tax on the grounds it would make Norwegian industry less economically competitive (NOU, 1996: 77 ff.). Still, this faction did not overcome an alliance of representatives from research institutions and the Nature Conservation Society, and the committee's report pointed to the efficiency of green taxes and their capacity to reconcile economic and environmental vales (a key aspect of ecological modernization, which we will discuss in

Chapter 7). Green taxes, including a limited carbon tax, began to be implemented in 1991, despite continuing resistance from industry, especially the oil industry. But some energy-intensive industries managed to secure exemptions for themselves from the carbon tax (Kasa, 2000). The green taxes issue shows that, despite industry reluctance, the balance of forces within the state perceived that there was no conflict between environmental protection as promoted by such taxes and the core economic imperative of the state.

The pervasive danger, of which environmental groups are aware, is that groups will end up hostage to their desire to participate in policy formation. The fisheries case shows that environmentalists were kept away from the state's economic core. However, the case of green taxes reveals a very different story, in which environmentalists managed to enter the core of the state, even if the content of policy (especially given industry resistance in implementation) fell short of their target. A comparison with Germany puts the Norwegian process of committees in a more positive light. In Germany, consultation with groups is confined to an Environment Ministry which is itself excluded from the most important decisions. In Norway, environmental groups have managed to escape such confinement, and make their presence felt in committees on the most economically and environmentally important issues.

Thus it is easy to conclude that inclusion in the state has been less co-optive and more effective in Norway than in Germany. Norway also compares well in these terms with Britain. The comparison with the United States is harder to make because, as we pointed out, it is less easy to identify the reach of the state's zone of necessity there. But however positive matters look in comparative terms, in Norway there is still a zone of necessity where environmentalists cannot easily step without being co-opted. This is illustrated historically by the strength of the hydro-power complex, more recently by the fisheries committee we discussed.

Conclusion

We have argued that truly effective inclusion in the state is possible only when the environmental movement (or sections of it) can align its interests with one or more of the imperatives that define the core of the state. When this connection cannot be made, inclusion is co-optive, requiring a great deal in terms of the time and energy of environmentalists but delivering very little in terms of policy substance.

The possibility of clear and effective connection to a state imperative is demonstrated most effectively by the case of the United States around 1970, when a general legitimation crisis induced the state to embrace environmentalism.[9] A head-on clash between environmentalism and the economic imperative is illustrated by energy policy in all four of our cases in the 1970s, and though matters played out somewhat differently in each case, the economic imperative determined the policy outcome. The security imperative also inevitably overrules environmental interests, at least in the United States, United Kingdom, and Germany prior to 1989 and the fall of the Berlin Wall.

We have found much in the way of co-optive inclusion as we examined the environmental history of the four countries in depth. Of the four countries, this story is perhaps most pervasive and persistent in the United Kingdom. In each country we can identify instances of co-option resulting from environmentalists being included in the state but systematically shut out of the core. Of course, there are also instances of co-option that cannot be accounted for by this mechanism—co-option can also occur when no imperatives are at issue. In Britain it seems to go along with administrative habits.

---

[9] This combination of circumstances while unusual is not completely unique. A similar sort of situation prevailed in New Zealand in the late 1980s, operating to include environmentalists effectively at the very time a government was otherwise targeting organized interests (except for business) for active exclusion. The connection of the nuclear weapons issue to security imperatives long frustrated movements in Germany, Britain, and the United States. The experience of New Zealand's anti-nuclear movement provides a startling contrast. New Zealand became the world's first country to adopt a nuclear-free policy. To some degree this was made easy because New Zealand had no need for nuclear energy (like Norway, it has abundant hydro-electric resources) and no nuclear weapons of its own. But the policy not to allow nuclear weapons—including those on US ships—into New Zealand and its waters adopted in the mid-1980s undermined New Zealand's most important security alliance, to the United States, which threatened suspension of military ties. The anti-nuclear movement could prevail, even in the face of wavering by Prime Minister David Lange, because it could make a positive connection with legitimation imperatives. The movement was not in itself capable of destabilizing the Labour Government. But this government had implemented an extreme market liberal economic policy without an explicit electoral mandate—a position which threatened to alienate its traditional centre-left constituency. The anti-nuclear issue had been the catalyst for the election that brought Labour to office and formed a key part of Labour's election campaign (a National MP crossed the floor to vote against nuclear warship visits, undermining the Government's majority and prompting Prime Minister Muldoon to call an election). By introducing anti-nuclear legislation in 1987, Labour appeased an influential part of its constituency and so headed off a critical legitimacy challenge. Continued public support for this legislation prompted the opposition National Party to later accept the anti-nuclear position. After 1987 anti-nuclear movement leaders were incorporated into and controlled a Public Advisory Committee on Disarmament and Arms Control (PACDAC), which also constituted a response by the government to movement pressure for greater involvement in government decision making and improved accountability (Boanas-Dewes, 1993: 82). PACDAC had statutory responsibility to oversee the implementation of the anti-nuclear policy, reporting to the Minister of Foreign Affairs and the Prime Minister. From this institutional platform movement leaders extended their influence to international nuclear politics, lobbying government officials to sponsor a UN resolution seeking an International Court of Justice ruling on the legality of nuclear weapons (Boanas-Dewes, 1993: 85). Under the National Government elected in 1990 PACDAC's composition was changed, and all but one of the original members were replaced with National Party functionaries, academics, and ex-military staff (Boanas-Dewes, 1993: 101–2).

The pervasiveness of co-option as we approach the state's core should not lead us to conclude that environmentalist action is generally futile. First, action in the state's periphery is not completely without impact. Second, as we will see in succeeding chapters, there are ways for environmentalism to have an impact that do not involve inclusion in the state. Third, it may just be a matter of time: that environmentalism's time will eventually come, just as the time eventually came for effective inclusion of the bourgeoisie and the working class in previous eras. But before turning to these questions of impact, the next chapter will dig more deeply into what inclusion does to included groups.

4

The Perils of Political Inclusion:
Moderation and Bureaucratization

Inclusion in Question

Inclusion in the state is widely presumed to be a good thing from the point of view of both a movement's interests and the democratic health of the political system. After all, the state is society's primary collective decision making body, and walking the corridors of its power surely means that a movement's interests are being taken seriously. Access to the state means enhanced credibility and legitimacy for movement groups, perhaps even direct influence on public policy. This presumption explains the howls of anguish when (say) environmentalists are expelled from the state in Thatcher's Britain, or from the Reagan and the Younger Bush administrations in the United States; and the sighs of relief when the doors are reopened, be it to the US EPA in 1983 as early Reagan zealotry waned, to the Clinton White House, or to the sustainable development process set up in Britain after 1989. In Germany, many Greens have devoted their lives to the long march through the institutions, obviously believing that the march leads somewhere.

Scholarly observers concerned with the health of democracy also welcome inclusion. Such observers include pluralists who see this as a sign that lingering inequalities are at last being corrected (as when African-Americans became an effective voice in Washington in the 1960s), corporatists who want the state to be more expansive (Cohen and Rogers, 1992; Schmitter, 1992), and even difference democrats, who want the state to validate the claims of the variety of oppressed groups in society (Philips, 1995; Young, 2000: 141–53).

In this chapter we question this seemingly widely-shared consensus about the desirability of inclusion. In the previous chapter we elucidated the circumstances under which inclusion can be co-optive rather than genuine and effective. Our implicit assumption was that groups themselves did not change their values or their internal structure as a result of their inclusion. In this chapter we will show that groups themselves can change in two ways as a result of being included within the state. First, they may have to moderate their positions substantially in order to be more consistent with the political mainstream—especially as conditioned by state imperatives. Second, they may have to develop a much more professional and bureaucratic character, entailing a large full-time staff, internal hierarchy and division of labour, and specialists in fund-raising, organizational maintenance, and management. These sorts of developments compromise the 'social movement' character of groups. While it is necessary here to document their occurrence in each country, more instructive is comparison over time and space in the character and degree of such developments, and the possibility of movement resistance to them.

Within each country there are of course environmental groups with very different origins and orientations, not all of which ever fit very easily under the social movement heading. It is necessary to distinguish between, first, environmental groups unconcerned with the state; second, those that in their beginnings sought a close and co-operative relationship with government; and third, those social movements initially based in oppositional civil society.[1] Lifestyle groups and more romantic greens (such as those that long dominated the green fringe in the United States) can be set aside for the moment. Even though they may exercise influence over collective outcomes, they are unconcerned with the state and so do not encounter the perils of political inclusion.

Groups traditionally oriented to co-operation with government are significant in that they often have large memberships. They tend to dominate mainstream environmental politics in states like Norway and the United States that have numerous institutional openings for such groups, but also feature prominently in countries such as Germany and the United Kingdom where openings are fewer. It is not surprising that with time such groups in all countries have become increasingly professional when they had the resources to do so, for they never had any ideological objection to professionalization. So in Germany, the NABU around 1990 changed from an amateurish conservationist group to an organization capable of handling scientific research, public education, and engagement in legal and administrative procedures on a broad range of issues related to sustainability. The BUND similarly developed a capacity to provide expert opinions on environmental issues and adopted a multi-focused strategy including research, education, and lobbying (Bluhdorn, 1995). Britain's RSPB fulfils a similar role to the NABU as a mainstay of the conventional movement. The RSPB sought to modernize in the 1990s, appointing a new Director, Barbara Young, who had a professional background outside the NGO community. The WWF, which in all countries has traditionally avoided confrontation and maintained close links

---

[1] A fourth category could be identified as the newly emerging professionalized organizations which in ecological modernist terms seek to bridge the movement, government, and industry. We leave our discussion of these groups to Chapter 7.

with industry (Bluhdorn, 1995), has since the 1980s broadened its agenda beyond wildlife advocacy to policy development, lobbying, and research.

While professionalization has enhanced the stature and effectiveness of these organizations that have always sought to engage directly with the state and industry, it is more problematic for new social movement-derived groups. Our special (though not exclusive) concern in this chapter is with such movement-derived groups. New social movements burst on the scene in the late 1960s and 1970s promoting post-materialist values and developing unconventional, oppositional tactics. Scope for individual expression and empowerment has been embodied in their informal and participatory workings. For some individuals, decentralized participatory organizations provided a microcosm of the political structures they ultimately desired for the broader society. Movement groups cannot easily put aside the ideological baggage with which they began their journey, particularly those groups whose identity is forged upon ecological values and grassroots democratic practices.

We will show how political inclusion places strains upon movement groups in a way that undermines participatory and decentralized structures, even among groups aware of these dangers and how they have played out in all kinds of movements in the past. Indeed, one very large question is whether the new social movement interpretation is still valid anywhere, in light of the more inclusive state politics on offer in Germany and the United Kingdom in comparison with the heyday of these movements.

These sorts of developments can have negative consequences for the vitality of civil society and ultimately the democratic well-being of the polity as a whole (even if the consequences for democratization of the state are positive), which we will explore in Chapter 5. An informed and empowered citizenry strengthens civil society and adds a democratic safeguard against the abuse of state and corporate power. The vitality of civil society can be used as one measure of the democratization of the polity. We are interested in how all these processes play out in our four states, with special reference to the effects of the particular kinds of inclusion on offer. We should emphasize that the kinds of developments we examine in this chapter can happen even when inclusion is genuine rather than co-optive.

Does Inclusion Have to Mean Moderation?

Sorting out the effects of inclusion on moderation is not easy, because it is plausible that all radical groups have a tendency to moderate with time anyway, simply because radical energies are hard to sustain. Groups often encounter occasions where they 'face a choice between being pragmatically successful (in broadening their popular base and reaching more modest policy goals) and being true to their fundamental beliefs' (Kuechler and Dalton, 1990: 288). Rochon (1990: 106) refers to this as a 'classic dilemma between maintaining ideological purity within a movement and diluting that purity in order to widen the breadth of movement support', though such statements beg the question of why exactly groups should take the moderate path when such choices arise.

It is here that comparison across both time and space is instructive. Over time, if periods of inclusion coincide (or are immediately followed) by accelerated moderation, we should suspect that inclusion causes moderation. Over space, if we find that more inclusive states feature more moderate groups, then again we might conclude that the relationship is a causal one. Germany and the United Kingdom deserve special attention because they feature more substantial changes over time than our other two countries in the kinds of inclusion their states make available.

Inclusion amid Scientism in Germany and the United Kingdom

Germany's environmental movement has unquestionably moderated since the epic confrontations of the 1970s and early 1980s, which had given the emancipatory ideas of 1968 a new lease on life. Since then, more pragmatic sorts of environmentalism predicated on working with rather than against Germany's social market economy have predominated, and the 'lifestyle' aspect of the movement has declined. The story of the Green Party is well known, and need not be repeated in depth here. With time, the *Realo* wing of the party, driven by the desire for electoral success and participating in coalition governments at city, *Land*, and ultimately federal levels of government, gained dominance (though not without some spectacular fights) over the *Fundis* who spurned compromise. Radical critics of the Greens argue that parliamentary representation has brought mostly symbolic gains at the cost of taming their zeal. They accuse the party leadership of viewing environmental issues through the lens of electoral politics (though voters who remember the party's ill-fated proposal to triple the price of gasoline may have doubts about the Greens' electoral savvy). Over the years, eco-radicals lost leadership battles or left the party altogether. The pragmatists who replaced them embraced the aim of 'ecologically modernizing' the country's social-market economy, about which we will have much more to say in Chapter 7.

The more moderate German environmental groups had long believed that working with rather than against the system makes sense, even when it brought them little in return, but in the 1980s the perception that the state and some business sectors have become more open to change became more universal among environmental groups. Let us attempt to trace the degree to which this perception and ensuing moderation stem from the (limited) possibilities for inclusion that the state eventually started to offer to environmental groups.

Opportunities for inclusion in the traditionally passively exclusive German state really only opened up for environmentalists in 1986 with the creation of the federal Ministry for Environment, Nature Conservation, and Nuclear Safety. In Chapter 3 we concluded that this ministry functions as a classic co-optive device, given that the participation it allows keeps environmentalists away from the core corporatist ministries which are ultimately more consequential in determining the content of policy. But we did not address the possibility that inclusion for environmental groups in the Environment Ministry or elsewhere necessarily leads to these groups moderating their positions. Federal environmental officials and environmental activists alike deny that public funding for environmental research and education projects hinges on the funded organizations toeing a particular political line.

However, there is a more subtle mechanism that operates so as to condition the kinds of representations that groups can make in the policy process. This mechanism is a consequence of what Dyson (1982) has termed the legalistic, science-based style of reasoning about public affairs favoured by the country's politicians and bureaucrats. An emphasis on environmentalists' technical competence as a condition for participation in state-sponsored policy deliberations is pervasive. As a federal official explains:

To have a reasonable concern means to have a proposal to solve a real problem. This type of reasonable concern is legitimate in Germany. NGO representatives with a reasonable concern have opportunities for access to the ministry's political leadership; that they have access to the bureau level goes without saying. . . . However, if conversations with the political leadership are to take place, some artists' collective expects to make recommendations on wastewater treatment. The association must recently have shown a certain competence in the area it wants to address. (Interview, 1999)

Moral objections are more or less irrelevant in the political sphere, and inasmuch as environmental advocacy groups can hope to have any political influence at all they must press their claims on the basis of technical expertise. Given this technical orientation, eco-radical groups such as Robin Wood and Greenpeace Germany do not try to gain access to government agencies through conventional channels (though Greenpeace now has a few lobbyists on its payroll).

By engaging in this technical discourse, movement groups can become complicit in relocating and containing issues of public debate. This has been a challenge to the movement in Britain as well as Germany, for in Britain too scientific expertise is highly valued within bureaucratic agencies. Thus those environmental issues that did attain governmental attention were often framed within an exclusionary scientific discourse and environmental movement claims were often dismissed as 'unsound science'. Hajer (1995: 142) shows that in the governmental response to acid rain during the early 1980s 'the dominant role for science was legitimized as a way of keeping pollution control out of the sphere of corporatism and pressure-group activity'. When environmental groups became more acceptable to the British government after 1989, issues remained framed in terms of the need for sound science as the basis for action.

As we pointed out in Chapter 2, any openings to the British state that did exist in the 1970s came with a stipulation for moderate and responsible behaviour. Despite the modest rewards on offer, traditional mainstream groups took the bait, perhaps because they saw no realistic alternative. With the blocking of these limited channels of access after 1979 and the arrival of Thatcherism, many environmentalists began to question such moderation as a failed strategy. Blowers (1987: 293) argued that the effect of the Thatcher Government's explicit developmentalism 'has been to nurture debate to the point where the environment is now a significant issue in national politics'. Robin Grove-White similarly considers that an unintended side-effect of the Thatcher Government's approach was that

Environmental [issues] emerged as points of shared concern in a way they couldn't have done in the 70s. Because so many props were kicked away you began to get a sense of what was really important to people collectively, and environment was one of them. (Interview, 1999)

Even conventional mainstream groups such as CPRE and RSPB explored more populist strategies and better communication with their members, though they never quite let go of the hope of constructive relations with government (Lowe and Flynn, 1989: 271).

In keeping with the continued governmental emphasis on the need for 'sound science', mainstream environmental groups responded to the increase in political openings to the state after 1989 by developing specialized and professionalized approaches, which we will discuss later in this chapter. However, the case of Greenpeace UK shows that it is possible to professionalize without moderating, at least in a national context where the inclusion on offer remains limited and conditional. In the late 1980s the organization employed a consultant to analyse its prospects, who argued for steering a middle course between dangers of co-option and marginalization (Rose, 1993: 289). Greenpeace subsequently applied a judicious mix of radical strategies and policy specialization by developing expertise in scientific, legal, media, and political areas (Rose, 1993: 289). But Greenpeace is the exception. In the late 1980s UK Friends of the Earth also subtly changed its campaigning approach. This was in part due to an increasing pressure to make public campaigns newsworthy, especially in comparison with Greenpeace's dramatic media stunts. FoE shifted its emphasis to developing constructive solutions consistent with sustainable development principles, meanwhile enhancing its research and scientific capacities (Lamb, 1996: 75). This more moderate approach was explicit in its 1989/90 Annual Report, which proclaimed the organization's progression from 'opposition to proposition' (in Wall, 1999: 121).

After a network including RSPB, WWF, FoE, Greenpeace, and Wildlife Trusts had produced a document entitled Biodiversity Challenge, groups such as RSPB and Wildlife Trusts became involved in the drafting of a Biodiversity Action Plan in 1994. They proceeded to liaise with government agencies on technical aspects of biodiversity and to draw up Species Habitat Plans under government grants. Opportunities for direct policy influence increased further with the return of environmental responsibilities to local government. Grant (1995: 95) points out that this decentralization has resulted in 'more emphasis on partnerships with the private and voluntary sectors, [which] creates a new class of "insider" groups whose involvement in service delivery gives them a special opportunity to influence policy development'.

The experience of Germany, especially after 1986, and the United Kingdom, especially after 1989, suggests that inclusion does entail moderation. Correspondingly, exclusion of the sort that operated in the Thatcher years in Britain meant (limited) radicalization. For Norway and the United States, there is no real turning point when possibilities for inclusion changed quite so substantially. Still, it is instructive for comparative purposes to examine these two persistently inclusive cases.

Moderation Under Persistent Inclusion: Norway and the United States

When it comes to the balance of radical and moderate environmental action, the Norwegian story is, as we pointed out in Chapter 2, a case of the dog that didn't bark in the night, in the face of issues that might to an outsider look ripe for protest. Thus there is little history of radicalism that could ever be moderated, outside the Mardøla and Alta Dam protests around 1970 and 1980 respectively. Neither protest spawned a social movement that outlasted the specific issue. Certainly, Norwegian environmentalists themselves are not aware of any problem here. In our interviews, no group representative accepted that state funding compromised the independence of the group. And it is possible to point to instances such as a 1999 court case where the Nature Conservation Society, the Norwegian Society for the Protection of Raptors and Carnivores, and WWF challenged (and beat) the government over wolves. However, some of our interviewees admitted that their organization had made some marginal adjustment in order to receive project grants, though they argued that core group values remained unaffected.

Project grants weave tight bonds with the state, as they are given in return for the group promising to meet some need of the state, though the group has some leeway in terms of how it writes the grant application. The system of grants is not neutral in terms of the kinds of groups it favours. The operating grant system began as a 'lex naturvernforbundet', an arrangement for the Nature Conservation Society. Despite expansion of the system over the years, groups not backed by a nationwide organization are not covered by it. The favoured large groups, notably the Nature Conservation Society and Mountain Touring Association, are co-operators. Moreover, the groups most critical of Norwegian environmental policy, such as (small) animal welfare groups, are not included.

In the United States, unlike Norway, the excessive moderation of long-included groups did by the 1990s itself become a contentious political issue. The critics argue that inclusion has changed the nature of the groups and the people within them. Jeff St. Clair jokes that 'there's an old adage that when you go to DC only take two clean shirts because if you stay any longer than that, you're going to succumb to DC-itis or something' (interview, 1999). 'DC-itis' is a shift in attitude, not just organizational professionalization (which we will address later in this chapter). With time, environmentalism became a business, and the major groups moved away from their roots. Inclusion means participation in a constrained discursive arena. Curtis Moore, a former Republican counsel to the Senate Environmental Affairs Committee, notes that '[i]f I represent an industry, I can always get into the argument . . . But if you're an environmentalist, you can't get into the argument unless they want to let you in. And they're not going to let you in if they think you are crazy, if you don't think in the same terms they do. You have to sound reasonable or you don't even get into the room. So you don't find many people in major environmental groups who are willing to be seen as unreasonable' (quoted in Greider, 1992: 216). As Brian Tokar notes, 'In order to play that kind of role, organizations need to be willing to moderate their demands' (interview, 1999). The case holds not just for organizations, but individuals as well. 'The American system is very effective at co-opting and moderating dissidents by giving them attention and then encouraging them to be "reasonable" so their ideas will be taken seriously,' says Dave Foreman (1998: 360), a former Wilderness Society staffer and one of the founders of Earth First!.

Jon Margolis, a journalist who has covered the environmental scene in Washington for years, reflects:

I think when you come to Washington you learn to play the game and there are people for whom that's a bad thing. I don't think it's a bad thing. I mean democracy is a conversation. . . . You get to know people and they're not such bad guys. You know, you go out and have a drink with them after the session in a congressman's office [and see] they have a legitimate constituency also. . . . Somebody has got to come to Washington and cut a deal at some point. Former Governor Hickel of Alaska once said to me, at some point somebody's got to say yes, otherwise nothing gets done. And what gets done may not be entirely what an environmental group wants, but . . . it's better to save half a million acres than to save no acres. (Interview, 1999)

Compromise and negotiation, then, are seen not as co-opting, but as a way to get things done.

Once inside, the major organizations often come to accept the strength, if not the validity, of other players and values at the table. William Meadows of the Wilderness Society notes that a Secretary of Interior is

not only trying to manage for conservation values, he also has responsibility for managing for oil and gas, wildlife, [and] mining interests. . . . [A]t any given point in time, someone sitting in the Department of Interior is going to have to juggle a lot of different values and a lot of different needs and a lot of different interest groups . . . We get into situations where . . . he may come to us and say 'Listen, we can protect a million acres, but I'm going to have to let the oil company have access to these 3 places. Are you willing to accept that?' And so we have to make those decisions, almost on a daily basis. What are we willing to give up to get something protected. (Interview, 1999)

In this sense, argues Meadows, 'I don't see as much co-optation as I do compromise.' John Adams of the NRDC makes a similar case about the give and take of compromise and co-optation:

Sometimes there's an effort to say give me a break in one way or the other. Don't press me too hard yet, but I will get you there given some time. Is that being co-opted? I suppose that is. So I think you get some of all of that, but our job is to see through the co-opting and to see through for what is realistic for us to achieve at any given time and there is no sense just screaming about failed policies day in and day out. (Interview, 1999)

Again, the bottom line for these leaders of the environmental mainstream is getting *something* done within the context of legislative negotiation— co-opted or not.

Leslie Thiele argues that 'The word *co-optation* has acquired a negative connotation, often signifying a caving in, a selling out, or a perverting of ideals. But co-optation has a more neutral meaning, denoting an appropriation, assimilation, and incorporation into an established order. To be co-opted, in other words, simply means to become part of the mainstream' (1999: 19–20). For Thiele, this is desirable—inclusion of the environmental movement came with a popularization of environmental concerns and values. But there was a downside as well; the integrity of the movement came into question.

Generously interpreted, the co-optation of environmentalism that began in the 1980s produced increased support from a wider cross-section of the general public and initiated a constructive engagement with former antagonists in business and government. Critically interpreted, it signalled a crass commercialization, a self-serving professionalization, and a caving in to the powers that be. (p. 29)

The bottom line for Thiele is that inclusion of the environmental movement enabled appeal to a broader section of society (which we think is debatable) and greater access to economic and political institutions (which is true). For the critics, gradual shift from confrontation to compromise has co-opted the soul and values of the movement, made it settle for less than it would have in the past, compromised its effectiveness, and undermined regional and grass-roots groups. Dowie (1995: 6) represents this view:

In a desperate drive to win respectability and access in Washington, mainstream leaders politely pursued a course of accommodation and capitulation . . . Compromise, which had produced some limited gains for the movement in the 1970s, in the 1980s became the habitual response of the environmental establishment. It is still applied almost reflexively, even in the face of irreversible degradations. These compromises have pushed a once-effective movement to the brink of irrelevance.

Moderation in Comparative Perspective

Our comparisons over time and space show that almost invariably inclusion means moderation; and, as the case of Thatcherite Britain shows, exclusion can cause at least a modicum of radicalization. If a group wants to maintain its radicalism, it has to resist inclusion. Where inclusion is meagre to begin with, as in Britain and Germany, it is easier for a group like Greenpeace to resist inclusion and maintain its radicalism, while other groups co-operate with the state and moderate. In more inclusive Norway and the United States, such resistance is harder to sustain; though in the United States, newer groups can step in and fill the radical niche, while in Norway apparently they cannot.

Inclusion has brought comparatively few returns at substantial cost in Britain and, until the onset of ecological modernization, in Germany. The returns have apparently been greater in both the United States and Norway, though in the United States it became a matter of great controversy—unresolved at the time of writing—as to whether the gains were worth it. Also, a comparative perspective would add grist to the arguments of the critics of the inclusion of US mainstream groups, for clearly the United States has slipped from leader to laggard in environmental policy since the 1970s, suggesting perhaps that the gains are not worth the cost.

Are the policy gains worth the degree of compromise of core environmental values? This is an extraordinarily difficult, but not impossible, question to answer. It is a difficult question because there is no common metric on which policy gains and loss of core values can be measured. Even on the policy gains side of the calculation alone, many moderators will say that ultimately public policy is the only game in town, such that there is no opportunity cost involved. However, in Chapter 6 we will show that even if policy is the only game, then it can still be influenced by groups that do not accept the embrace of the state. Moreover, we will show that collective outcomes can be influenced by action in civil society that does not target the state. And adding a temporal dimension may indicate that groups facing the possibility of inclusion should bide their time; that in the long run, greater gains can be made by waiting until the time is ripe, most notably when an emerging state imperative looks to be consistent with the movement's defining interest. In Chapter 7 we will show that Germany's history can be interpreted in exactly this light.

Does Inclusion Have to Mean Hierarchy and Bureaucratization?

Some—but by no means all—environmental groups were in their early years opposed to hierarchy and institutionalization, favouring instead looser, more participatory structures. This disposition is especially true for groups that began in new social movements in the 1970s and 1980s. But can these groups maintain their participatory values if they enter into state processes? We suggest that generally they will not, and instead face a traumatic transition toward hierarchy and stable leadership. In the following discussion we consider how this transition has played out in our four kinds of state. The transition itself is common, though not universal;[2] the severity of its consequences for the character of groups and the movement as a whole is not.

Before we address the impact of political inclusion upon hierarchy and bureaucracy in movement groups, the effects of time and organizational growth need to be controlled. In the 1980s a series of environmental disasters increased the membership of existing environmental groups throughout the developed world. In the United States, *Time* magazine placed the Planet Earth on its cover in place of its traditional 'Man of the Year', its publisher explaining the decision as prompted by 'the scorching summer of 1988, when environmental disasters—droughts, floods, forest fires, polluted beaches—dominated the news' (cited in Dobson, 1990: 1). The explosive growth of many organizations from the mid-1980s until the early 1990s placed considerable strain on existing organizational structures.[3] Offe (1990: 238–40) argues that a degree of institutionalization within movement groups is inevitable with time, as oppositional movement groups become vulnerable to organizational difficulties, a decline in 'highly visible events' around which to mobilize protest, and fatigue on the part of erstwhile protestors. To arrest

---

[2] Van der Heijden (1997: 36) observes a common pattern of institutionalization in a comparative study of environmental movements in France, Germany, the Netherlands, and Switzerland, involving 'marginalization of the local grassroots level'.

[3] Membership generally declined somewhat in the 1990s. In Britain, for example, there was a decline in organization staff numbers in 1992–3 due to the combination of economic recession and 'doom fatigue' (Grant, 1995: 145).

decline, activists develop organizational structures, finding it hard to avert 'bureaucratization, centralization, alienation and deradicalization'.

Offe's observations on institutionalization were formed with the German Green Party in mind, where initial concerns about hierarchy saw a resistance to an established leadership, a policy to feed portions of parliamentary members' salaries back to the party, and a rotation of parliamentary members. All these features have since fallen by the wayside. Over time Die Grünen has shifted from Petra Kelly's hybrid 'half movement half political party' in the early 1980s to a more conventional political party, shedding along the way many of its self-imposed safeguards against institutionalization. Later we will link these developments to the kinds of inclusion Die Grünen has engaged.

Resisting Bureaucratization in the United Kingdom

Two cases from the United Kingdom do however partially contradict Offe's thesis about the life cycle of movements. Britain's Friends of the Earth (FoE) traditionally encourages its members to engage in political action, and has maintained a decentralized structure with a high degree of local autonomy (Byrne, 1997: 132–3). Its mission statement declares a commitment 'to increase public participation and democratic decision-making', a commitment reflected in the organization's consensual and non-hierarchical decision making processes (Byrne, 1997: 133). An early disillusioning experience at the Windscale Inquiry in 1977 was followed by a push within the branch structure to reverse a tendency towards centralization, and until 1981 FoE's commitment to equality was reflected in a 'parity' pay structure amongst all its staff (Lamb, 1996). However, organizational growth and greater access to government since the late 1980s posed a greater challenge. After 1987 there was renewed centralization (Wall, 1999: 121). By the 1990s FoE had developed a much broader membership base which was less supportive of a protest culture and more disposed towards constructive engagement on environmental issues (Doherty, 1999: 282). Jordan and Maloney (1997: 190) argue that as a mass organization FoE had by the mid-1990s lost touch with its membership and now 'is nearer something that can be termed a *protest business* than a new social movement organization'. Weston (1989, in Wall, 1999: 37) similarly observes that FoE have 'moved from being the amateur, evangelical, fundamentalist ecocentric pressure group of the 1970s to a professional pragmatist organization which is run almost like any other modern company'. Thus in the end FoE confirmed Offe's prediction about institutionalization, despite having tried to resist and indeed move in the opposite direction along the way.

Britain's Green Party presents a much clearer refutation of Offe's thesis. The party attempted to restructure its organization and set strategic goals following its surprising performance in the 1989 European elections where it attracted 15 per cent of the vote. The Greens 2000 professionalization initiative was initially successful, although the reformist drive within the party lost momentum following the departure of Jonathon Porritt and Sara Parkin in the early 1990s. In recent years activists within the party have reasserted participatory values and maintained internal decentralization, even though the party has now secured parliamentary representation in both the European and Scottish parliaments. To their critics, the triumph of fundamentalism is seen to hold back the party from greater electoral success. However, another way of reading this history is that the first-past-the-post voting system used in most British elections makes it impossible to win a seat anyway, thus denying the party the possibility of inclusion in the state, thus removing the main cause of professionalization.

Embracing Professionalization in the United Kingdom

Outside the Green Party and to a lesser extent FoE, there began in the 1980s a transformation in the character of British environmental organizations and in particular their relationship to their membership. Robin Grove-White (1991: 35) explains this shift in Britain:

In the mid-70s, it was realistic to conceive of most UK NGOs as consisting of—and being run by—their members, with the assistance of paid staffs. By the late 80s, the mode had changed. The fastest growing, and most influential, groups . . . were better pictured as groups of campaigning specialists on the staffs and executive boards, offering programmes of action for public support.

The British branch of Greenpeace is interesting in this respect because although it has resisted moderation, it led the way in professionalization. Until the mid-1980s, Greepeace UK was 'little more than a small, anarchic group of individuals—with no formal membership structure—specialising in the provision of spectacular, symbolic David and Goliath images to TV and press, and making minimal attempt to engage in routine lobbying, participation in public inquiries, etc' (Grove-White, 1991: 28–9). By the 1990s it was a slick organization capable of deploying technical expertise (for example, in promoting a CFC-free refrigerator) and raising funds—but still organizing radical actions such as the Brent Spar occupation in 1995.

Beyond time and membership growth, the enhanced opportunities for inclusion presented to movement groups in the traditionally exclusive states of Germany and the United Kingdom in particular in recent years has brought these issues into sharper focus. To engage successfully with the state, groups require very different qualities than the open expression of ideas and diverse, unpredictable forms of action found in new social movements. Groups engaging in consultations and negotiations with state actors need to carry their membership with them toward an agreed outcome, and having them engage in uncontrolled protest is a hindrance here. Because new social movements were averse to formal, hierarchical decision making structures, Offe (1985: 830–1) doubted any leaders could claim the authority to commit their members to the outcome of their negotiations with government. Kuechler and Dalton (1990: 288) similarly observed that participatory structures worked against the ability to work with governments, because 'movements value openness and immediate participation, which at the same time seriously restrict their effectiveness and efficiency in reaching policy-oriented goals'. We will demonstrate that movement-derived groups have in fact adapted to emerging opportunities for inclusion, and consider the challenges this has presented to both these groups and the broader movement.

Far from providing fresh impetus to the movement, the increased opportunities for inclusion that accompanied the Thatcher Government's sudden conversion to an environmental agenda in the UK in late 1988 and subsequent reopening of bureaucratic channels of consultation caused a kind of paralysis. Jonathon Porritt, Director of FoE at the time, reflects on the changing political circumstances for his organization:

FoE spent a lot of time beating at doors because people didn't want to let us in. We had to work hard to get the attention of ministers . . . Now we just have to nudge the door, it opens wide, and we fall flat on our faces, not really knowing what to do when we get there. (McCormick, 1991: 117)

According to Rose the increased resources available to organizations combined with enhanced opportunities for engagement with government meant that 'by Rio, 1992 . . . these groups were not so much muscle bound as barnacle encrusted with all these commitments' (interview, 1999).

Hierarchy and Centralization in Norway and the United States

Not coincidentally, hierarchy and centralization are most prevalent amongst movement organizations in Norway and the United States where there exist institutional opportunities for movement engagement with the state. We have already described how in Norway the system of operating and project grants encourages group moderation. With time the grant system expanded to cover more groups, which the Environment Ministry justifies in terms sustaining a broad movement of democratic organizations (Miljøverndepartementet, 1999–2000: 114). But the consequences for democracy may be precisely the opposite of that intended. Only national groups receive operating grants, putting local groups with flatter hierarchies at a disadvantage. In order to qualify for project grants, there is every incentive for environmental organizations to become more professionalized, a trend evident since at least 1980. Organizations neglect their membership, even as a mere source of income (in this they differ from the mainstream groups in the United States); and the size of that membership declines. The Nature Conservation Society in particular has become heavily and increasingly dependent on state funding with time. There has been a shift from large, supporter-, branch-based national organizations to small organizational elites adept at gaining media attention (Klausen and Opedal, 1998; Selle and Stromsnes, 1998*b*). Selle and Stromsnes (1998*a*: 17) consider that government financial support to environmental organizations has served to 'gradually debilitate the genuinely voluntary'. Groups are funded because they are seen as instrumental in the implementation of government policy, and internal democratic challenges within groups cannot be allowed to obstruct implementation.

The other half of Norwegian inclusion, participation in the committee system central to government, also acts to strengthen the hand of the leadership and reduce the influence of ordinary members (Nordby, 1996: 287 ff.) Committees generally operate behind closed doors, open for public comment only after key decisions have been made. Committee work does not involve the environmental organization *per se*—only individuals from the organization. Thus groups cannot discuss within themselves the ongoing work of a committee on which they have a representative. In a sense, the inclusive state fails to deliver on its promise, because the group as a whole is not included, only a few leaders.

In the United States we see professionalization and hierarchy growing with time ever since the initial inclusion of a raft of environmental groups around 1970, but for reasons very different than in Norway. The large Washington-based organizations increasingly sought to secure deals and 'carry' their largely passive membership. Dowie (1995: 61) argues that beginning in the 1980s, the major groups became 'the domain of list managers, marketing directors, and organizational development specialists'. Groups hired lawyers to cope with the growing complexity of environmental law and policy, and MBAs to raise and manage money. The NRDC led the way in these developments (Gottlieb, 1993: 143). Offices in Washington were expanded to the detriment of regional centres. At the top of the movement, impassioned amateurs fuelled by moral outrage were replaced by professional directors and presidents: thinking like a manager replaced thinking like a mountain. And it was the membership that needed managing, seen as a source of funds rather than ideas.

Dowie (1995: 61) argues that

during the high-flying eighties . . . mainstream organizations created institutions. They continued a 1970s trend toward adding programs and expanding staffs. They spent more effort and resources on developing entrepreneurial and organizational enhancement skills than on environmental issues. The unfortunate end result is a bland, bureaucratic reform movement devoid of passion or charismatic leadership.

Jeff St. Clair (1995) was a bit more acerbic in his characterization:

Somewhere along the line the environmental movement disconnected with the people. Rejected its political roots, pulled the plug on its vibrant tradition. It packed its bags, it starched its shirts and jetted to DC where it became what it once despised: a risk aversive, depersonalized, overly analytical, humorless, access-driven, intolerant, statistical, centralized, technocratic, deal-making, passionless, sterilized, direct-mailing, jock-strapped, lawyer-laden monolith to mediocrity.

Other criticisms were levelled at professional 'envirocrats' who moved through the revolving door between the major environmental groups, governmental agencies, and industry, and at groups that took on the same organizational form as business and government. At any rate, the overall pattern is clearly one of growing hierarchy and professionalization with time, which can be traced quite directly to the kinds of inclusion that the mainstream groups have accepted with such alacrity.

There is of course a story to be told about segments of the movement that resisted these developments by refusing to accept the sorts of inclusion on offer, to which we will return in the next chapter. However, the pull of passive inclusion is hard to resist, as indicated by the persistent yet in the end unsuccessful attempts to resist it on the part of the leading American environmentalist of the twentieth century, David Brower. As executive director of the Sierra Club in the 1950s, Brower transformed the Club from a staid group of outdoor enthusiasts into an effective campaigning organization. He went too far in this direction for the tastes of more conservative members, who eventually ousted him from the leadership. Brower's reaction was to found Friends of the Earth in 1969, with its headquarters symbolically in San Francisco, not Washington, DC. Friends of the Earth grew and prospered, both nationally and internationally. But in 1985 Brower found himself in an internal battle within Friends of the Earth. He wanted to maintain an emphasis on grassroots campaigns, a participatory style of management, and a distance from the centres of power in Washington. His opponents believed the organization could only hold its own and flourish if it adopted a more professional kind of management. His opponents prevailed—and Friends of the Earth moved its headquarters to Washington, to consolidate its position as one of the majors. Again Brower responded by founding a new organization based in San Francisco, Earth Island Institute. But this time the Institute remained small, focused on particular projects, but remaining a marginal player on the national scene.

Bureaucratization in Germany

Inclusion in Germany remains less thoroughgoing than in Norway and the United States, but German groups have not escaped the effects of inclusion.

The 1980s were in many ways a high point for environmental group activity in Germany, as old and new groups alike extended their concerns beyond the confines of nature conservation toward a more expansive conception of environmental protection (Hey and Brindle, 1994: 133–5). There was considerable growth in membership. With this expansion groups took on more full-time staff. Since the early 1990s, however, membership and funding levels have stagnated. Many groups have developed more bureaucratic organizational structures, and a growing proportion of personnel is concerned with internal maintenance rather than activism. Given that a high proportion of their revenues comes from donations and membership dues, a significant share of staff resources must be devoted to fund-raising and member recruitment (Hey and Brendle, 1994: 135). Environmental interest groups developed professional public relations departments and communication strategies that utilize these organizations' presidents as their main public spokespersons. These organizational and leadership trends, which reflect a more general trend toward greater professionalization among German interest groups (Sebaldt, 1997), make environmental groups look more like conventional advocacy groups than new social movement organizations (Lahusen, 1996).

These developments are not a consequence of increased inclusion *per se*; however, there is a subtle link. Environmental issues slipped down the political agenda in part because they became cast in technical problem-solving terms rather than epic confrontation. As a result it becomes harder to attract and retain members and donations, and groups must then devote much more of their time and effort to fund-raising and recruitment. When recognition of movement groups as 'legitimate' participants in environmental policy making depends upon their scientific expertise, as it does in the United Kingdom and Germany, it is unsurprising that groups seek to enhance their scientific research capabilities, which again requires money. Organizations such as FoE, WWF, and RSPB in Britain and BUND and NABU in Germany pride themselves on their effective research capacity that allows them to participate constructively in technical policy debates. But there is a downside—by engaging in technical debates they are drawn into what Pakulski and Crook (1998) describe as the 'routinisation' and 'scientisation' of environmental issues. This conveys the impression that issues are complex and necessarily resolved beyond the public gaze. On the face of it this is an unattractive formula for reaching out to organizations' membership and the broader public, which groups then have to remedy by increased effort devoted to raising funds and recruiting and retaining members.

Groups that spurn the state are not quite so subject to this dynamic, though neither are they insulated from it—because they too suffer if the environment falls down the public agenda. Notably, the German branch of Greenpeace, founded in 1980, is the only substantial German environmental group that does not accept any government or business funding, perhaps because its successful fund-raising from over half a million financial supporters long meant it did not have to. Its budget (DM 71.5 million in 1998) is by far the largest among German environmental groups. Greenpeace has maintained a largely confrontational stance towards big business, and continued its media-savvy actions and exposés of environmental scandals in the 1990s. Greenpeace did, however, begin to engage small and medium-size businesses in a 'critical dialogue' in the 1990s. German observers sometimes use the term 'environmental enterprise' to capture the corporate outlook of Greenpeace and sustainable energy companies created in the 1990s. New social movement groups that have been less willing to compromise on participatory values and engage in instrumental politics have withered over time. In Germany the BBU does not enjoy the membership or visibility that it achieved through mass campaigns in the 1980s. One representative reports he is seldom now asked to lecture on alternative energies, an area of expertise claimed by 'green' consultancies and alternative energy trade associations such as Eurosolar and others.

Developments in Germany's environmental group sector largely confirm the proposition that engagement with the state means the development of a hierarchical structure within a group for government officials to recognize and deal with. True to corporatist form, the federal government seeks to structure its relationship with environmental groups by helping to fund a peak organization that includes the most important environmental groups active at the federal level. The DNR, which receives part of its operating budget from the federal government, became the government's designated point of contact with the environmental movement. Officials complain that leaders who represent environmental groups on a voluntary basis seldom have the same level of expertise they have come to expect from other interest groups. The quality of environmental group participation, officials say, improves where full-time professional environmental scientists represent groups in official policy deliberations, which confirms our earlier point about the subtle effects on included groups of German policy discourse framed as a search for the truth. Environmental group representatives agree with this assessment of the demands of formal participation. However, some public officials and environmentalists believe that the internal structure of most environmental groups is still not hierarchical enough for corporatism to function properly. In 1999 a Green MP and BUND board member, for example, vented her unhappiness with BUND's inability to formulate a position supporting the government's plan to phase out nuclear power (Hustedt, interview, 1999).

Any contemplation of the effects of inclusion on the form taken by the movement and groups in Germany must of course highlight the parliamentarization and subsequent entry into government of the Greens. While the party emerged from within the movement and vowed to maintain close ties to its members (Guggenberger, 1980), Green MPs have gained considerable autonomy from the party's rank-and-file members. The Greens arguably remain somewhat less elite-dominated than older political parties, but with time these differences have decreased and often look more like symbols (Raschke, 1993; Mayer and Ely, 1998; Tiefenbach, 1998). This movement toward organizational pragmatism occurred whenever Greens entered local or regional parliaments and then coalitions, and accelerated in 1998 with entry into the federal government.

In keeping with this transformation, Green MPs by 2001 had a more polished look than the diverse group of nonconformists who wore jeans and sweaters on the floor of parliament in 1983. The erstwhile 'anti-party' has changed parliament while having absorbed the institution's norms and values. *Fundis* view the party's professionalization as evidence for the iron law of oligarchy in action (Tiefenbach, 1998), while *Realos* welcome the same trend as a prerequisite of political efficacy and electoral success (Offe, 1998; Raschke, 1993).

The Greens' parliamentarization and participation in the national government have forced environmental groups to negotiate a brave new world characterized by improved access to government officials as well as growing public complacency about the state of the environment. Thus the effects of green penetration of the state extended beyond the party itself and into environmental groups.

Comparisons and Conclusions

At the most general level, our main finding in this chapter is that inclusion causes moderation and bureaucratization of included groups (and sometimes the influence may extend to groups that are not included). This effect remains important after we control for the effects of time and membership growth. The persistently inclusive states of Norway and the United States feature earlier and more extensive professionalization than the more tenuously and belatedly inclusive United Kingdom and Germany. The latter two cases show that when the state becomes more inclusive then moderation and professionalization on the part of the movement follow. Correspondingly, a shift toward exclusion produces some radicalization, as shown by the United Kingdom after 1979. Inclusion can also help cause professionalization on the part of groups that are not included and maintain their radicalism. The best example of this is the case of Greenpeace in both the United Kingdom and Germany. Perhaps Greenpeace is, paradoxically, immune to the moderating effects of inclusion because it was never a new social movement to begin with (because it was never internally participatory).

The idea that inclusion causes moderation and professionalization is consistent with a school of thought that sees 'political opportunity structures' as the most important explanation of the form taken by social movement activity. Van der Heijden (1997: 27) defines political opportunity structures in terms of the strategies that elites adopt toward challengers and the pattern of alliances within party systems as well as the enduring institutional structure of the state.[4] Our exclusive/inclusive distinction resembles that of Kriesi et al. (1992: 222) between state strategies that are 'either *exclusive* (repressive, confronting, polarizing) or *integrative* (facilitative, co-operative, assimilative)'. (Kriesi, 1995, uses the term 'inclusive' instead of 'integrative'.) Analysts in this tradition believe that structural opportunities and elite responsiveness affect movements' 'decision to mobilise or not, their choice of form of mobilisation' (Kriesi et al., 1992: 220). Thus there is likely to be 'a curvilinear relationship between openness and movement mobilization, which shows that very closed regimes repress social movements, that very open and responsive ones assimilate them, and that moderately repressive ones allow for their broad articulation but do not accede readily to their demands' (Kitschelt, 1986: 62, whose analysis is based on anti-nuclear protests in France, Sweden, the United States, and Germany).

However, we can tell a more nuanced story than political opportunity structure theorists by distinguishing between actively and passively inclusive states, which have quite different consequences for the kind and degree of movement professionalization and bureaucratization. Actively inclusive Norway yields groups whose professionalism is oriented very much to securing state funds and participating in committees, enabling groups to neglect their membership. The passively inclusive United States, in contrast, produces a kind of professionalization in which political and legal skills are in greater demand, and which requires much more in the way of internal management of the group's membership, vital as a source of funds. The kind of professionalization that occurred in the United States became controversial, while that in Norway did not. The modicum of inclusion available in the traditionally more exclusive states of Britain and Germany has been different in kind than in Norway and the United States, hinging as it does on the scientific expertise that a group can demonstrate. In Britain, limited inclusion does not extend to a Green Party that can therefore maintain its participatory and radical aspects, while in Germany the electoral system meant that inclusion could beckon the Greens, who eventually accepted the embrace, moderated, and professionalized. A further point of contrast is that political opportunity

---

[4] Structural influences tend to be ignored by the major competing schools of thought on social movements, resource mobilization (which stresses the social sources of group strength) and new social movement theory (which is preoccupied with ideology and identity).

structure theorists generally argue in deterministic terms; we believe, in contrast, that groups can reject the political opportunity structure with which they are faced in light of its insidious effects. This explains, for example, the development of alternatives to the mainstream in the United States environmental movement since the mid-1980s, and the strenuous (if finally unsuccessful) efforts on the part of UK Friends of the Earth to resist professionalization.[5]

In light of the moderations and professionalizations we have charted in this chapter, one large question is whether the new social movement interpretation of environmentalism remains valid. Certainly by the 1990s this interpretation did not capture environmentalism as a whole in any of our four countries. In Norway it captures absolutely nothing about the movement. In a search for remnant new social movements, we can see at the turn of the millennium the following sorts of movements that have resisted the moderation/professionalization nexus:

- Protest businesses or environmental enterprises such as Greenpeace in the United Kingdom and Germany and the Bellona Foundation in Norway that are highly professional but keep their distance from the state. In the case of Greenpeace at least, a capacity for radical action has been retained.
- Unstructured radicals exemplified by Earth First! in the United States in the 1980s and the anti-roads movement in Britain in the 1990s. These groups lead a fugitive organizational life, which whether by design or happy accident helps them, in the UK, to elude an asset-seizing state.
- The broad and diverse, yet equally unstructured transnational anti-globalization movement that revels in a carnival spirit and lack of unifying ideas, a search for which in the 1970s cost social movement activists many an evening. In eschewing singular political programmes and metanarratives, such networks have used mutual recognition and agonistic respect to construct a united—though not uniform—movement.
- Tactically opportunistic networks that join together loosely connected local actions but have no single comprehensive program for political change.

---

[5] To further contrast our view with that of political opportunity structure theorists, we agree with them that group calculations generally proceed as though structures were fixed (Kriesi et al., 1995: 168), but that occasional moderate change in structures with real effects is possible (as in Germany in 1986 and the United Kingdom around 1989). Kitschelt (1986), Kriesi et al. (1992), and Kriesi (1995: 168) all allow that political opportunities can change with time, but in practice their comparative analyses fix countries in particular categories, and they have no theory of change. We link more substantial change in the real possibilities for inclusion to changes in state imperatives. We argued this case historically in Chapter 3, and in Chapter 7 will show how matters play out in the context of ecological modernization and challenges to the legitimacy of the political economy associated with environmental risks. This linkage did of course enable us to distinguish between co-optive and genuine inclusion in Chapter 3. Finally, we disagree with these theorists' presumption of lack of group influence when inclusion does not occur (see Chapter 6).

Rather, the focus is on the sum of local, regional, and national actions and the internal politics of participation and empowerment that the network itself embodies. Within our four countries the best example is the United States environmental justice network, though transnational networks such as those concerned with biopiracy, GMOs, and oil refineries are equally instructive.

None of these four categories embodies the full new social movement repertoire of self-limiting radicalism, preoccupation with identity issues, fluid and participatory organizational style, unconventional tactics, and lack of class basis (as we outlined in Chapter 1). Networks are not self-limiting, and the unstructured movements appear to be happy with different and perhaps contradictory identities. The existence of these four types perhaps makes sense against the background of the moderation and professionalization of a previous generation of activist groups, which the new generation can recognize and resist (though of course protest businesses are interested in resisting only moderation, not professionalization). Their existence also underlines the point that political opportunity structures presented by states can be recognized and resisted in a fashion consistent with the idea of a reflexive modernity, which we will address in Chapter 7.

The professionalization which has accompanied, and indeed helped secure, the entry and effective engagement of movement groups with the state has often come at the expense of movement vitality. From this perspective political inclusion may not be as benign an influence upon the democracy of the national polity as a state-centric interpretation suggests. In addition, wholesale group moderation may adversely affect the quality of democracy because it narrows the available range of positions capable of expression and response in the polity as a whole, thus restricting democracy's scope. We will address such questions of the relationship of social movements to democratic development in the next chapter.

5

The Dynamics of Democratization

Democratic history cannot be understood without reference to the crucial roles played by social movements. In the previous three chapters we have circled around the edges of democracy, coming ever closer to its heart in the previous chapter when we addressed the negative consequences of inclusion for the degree of democracy prevailing within environmental movement groups. In this chapter we broaden the focus in order to consider the consequences of patterns of movement activity, inclusion, and exclusion for the degree of democracy obtaining in society as a whole. Note that we say *society as a whole* here. Our conception of democracy extends beyond the state. Obviously what happens within the state is of crucial importance when it comes to democracy. But this should not blind us to the consequences of state structures and state actions for democracy beyond the state. In particular, we should be alive to the counterintuitive possibility that changes promoting democracy within the state may have actually undermined democracy in society; and, correspondingly, that changes reducing democracy within the state have actually promoted democracy in society at large. This does not mean we are promoting the right kind of exclusive state as some kind of normative ideal, for we doubt that such states can be designed: it is implausible to postulate a state whose main task is to organize opposition to itself.

This broad focus on democracy within society as well as the state is further justified to the extent that the core of the state itself is under sway of the imperatives we introduced in Chapter 1, for such imperatives constrain democracy within the state because they predetermine the outcomes of collective decision processes (Dryzek, 1996*a*). Civil society where social movements operate beyond the state is less constrained in these terms, and as such is an important site in its own right for democratic activity and innovation.

In this chapter we intend to demonstrate that:

1. Inclusive states are capable of undermining democracy in society as a whole by depleting civil society.

2. Passively exclusive states that for the most part ignore social movements and provide no points of entry for them can be surprisingly, if unintentionally, beneficial for the democratic vitality of society.

4. Actively exclusive states such as those induced by contemporary market liberalism undermine the conditions of association for social movements, and so weaken democracy in civil society.

5. Diversity in the movement, itself a resource for democratic communication and innovation, is inhibited by states that actively intervene to affect the pattern of interest representation, whether that intervention be designed to incorporate groups or exclude them.

As stated, these propositions seem to imply that we can compare the degree of democracy prevailing in a country across time and place. Substantial ink has been spilled on measuring democracy in these terms (see e.g. Inkeles, 1991, or the efforts of Freedom House, 2000, to assess countries on the basis of whether or not they qualify as democratic). However, we believe that such measurement is impossible. Thus we cannot evaluate 'degree of democracy' in a comparative inquiry except in very crude terms. For the precise meaning of democracy is something that will always remain contested; as we pointed out in Chapter 1, democracy is an 'essentially contested concept' in that disagreement about what democracy means is intrinsic to the very idea of democracy. These difficulties notwithstanding, we believe that the three propositions concerning the impact of state forms on democracy can in fact be evaluated.

Following Dryzek (1996a: 6–9), we believe that it makes much more sense to focus on processes of democratization than on models of democracy (See also Cunningham, 1987: 26–7; Hyland, 1995). In other words, even though it is not possible to specify the ideal democracy, or how far a political system is from that ideal, we can recognize democratic advances and retreats. Democratization in this light consists of advances on any one of three dimensions:

- Franchise: the number of people effectively participating in collective decision making. Franchise here is not simply minimal citizenship rights, such as the right to vote, but rather the *effective* participation of categories of people, whose continued exclusion formal citizenship rights can mask.
- Scope: the areas of social, economic, and political life brought under conscious collective control.
- Authenticity: the degree to which participation in collective control is effective rather than symbolic, and engaged by competent actors.

In addition, it is crucial that advance on one dimension never be purchased at the expense of loss on another dimension. We have no common metric to decide whether or not (say) an increase in the franchise is worth a loss in scope. In fact, reckless pursuit of any one dimension at the expense of the others can be quite destructive. For example, republican thinkers such as Hannah Arendt (1958) are often accused of pursuing democratic authenticity for the privileged few (such as the ancient Athenian *polis* that Arendt so admires) at the expense of a severely restricted franchise. On the other hand, expanding scope and franchise—for example by instituting a referendum—can lead to wholesale loss of authenticity if the referendum campaign features mainly television advertising, with wealthy interests and their public relations experts to the fore. The problem with referenda, as with ordinary opinion polls, is that they generally register unreflective preferences.

A further constraint when it comes to recognition of democratization on one or more of these three criteria is that positive movement in the long term should never be purchased at the expense of negative movement in the short term. This would open the door to the (bad) arguments of dictators who claim to be stabilizing the current situation in the interests of a future democracy, or Leninists who are ruthless in the short term in the interests of a supposedly free and democratic long term. Again, the state of our knowledge is such that we never know whether such short-term sacrifices will indeed pay off in the long run; but we do know they are dangerous.[1]

The fact that we are looking at the *history* of the environmental movement and its relation to the state means that we are well placed to analyse democratization in the form of advances and retreats on the three dimensions of franchise, scope, and authenticity. And it is these advances and retreats that we will compare across countries, rather than 'degree of democracy' as such. Thus we are not in the end interested in whether or not (say) Norway is a more democratic country than the United States as of the year 2001. But we will be able to address the issue of whether or not democratization has been pursued more or less effectively in Norway than in the United States in the last three decades of the twentieth century.

Before we move to our substantive analysis, one further conceptual issue needs attention. Democratic advances and setbacks are charted most meaningfully for the state as a whole or the polity as a whole, rather than for the environmental sector of each of these three arenas in isolation. If our focus is restricted to the environmental movement, what can we really say about democracy in these larger entities? We believe that in fact we can say a lot, because in this chapter we will be using the experience of the environmental

---

[1] Later we will show that the democratic benefits of passive exclusion can take years or even decades to take effect when it comes to democratization of the state. However, passive exclusion is never justified by the excluders in these terms. If they justify exclusion at all in democratic terms (often they will not), it is in terms of protecting the constitutional processes of liberal democracy against destabilization.

movement as a lens through which to examine the larger democratization tra-jectories of states and societies. The environmental movement is uniquely suited to play this role. In terms of the sheer numbers of people it has involved in all developed countries, and in terms of the post-materialism it embodies, the environmental movement is (as we argued in Chapter 1) emblematic of late twentieth-century social movements in general. Moreover, it is the most prominent candidate for assimilation to dominant state imperatives, a theme we will develop in Chapter 7. This candidacy means that if we are interested in the democratic benefits of passively exclusive states, the environmental movement constitutes an especially hard case for demonstrating this thesis. On the other hand, this same situation may mean that the environmental movement has historical significance in relation to the state that other contemporary social movements have yet to demonstrate.[2] These qualities of the movement notwithstanding, we will be sensitive to occasions when the experience of the environmental movement does not mirror that of social movements in general.

Inclusion and the Depletion of Civil Society in Norway and the United States

In Chapter 4 we pointed to the effects that inclusion in the state has on the internal organization of groups, especially in terms of the kind of profession-alization, centralization, and bureaucratization it often entails. Here we wish to broaden the analysis from what goes on inside particular groups to the con-sequences for civil society as a whole. Specifically, we will argue that while inclusion may mean a more democratic state—for effective franchise in the state is expanded—it can mean a less vital and democratic society. For if a group migrates from oppositional civil society to the state, then by definition the oppositional public sphere in question is depleted. Now, if this migration completely empties the public sphere in question, then we should worry a great deal about democratic authenticity. The public sphere is both a rela-tively unconstrained setting for democratic debate and a reservoir for future democratization of the state (in terms of extension of the effective franchise in the state). So even though it may be irrelevant from the point of view of the group's substantive goals, from the point of view of democracy it matters a great deal whether or not a group's movement from civil society to the state leaves behind a flourishing public sphere.

---

[2] The civil rights movement in the United States had such significance in the 1950s and 1960s. Aspects of feminism, especially liberal feminism, are also candidates for assimilation both to the state's legitimation imperative and to the state's economic imperative to the extent it can be shown that equal employment opportunities for women are conducive to economic growth.

The case of Norway highlights this problem. As we pointed out in earlier chapters, Norwegian movement groups have for the most part been thoroughly assimilated into the state from the very beginning of the environmental era. Such active inclusion is true for all kinds of groups, not just environmental ones. This inclusion leaves very little in the way of a democratic civil society; oppositional public spheres hardly exist at all in Norway, outside of the two transient anti-dam protests peaking in 1970 and 1980 respectively. Moreover, the membership of environmental groups is very small in Norway in comparison to its Scandinavian neighbours (see Chapter 2).

We may summarize Norway's democratization trajectory as follows. If we begin with a narrow focus on the state, there are many positives. Scope and franchise underwent substantial increase at the beginning of the era of environmental concern in the early 1970s, with the scope of public control expanding into an additional set of issues, and effective franchise in Norway's corporatist system extended to environmental groups. The later decline of the dominance of the hydro-power complex meant a further increase in democratic scope, because as we saw in Chapter 3, hydro-power policy had traditionally been an area off limits to popular control of any sort. Scope increased once more as the era of sustainable development began in the late 1980s. However, a cross-national perspective highlights the limits to scope's expansion in Norway; the enforced moderation of environmental groups means that a number of issues that ought to be on the public agenda (e.g. commercial whaling, animal welfare) are just not there.

Franchise within the state was further extended as government recognized and funded an ever-increasing number of groups. Authenticity is more questionable; arguably there have been no substantial advances, as included groups have had to adapt to the prevailing style of political interaction within the state. Their inclusion has also meant enforced moderation, such that debate proceeds within a comparatively narrow range. This constriction of deliberation is itself an impediment when it comes to authenticity.

If we expand this assessment to society as a whole, then the weakness of Norway's civil society comes into play. In Chapter 2 we pointed out that civil society in Norway is little more than a reference point for groups that are really quasi-governmental. Despite the number of voluntary groups, there is very little in the way of group life autonomous from the state. In the environmental area the exception is the Bellona Foundation, itself hierarchical, professionalized, and with no democratic credentials. When it comes to franchise, there have been two major retreats. The first occurs after the peaks of mobilization achieved around Mardøla in 1970 and Alta in 1980. The second is seen with the falling membership of the included environmental groups, and the effective disenfranchisement of ordinary members by group leadership that can rely on government grants as the main source of income, and can participate in government committees only as individuals from the group, not by involving the groups as a whole in decision making. There are no *grassroots* groups that have resisted the state's embrace. Thus increase in franchise within the state has been bought at the expense of loss of franchise within the larger society, as group members are marginalized from any kind of political process, be it within or beyond the group.

Mardøla and Alta also signify high points of authenticity in democratic interaction encompassing the public sphere and state that have not been approached since 1980. In short, if we broaden the focus beyond the state, we find that the withering of the grassroots largely vitiates the apparent increase in franchise accompanying the inclusion of environmental groups. However, the gradual increase in scope since 1970 is undeniable, and so a positive assessment on this dimension is unqualified (except for the question marks about issues that have not made the political agenda).

To summarize radically, when it comes to the three dimensions of democratization for the Norwegian polity as a whole:

- Scope advances in a series of steps between 1970 and the 1990s.
- Franchise within the state increases over this same period, most especially in its earlier part. However, once we consider society as a whole, a decline in franchise outlasts this initial period of state-associated gain.
- Authenticity declines after peaks around 1970 and 1980.

Have the undeniable advances within the Norwegian state on scope and franchise been worth the losses when it comes to franchise and authenticity once we expand our purview to encompass civil society? Given the absence of a common metric this is a hard question to answer. The fact that one of the three dimensions—authenticity—is a clear casualty means that one of the principles elucidated at the beginning of this chapter, that advances on one dimension of democratization should never be achieved at the expense of retreats on another, has been violated. Moreover, advances in franchise in the short term seem to have been purchased at the expense of franchise in the longer term, thus violating another principle. Beyond these observations, the depletion of the democratic qualities of civil society has been so complete that serious problems have been caused for democracy in Norway—especially when it comes to the prospects for continuation of democratization as an open-ended project.

To what extent does the United States share such problems as a result of the inclusive character of its state absorbing groups from civil society? Our prediction here is that matters should be somewhat less problematic under passive inclusion, simply because in its early phase a movement or group may have to establish its credentials and mobilize support in civil society before it can make a serious move into the state. It may take some time for a group to decide what sort of political strategies to pursue; in Norway, groups do not have this breathing space, as they are quickly absorbed into the state. Moreover, under passive inclusion a group cannot simply ignore its membership base in the way that Norwegian groups do; communication with members is required, if only in the interests of fund-raising.

We will show in the next section that the United States is capable of generating forms of exclusion that can lead to the at least temporary revitalization of civil society, though perhaps these are best thought of as deviations from the passively inclusive ideal type, rather than consequences of passive inclusion *per se*. But American passive inclusion too causes substantial problems for civil society. Let us now examine these.

The environmental era in United States politics began in the late 1960s with at least some aspects of environmentalism in association with the radical counter-culture—though, as we pointed out in Chapter 2, parts of the movement never had counter-cultural connotations. As we demonstrated in Chapter 3, the Nixon administration in the early 1970s succeeded brilliantly and comprehensively in incorporating environmental groups genuinely and effectively in the state. From those days forth, the movement could be interpreted as a set of interest groups pursuing thoroughly conventional strategies, taking advantage of the multiple channels of access that the United States political system allows. The new social movement form that is so striking in several European countries, Germany foremost among them, in the 1970s and 1980s simply fails to register in the United States.

There are however many positive developments in environmental democracy in the United States from the 1970s to the 1990s. Indeed, the environmental area leads all others in terms of institutional innovations that promote opportunities for consultation and broader participation in policy making. These innovations include public hearings, impact assessment with mandated opportunity for public comment, mediation of disputes, regulatory negotiation, advisory committees, and policy dialogues (see Paehlke, 1988; Rosenbaum, 1989). Most of these innovations are creatures of the 1970s, though more recently they have been joined by a new opportunity for comment on proposed regulations via the Internet (see Chapter 2; Shulman, 2000). All these innovations supplement the traditional avenues of interest group influence via lobbying in the legislative and executive branches of government and litigation in the courts. So if we focus narrowly on the state, we see an upsurge of scope, franchise, and authenticity that begins in the 1970s. Scope increases with the addition of a range of environmental issues to the government's agenda. Franchise increases with the entry of environmentalists into the state—and in the early 1970s, as we established in Chapter 3, they got as far as the state's core. And authenticity increases with the addition of all the participatory innovations that were pioneered in the United States. Though we see stagnation after the 1970s, there is no denying the US status as a pioneer when it comes to environmental democratization of the state, to match its status as an environmental policy pioneer that we analysed in Chapter 3.

However, just as in Norway, there was a democratic loss in civil society to match this democratic gain in the state. From the early 1970s to the 1990s, the major environmental groups constituted a well-defined set, and, as we established in Chapter 4, all succumbed to moderation, professionalization, and bureaucratization as the price of their inclusion. One major difference with Norway is that they had to attend to their membership base, because that was their main source of funds, not government grants as in Norway. Ultimately, though, this leads to a different sort of professionalization in membership management and fund-raising. To the degree the majors under the sway of passive inclusion captured the entirety of environmentalism, no oppositional green public sphere was evident in the United States. However, opposition did begin to take root, especially at the local level, in the mid-1980s, and we will return to the reasons for this later in this chapter.

Can we reach any summary judgment about whether or not the undeniable advances on scope, franchise, and authenticity within the state compensate for this absence of an oppositional sphere? This is a hard question which can however be answered in the negative in light of an analysis of the *dynamics* of democratization. For these advances within the state were largely complete in the 1970s; little real progress is observable since then. So if these advances were bought at the cost of a subsequent halt to democratization within the state and a prevention of democratization (on any of the three dimensions) in civil society, we can conclude that the initial gains were not worth the subsequent costs. However, this judgement must be suspended pending an examination of the implications of the rise of the environmental justice movement in the United States that begins in the late 1980s, to which we will turn shortly.

Germany has of course seen much less inclusion than either the United States or Norway, and in a moment we will analyse it as an exemplar of democratization in the presence of passive exclusion. But a German case shows that even a successful challenge by a movement can make democracy a victim of instrumental success if the challenger accepts even partial embrace by the state. Carol Hager's (1995) study of citizen opposition to the construction of a coal-burning power plant in Berlin describes this dilemma. Using mass protests, legal challenges, and state parliamentary elections to articulate their demands, citizens' groups forced the city's utility company to accept higher emissions standards, a less controversial site, and a much smaller facility than the one first proposed. However, their political concerns went beyond technical issues to include a critique of the way energy policy was being formulated in collusion between the public bureaucracy and the utilities. They

championed an alternative politics based on popular participation and deliberation among the citizenry. The citizens failed in this endeavour because in
making arguments about particular policies they accepted a technical conception of deliberation as a collective search for the truth. This framework
misled them to mistake political for scientific disputes, which in turn undermined their democratic aims by suppressing the diverse forms of political
expression originally present in the movement. Public officials seized on those
elements of the movement they found most congenial and ignored the others.
Ironically, the citizens' attempt to rely on technical expertise to beat the
authorities at their own game—though crucial for succeeding on the policy
dimension—limited their ability to sustain a mass movement and detracted
from their broader concerns with democratic scope, franchise, and authenticity. Such inclusive episodes notwithstanding, Germany provides more in the
way of illustration of the consequences for democracy and democratization
of a passively exclusive state, so let us now turn to these.

Democratic Benefits of Passively Exclusive States, with Special Reference to Germany

To point to the democratic benefits of an exclusive state (albeit a particular
kind—*passively* exclusive) seems on the face of it outrageous, not least to
those political activists who are excluded, and likely to rail against such a
state's undemocratic character. However, that very critical distance on the
part of activists can itself help constitute a more democratically vital society
in the short run, and, in the longer run, even a more democratically vital state
(as we will argue latter). This sort of empirical argument also pours cold water
over political theorists who see the main democratic task of the state in terms
of effectively organizing groups—especially disadvantaged groups—into the
state (for example, Cohen and Rogers, 1992; Young, 1992). Our analysis of
Norway in the previous section suggests that these theorists ought to think
about the depletion of oppositional civil society that would accompany such
moves; in this section we examine the other side of this coin, the vitality in
civil society that exclusive states can inadvertently promote.

Staying for the moment with the short run, political activists excluded from
the state can constitute a public sphere where political action is relatively
unconstrained (in that it need not be subordinated to the kinds of strategic
calculations that we discussed in Chapter 4 in the context of the moderation
and professionalization that accompanies inclusion in the state). Thus democratic authenticity may be achieved more straightforwardly in the public
sphere than in the state. Of course, constraints such as the influence of ideology, competition for prestige and members, the 'tyranny of structurelessness'

in which nominally egalitarian settings act to induce conformity (Freeman, 1975) can operate in the public sphere, so there are threats to authenticity. All we are saying is that one major set of impediments—those associated with action within the state—are less constraining when it comes to deliberation and interaction within the public sphere.

One reason new social movements could develop in countries like Germany in the 1970s and 1980s is that they had to develop an unconventional kind of oppositional politics because they were excluded from the more conventional politics associated with the state (Kitschelt, 1988).[3] A similar kind of politics could be observed fleetingly in the United States around 1970. However, its activists found it hard to resist inclusion, thus the public sphere in question had nothing like the staying power of its German counterpart. In both cases movements had their origins in the counter-culture for which the year 1968 is a symbol. But while movements in the United States peaked in terms of numbers of people mobilized around 1968–70, in Germany the peak came much later. The high point of new social movement activity in Germany was 1983, when 9,200 protests could be recorded (Balistier, 1996).

The prolonged agony of internal Green Party strategic debates illustrates the awareness of *Fundis* and *Realos* alike of the relative freedom of action in the oppositional public sphere, even as they debated whether or not to renounce it. While *Realos* believed that abandoning the politics of protest was a price worth paying for success in elections and participation in coalitions, *Fundis* believed that such abandonment was a betrayal of green principles pertaining to both political process and the substance of positions taken. But both wings of the party recognized the reality of the trade-off.

After the high points of the 1970s and 1980s, the vitality of the green oppositional public sphere in Germany declined along with somewhat increased opportunities for inclusion in the state. We pointed out in Chapter 3 that these opportunities remained quite limited in comparison to those in other countries (such as Norway and the United States), but they look significant within the German context. Notably, the creation of the federal Environment Ministry in 1986 gave movement groups a point of access to the state bureaucracy previously denied to them. As our analysis of passive exclusion would predict, such limited inclusion was accompanied by professionalization and moderation of groups. This effect persists once we control for the influence of time and organizational growth (as we did in Chapter 4), suggesting the relationship is causal, and corroborating our theoretical expectation concerning the positive influence of passive exclusion on democratic authenticity in the public sphere.

---

[3] Similarly, oppositional civil society could flourish as a parallel polity in East European states in the 1980s where Stalinism had waned, notably Poland and Czechoslovakia. See Dryzek, 1996a: 67; Bunce, 1992.

However, a comparative perspective on these developments shows that Germany was still largely a passively exclusive state in the 1990s, and remained so even after the Green entry into a Federal coalition government with the Social Democrats in 1998. For the Environment Ministry remained largely separated from the core of the state, and the anti-nuclear movement continued large mobilizations and protests, both before and after 1998. These required, for example, 30,000 police to be mobilized in 1995–7 to protect the route of trains returning spent fuel rods to Germany for long-term storage from reprocessing plants in the UK and France (Kolb, 1997). The protests persisted even after the Greens in government had negotiated a planned phase-out of nuclear power. Part of the bargain was that the Green Party would then acquiesce in renewed shipment of reprocessed wastes. But several environmental groups—not only the radical BBU, BUND, and Greenpeace, but also the more traditionally moderate DNR and NABU—refused to accept this position, and organized non-violent protests against the shipments in 2001. As we noted in Chapter 4, one Green parliamentarian expressed exasperation with the BUND's seeming inability to formulate a negotiating position when it came to nuclear power. While this could be seen as an example of organizational paralysis, another interpretation would highlight the persistence of 'movement' modes of politics under which internal democracy inhibits deal-making by the leadership.

In short, at the time of writing Germany remains a passively exclusive state, environmentalist participation via the Environment Ministry and Green Party presence in the Federal coalition notwithstanding. The phase-out of nuclear power was negotiated between Economics Ministry officials and nuclear industry leaders, with both the Environment Ministry and Green ministers on the sidelines. This situation confirmed Katzenstein's (1987) earlier observation concerning the remarkable continuity of Germany's legal-corporatist policy making structures and processes across changing governments. And as we would expect of a passively exclusive state, an oppositional public sphere persists. This sphere is now mostly specific to the anti-nuclear movement, and in that sense is more limited than that which existed in Germany in the 1970s and 1980s (see Rucht and Roose, 1999). But in comparative perspective, it remains large and vital.

This comparative analysis is however limited by the difficulty in comparing 'degree of democracy' across political systems that we noted at the beginning of this chapter. So for the reasons we stated, we must now turn to assessment of the extent to which passive exclusion in Germany has promoted democratization in terms of the three dimensions of scope, franchise, and authenticity—in the state, and in the polity as a whole. On the face of it, passive exclusion cannot by definition promote democracy within the state; but we will show that there is an indirect route that goes via civil society through which this can actually happen. However, because even this route goes first to civil society, in Germany we must start our dynamic discussion with civil society—unlike the case for Norway, where the state itself is the obvious starting point for such a discussion.

Germany begins the modern environmental era with the most passively exclusive of states (see Chapter 2). Environmentalism begins as a set of normative concerns, but as we have argued all along, the form the movement takes is influenced by the structure of the state (active or passive, inclusive or exclusive) as it is caught between a set of imperatives and the demands of the movement. In Germany in the 1970s, especially in the context of energy crisis that began in 1973, it is the economic imperative that dominates. Energy economics for the German state meant nuclear power, pursued in uncompromising fashion that completely excluded any opposition; which then had to create its own politics in a separate public sphere. In the 1980s the security imperative took centre stage with the renewal of the Cold War and associated deployment of new nuclear missiles on German soil. Again this core policy area was immune to any kind of critical questioning, and again opposition constituted a public sphere confronting the state.

We have claimed that democratic authenticity in the public sphere in Germany is facilitated by a passively exclusive state. If so, then when it comes to the *dynamics* of democratization, advances on authenticity are contingent upon the arrival of important issues that engage core state imperatives (in the German case, energy crisis and missile deployment) but shut out movement interests. Such issues do of course arrive from time to time in inclusive states too, but there they are likely to provide occasions for co-optation into the state's periphery rather than invigoration of the public sphere.

Now, any oppositional public sphere accompanying passive exclusion need persist only so long as the defining interest of the movement in question cannot be assimilated to a state imperative. The public sphere in question *can* outlast this conjunction—and the fact that old habits of legal corporatism die hard in Germany means that it does. However, it *need* not persist once the conjunction has happened, as the movement can then enter the state without merely being co-opted into the state's periphery. In Germany we do eventually see such conjunction, which we will explore in Chapter 7 when we discuss ecological modernization and the legitimacy issues that the risk society thesis highlights. But is then the only difference between a passively exclusive state like Germany and inclusive states like the United States and Norway that we just have to wait a bit longer for inclusion in the state?

We believe that the difference is much more significant than this. Consider the concise history of the state with which we began this book. Each historic wave of inclusions in the modern state—that of the bourgeoisie which produced the liberal capitalist state, that of the organized working class which produced the welfare state—was preceded by a large and lively oppositional public sphere where the category in question honed its arguments and political skills. We have argued that a passively exclusive state is much more conducive to the development of such a sphere than its more inclusive alternatives. So even if the members of the public sphere in question are destined for eventual inclusion in the state, it matters enormously whether they are included as former members of a vital social movement (as in Germany), or as individuals with a background only in a professionalized organization (as in Norway and the United States). So even democracy within the state will be more authentic in states with a history of passive exclusion because it is engaged by more critical and competent participants—those with a history in the oppositional public sphere. In Chapter 7 we will show how this dynamic plays out in the case of ecological modernization—and explain why Germany can therefore more readily experience, at this historical point, a much stronger and more democratic form of ecological modernization than the other countries in this study.

We are now in a position to assess the democratization of the German polity in terms of the three criteria of scope, franchise, and authenticity over the period since 1970. Starting with the state, scope increases very slowly in the 1970s (more slowly than in the United States), but key areas (the economy, nuclear power, then in the 1980s missiles) remain off-limits to enhanced democratic control in the legal corporatist system. Scope continues to increase in the 1980s and 1990s as the reach of environmental policy is extended into economic policy areas with the onset of ecological modernization.

In principle, this last development ought to enable extension of the effective franchise within the state to environmental groups. In practice, the state-related franchise does increase with the establishment of the Environment Ministry in 1986, but this expansion proves very limited, as this ministry itself is mostly excluded from core areas of policy making. The entry of the Green Party into governing coalitions, at first at city and state level, then eventually in 1998 at the federal level, might seem to symbolize further extension of the effective franchise beyond the traditional corporatist players. But we should not make too much of this development, because under legal corporatism the bureaucracy is in many ways more significant than parliament or even the composition of the governing coalition. As Rose-Ackerman (1995) observes in comparing US and German environmental policy styles, the German style of regulation does not permit adequate public and environmental interest representation because the legislature delegates to the bureaucracy the power to write ordinances that have the force of law but do not require parliamentary involvement or public consultations of any sort. One of Germany's major anti-pollution measures of the last ten years, the Large Plant Combustion Ordinance, for example, is not an Act of Parliament but an agency rule, as is much of environmental law. Of course, as the US example shows, interests can be represented in administrative decision making processes (Hunold, 2001; Kerwin, 1999). Not so in Germany. The problem, from the perspective of environmental NGOs seeking to influence environmental law, is that German administrative law does not allow for the sort of agency discretion that is needed to facilitate the gathering and use of comprehensive cross-media environmental impact assessment data in planning decisions. Famously, the German government took five years to transpose the EU's 1985 Environmental Impact Assessment directive into national law, and another six years to introduce the administrative provisions required for its implementation—largely because, as Kraak and Pehle (2001: 6) explain, the European directive 'is comparatively blind when it comes to internal German administrative structures'. By limiting the discretionary power of regulatory agencies in industrial licensing processes, German administrative law provides developers with a high degree of legal predictability, but looks askance at the sort of procedural and substantive flexibility necessary to accommodate greater public involvement. The European Commission has since sued the German government (successfully) over the inadequacies of the provisions it did manage to implement.

Authenticity within the state does probably advance with the entry into it in the 1990s of politically competent individuals with a background in the oppositional public sphere. However, so long as the dominant legal corporatist style of policy making persists, then advances on authenticity within the state remain limited.

Thus if we look at democratization of the German state alone, we find that over three decades advances in scope, franchise, and authenticity do occur—but they are very modest, especially in comparison with the United States in the early 1970s and Norway thereafter. If we stayed with the history of the state, our proposition about the democratic benefits of passive exclusion would seem to be falsified. It is only when we broaden the focus to the polity as a whole, encompassing civil society, that a different picture emerges. For even in the clearly exclusionary decades of the 1970s and 1980s, the oppositional public sphere played a vital part in German democracy, to the extent of securing some power over collective outcomes. For example, the anti-nuclear movement had some substantial successes in forcing the abandonment of plans for particular power stations (though not in terms of reducing the state's commitment to nuclear power). Thus the expansion of scope when it comes to the polity as a whole does reach into the nuclear energy area—if only to the limited degree of pressure from the public sphere forcing the cancellation of projects. By the late 1980s the mainstream parties were beginning to embrace ecological modernization, in large measure because of pressure from the public sphere—and the power of the ideas generated therein. So environmentalists were increasingly 'enfranchised', even though their activity was largely confined to the public sphere as a site of political activity. Momentum in scope and franchise in the public sphere was maintained in the 1990s with the development of 'paragovernmental' forms involving movement groups, eco-consultancies and green companies, which we will address in Chapters 6 and 7. But it is on the dimension of democratic authenticity that we see the most dramatic advances, as large numbers of citizens were mobilized into communicative political action in the 1970s and 1980s. The numbers involved may have declined since a peak in the early 1980s (and so there has been some retreat on the franchise dimension from that high point). But the German state remains passively exclusive, ecological modernization and the end of the Cold War notwithstanding. And the German public sphere remains a site of authentic political action. So we have confirmed the basic proposition that passively exclusive states that for the most part ignore social movements and provide no points of entry for them can be surprisingly, if unintentionally, beneficial for the democratic vitality of society.

At the time of writing this dynamic process is still playing itself out. But in long-term historical perspective, Germany appears much better placed than our other three states to embrace the kinds of modifications to state imperatives that the advent of environmentalism ultimately requires. The implication for democracy is truly profound: alone among our cases, the German polity as a whole may be able to accommodate the environmental movement in a way that preserves the movement's authenticity. If so, it is in Germany that the parallel with the earlier inclusions of the bourgeoisie and organized working class may be strongest—but with an added democratic twist. We will explore this possibility more fully in Chapter 7.

Accounting for an American Anomaly: Passive Exclusion in Disguise?

According to our explanatory framework, it is Germany where democratic authenticity grounded in the public sphere should find its greatest potential, and for the most part this expectation is confirmed. However, the re-emergence of locally grounded environmental activism that rejects moderation and professionalization in the structurally inhospitable context of the United States, beginning in the mid 1980s and expanding in the 1990s, is a seeming anomaly that threatens to undermine the framework. Organizations such as Earth First!, resource centres such as the Center for Health, Environment, and Justice,[4] and networks such as the Southwest Network for Economic and Environmental Justice—along with numerous local and

---

[4] Formerly the Citizens' Clearinghouse for Hazardous Wastes.

regional-based groups dealing with wilderness, toxics, indigenous issues, and much more—grew in numbers and in strength. If we are right in categorizing the United States as passively inclusive, these movements ought to have very quickly become interest groups of the conventional sort. Yet this is not what happened. The movements consciously resisted professionalization and bureaucratization, and organized instead as networks, with many nodes but no central leadership or head office (Schlosberg, 1999).

The environmental justice network in particular is an innovator in the field of democracy. Growing out of a series of local actions against polluters and toxic waste dumpers, the movement effectively enfranchised many people, often ethnic minorities and/or poor. The question of the distribution of environmental risks and hazards was put firmly on the political agenda for the first time, so democratic scope increases too. But it is from the point of view of democratic authenticity that the movement is especially interesting. Environmental justice networks bring together very different kinds of people, of different racial and ethnic backgrounds, incomes, and geographical locations (as different as Native American reservations and middle-class suburbia). To negotiate this radical variety, the movement has developed a kind of discursive democracy embodying strong principles of respect for the identities and positions of others, with no attempt to impose or develop any common ideology. To Schlosberg (1999), this is 'critical pluralism' in action: not a pluralism of interest group influence and accommodation, but a pluralism of agonistic respect across very different kinds of people engaged in common struggles against particular industries or companies. Variety in local interpretations, points of view, and political strategies always has to be accepted.

The US environmental justice movement and associated anti-toxics movement are, then, pioneers of the network form of organization in the public sphere. Is that sphere separate and distinct from the state? The answer here is 'partly'—less so than the opposing totalities of green public sphere and state that we see in Germany in the 1970s and 1980s, but more so than the kind of interest group politics engaged by the established major environmental groups in the United States. As befits a loosely connected series of groups and actions, the movements sometimes take oppositional form, sometimes looking more conventional. They are oppositional when organizing protests, demonstrations, and boycotts. They are more conventional when fighting legal actions or lobbying politicians and government agencies. The movements have managed to penetrate the state, quite formally in the Office of Environmental Justice of the Federal Environmental Protection Agency and the National Environmental Justice Advisory Committee, also associated with the EPA.

Such state-related developments notwithstanding, the degree to which the environmental justice and anti-toxics movements in particular have maintained a relatively autonomous sphere in confrontation with the state is indeed striking, and a seeming anomaly when it comes to our explanatory framework. The easy way out for us here would be to say that this situation is just an example of heightened reflexivity. In other words, activists have seen how the majors operate and what they have accomplished, are not impressed, and consciously try to be different—especially in avoiding the lure of Washington and in maintaining a grassroots character. Certainly, there is an element of this—and activists can be extremely scathing about the majors and what they stand for (see Chapter 4). But activists are also quite conscious of how they have been excluded from a policy process that has accepted the moderate majors, but excluded others. The inclusion of the major groups left a vacuum at the community level. Local groups concerned with issues the major groups were not dealing with felt left out of the environmental movement (see Dowie, 1995). Community activists were often just as upset with the major environmental groups as they were with government agencies and local polluters, to the point of refusing to categorize themselves as 'environmentalists' so as to distinguish themselves from the majors. They saw the mainstream populated with people who would compromise with government officials or negotiate over a meal with corporate executives, leaving communities without real participation or protection.

The bitterness that arose was exacerbated when the majors then decided to take on environmental justice issues, absorbing foundation grant money and making compromises with governments and corporations. Often a major group would appoint itself the environmental movement representative, with no respect for those dissenting from its position—the Natural Resources Defense Council played such a role in regard to the North American Free Trade Area issue in 1993. A similar situation arose in the campaign that Concerned Citizens in Action and the Citizens' Clearing House for Hazardous Wastes launched against McDonalds' use of styrofoam containers in the early 1990s. The National Environmental Defense Fund then appointed itself to the role of negotiator. Its eventual compromise with the multinational excluded the CCA and CCHW, denying them a say in the outcome (Dowie, 1995: 139–40). This sort of action taken by an established group or groups can be divisive and debilitating.[5] On the other hand, it can also be energizing in the degree to which it reinforces the need for the grassroots groups to maintain their distance from the majors.

[5] Environmental groups in New Zealand learned this lesson with the 1986 West Coast forestry accord. In a negotiated agreement with the forestry industry mediated by government, some major environmental groups accepted restricted native forest logging in exchange for conservation reserves. The agreement effectively removed an issue which had been the mainstay of environmental campaigns for over a decade from the political agenda, and the environmental movement was subsequently beset by internal division (Downes, 2000).

Thus the persistence of the oppositional public sphere associated with the environmental justice movement can be explained by a kind of passive exclusion, even though it is not a passively exclusive *state*. As such, the kind of exclusion operating is less thoroughgoing and durable than when it is a matter of state structure, as in Germany. The exclusion that operates in the United States could be attenuated by the established major groups taking up the issue of the distribution of environmental hazards that they had hitherto mostly ignored, by governments taking these issues more seriously, and by environmental justice groups themselves getting weary of the oppositional life and taking advantage of the kinds of access that always beckon in the US political system. The 1990s saw development on all three of these fronts. The established majors began to admit that action at the local level by grassroots groups had a place, and to take environmental justice concerns seriously, such that the kind of position that the Environmental Defense Fund took in the McDonalds styrofoam case is increasingly rare. Beginning in the early days of the Clinton presidency, the federal government gave institutional recognition to environmental justice, with an executive order to agencies to take these matters seriously, as well as establishing the EPA units we have mentioned. And the more high-profile networks such as the Southwest Network for Economic and Environmental Justice (SNEEJ) by the late 1990s found themselves criticized by activists dissatisfied with the fact that these organizations were monopolizing the limited amount of foundation money available for environmental justice issues, and becoming tied up with the institutionalization of environmental justice in universities. Some individuals have made the move from new activist groups to the majors or into government.[6] But at the time of writing the oppositional public sphere is still there. The passive exclusion that helped to generate it having now been reduced, its persistence really does depend on the kind of reflexivity we mentioned earlier.

At this point we can conclude that passive exclusion is actually beneficial when it comes to the enhancement of democracy, and especially democratic authenticity, in the public sphere confronting the state. Of course, there are by definition also associated democratic costs associated with the exclusion of groups when it comes to democracy within the state itself. Our discussion of the more strongly exclusive case of Germany shows that in the long run the democratizing benefits outweigh the democratic costs. In the United States, the plural and discursive politics invented by the environmental justice movement is a major advance in democratic authenticity, accompanied by increases in democratic scope and franchise. This politics also demonstrates

---

[6] One environmental justice activist we spoke with worked for two years in the NRDC, recruited as part of an outreach to the movement, but left the organization in frustration. One of the key figures in the environmental justice movement, Bill Lee of the United Church of Christ, was later employed by the Federal EPA.

the possibility of reflexive retention of an oppositional sphere in a system that is in the main passively inclusive.

Active Exclusion Undermining Civil Society? Britain

The third proposition with which we began this chapter was that actively exclusive states damage the democratic qualities of civil society, and so sap the democratic vitality of society as a whole. Here we intend to explore this point by putting Britain in the 1979–90 actively exclusive Thatcher era in comparative perspective.

In fact, British environmental groups grew in numbers of members and supporters during this time period. Between 1981 and 1991 total membership of the established groups doubled (Rootes, 2000). Most of this increase came in 1988–90 as environmental issues underwent an upsurge on the international political agenda, and after Thatcher's change of heart in her 1988 Royal Society speech (though it is implausible to see the latter as a causal factor here).

Thatcherism's active exclusions were not fatal for the environmental movement. Indeed, there developed stronger networks and joint campaigns than had previously been the case. Grove-White (1991: 34) reflects:

there was more and more personal interaction and symbiosis between activists, irrespective of the formal operating traditions of their organisations . . . [a]s political self-confidence developed—through principally the anti-nuclear, anti-motorway and agriculture/conservation campaigns of the late 70s and early 80s—new link bodies emerged. Thus, Wildlife Link, the Council for National Parks, Countryside Link, the Green Alliance, even (corporately) the UK members of the EEB, became increasingly significant in linking overlapping networks of full-time staff/activists in a wide range of NGOs.

These linkages paid off on the nuclear front. Greenpeace, which had been sceptical of the government's motives with respect to the 1985 Sizewell Inquiry and wary of the likely resource demands of participation, directed its campaigning against the dumping of nuclear waste at sea. In concert with the National Union of Seamen, in 1983 Greenpeace successfully pressured the government to relocate nuclear waste on land (Rudig, 1994: 84). Friends of the Earth in turn targeted the land sites, thwarting NIREX's proposed development of a nuclear waste reprocessing plant through community mobilization in potential site localities and by lobbying local politicians (Lamb, 1996: 109). Local protest at Billingham in 1985 also successfully dissuaded the government from constructing a nuclear repository (Blowers, 1987).

On the face of it, increasing membership of environmental groups and a determination on their part to find alternative strategies once access to the state was completely blocked contradicts our proposition about the deleterious effects on the democratic vitality of civil society of an actively exclusive state. But numbers of members and the continued search for ways to make a difference tell only part of the story. Much of the action was defensive. Tony Burton, Policy Director at CPRE, reflects on the difficulties encountered by his organization by the late 1980s:

I suppose it was best to describe it as 'fire-fighting'. We were in the business of damage limitation in relation to Government policy at the time . . . the opportunity to even think positively or over the long term was very very difficult . . . (Interview, 1999)

What is peculiar about the United Kingdom throughout the 1980s and into the early 1990s is the lack of anything resembling a new social movement form of environmentalism. Friends of the Earth and Greenpeace 'represented the radical end of the spectrum of British environmental groups at the beginning of the 1990s, but they were neither very democratic nor participatory in practice' (Doherty, 1999: 278). As Rootes (1992) points out, there is a British 'exceptionalism' that needs explaining here. Elsewhere in Western Europe, a low degree of protest politics was accompanied by either a very low level of environmental group membership (as in the Mediterranean countries) or a movement that had strong access to the state (see also Doherty, 1999: 278). Only in the United Kingdom do we see minimal protest politics coexisting with relatively high membership of environmental groups and no access to the state.

The plot thickens inasmuch as the breadth of support for post-materialist values was just as strong in the United Kingdom as elsewhere in Northern Europe. Moreover, given that the modest consultative channels that did exist for environmental groups were suddenly blocked in 1979, one might have expected groups to then explore more oppositional forms of action in the public sphere. As Philip Lowe explains:

By the mid-1980s there were people in conventional lobbying organisations who were much more prepared . . . to go public with their concerns. There had been an understanding amongst those that had come up through environmental politics in the 60s and 70s that you played by certain unwritten rules of the game, that once you had a degree of access you didn't 'blow the whistle'. . . but there was a feeling that the rules had really been rewritten by the mid-80s. (Interview, 1999)

Yet no radicalized oppositional sphere emerged.

Rootes believes that British exceptionalism can be explained by the fact that protest politics was still mostly class politics, which in turn was absorbed by a relatively radical Labour Party. Environmentalism for its part was associated with privileged group leaders with an 'establishment' background, whom any self-respecting radical would avoid. Doherty (1999) endorses this explanation. But it is not really an explanation at all, because its dependent variables (moderation and hierarchy in the environmental movement; a class-based politics of protest) are also its independent variables (moderation and hierarchy in the environmental movement; a class-based politics of protest).

In a comparative light, British exceptionalism when it comes to environmentalism in the 1980s is matched by the exceptionalism of its state. The United Kingdom in this era was the only European outpost of radical market liberalism, with an authoritarian liberal, actively exclusive state to match. Our argument here turns on the degree to which this kind of state undermined democratic authenticity in civil society in general, and in the environmental movement in particular.[7] In part this is a matter of the state increasing the costs associated with radical action. A more important factor is that the actively exclusive state undermines the conditions that enable collective interests to be felt and articulated to begin with. The operative mechanisms here include the radical individualization and marketization of society accompanying market liberalism, and the associated redefinition of citizenship in terms of obligation and responsibility as opposed to political involvement.

However, the case for the democratic damage caused to civil society is weak. There are several considerations that inhibit any more confident causal conclusion. First, the green public sphere was not especially strong in Britain prior to the Thatcher era. Thus in the 1970s, the United Kingdom already featured exceptionalism in its lack of the new social movement form as identified by Rootes. When it comes to democratic authenticity, the Thatcher era therefore saw little decline in civil society (though authenticity declined along with scope and franchise within the state). Second, it is always much harder trying to explain the absence of something—in this case, a new social movement—than a presence. Third, the Thatcher experience shows (along with contemporaneous experiments in market liberalism in other Anglo-American societies) just how hard it is to maintain a truly actively exclusive state for very long in a developed open society.

It is only when we put active exclusion in comparative perspective that its deleterious impact on civil society becomes apparent. Our other exclusive state, Germany, featured so much more in the way of advances in democratic authenticity in the 1980s than did the United Kingdom. Equally revealing is what happens when the exclusion is later ameliorated. In Britain after 1988, leaders and activists in movement groups heaved a sigh of relief and accepted governmental invitations to participate in renewed consultations, especially around sustainable development. In Chapter 4 we pointed out that this turn of events actually led to paralysis on the part of the mainstream groups as, in

---

[7] Hierarchy within groups such as Friends of the Earth and Greenpeace—and the effective disenfranchisement of ordinary members it connotes—is unhelpful to our explanation because we argued in Chapter 4 that it is an *inclusive* state that is likely to foster such hierarchy.

the words of one of our interviewees, they became 'barnacle-encrusted' as opposed to 'muscle-bound' with their new commitments. If anything there is a retreat in democratic authenticity in civil society at this juncture. Thus the major negative effect of active exclusion may be in just how little movement groups are prepared to settle for once it is lifted. In Germany, in contrast, we have pointed out that even after the waning of its confrontational phase, oppositional civil society leaves a strong democratic legacy.

The British story does not however end here. The 1990s witnessed a surge in radical protest, especially in connection with the anti-roads movement. Doherty and Rawcliffe (1995: 247) describe this activist resurgence as 'an eco-logical social movement' which, in contrast to the pressure group politics of the more established groups, engaged in direct action and developed a broad critique of industrialism in British society. The new activists avoided formal organization, not just because of their antipathy to hierarchy, but also because an identifiable decision making body would be vulnerable to legal prosecution and asset seizure. Reclaim the Streets, for example, relies on word of mouth and communication through the Internet to mobilize actions. The activist support base included some of the casualties of Thatcherite eco-nomic policies. As one activist put it, 'maybe it is Mrs Thatcher who should be thanked most because many of our activists were unemployed, early retirees or redundant and were able to give all of their time to fighting the campaign' (Charles Elstone, cited in Wall, 1999: 115).

Shane Collins, who was involved in the anti-roads campaign through Reclaim the Streets, emphasizes democratic empowerment as a motivating factor and point of distinction from the formerly more radical Friends of the Earth and Greenpeace:

We felt Friends of the Earth and Greenpeace were basically saying to people 'Look, join us . . . and we'll sort out the problem', and we felt that this was ultimately extremely disempowering for people, and the situation then and now is that it needs direct action, it needs people protesting, being passionate and upfront about it and making sure that the government, the roadbuilders, the globalisation capitalists know that we're in their face. (Interview, 1999)

This kind of perception is consistent with that of anti-toxics and environ-mental justice activists in the United States at the same time. That is, the established 'major' groups are seen as having entered into an association with government that is both exclusive and ineffective from the point of view of the activists' concerns. (Perhaps paradoxically, many of the radicals were or had been members of the more established groups such as Friends of the Earth, though not in leadership positions.)

Doherty (1999: 276) believes that this surge of protest signalled the first arrival in the United Kingdom of the new social movement form of organ-ization, embodying 'counter-cultural ideas, ideologically justified resistance to formal organization and non-violent direct action'. However, these groups featured less of the ideological agonizing that was one defining feature of such groups in the 1970s and 1980s elsewhere in Europe. The forms of activism were quite innovative, involving tree-sitting and tunnelling to prevent motorway construction in the countryside, and actions to 'Reclaim the Streets' in the cities. Actions were organized on a decentralized basis that made it hard for organizers to be pinpointed and targeted. The movement lacked formal structure—in part a matter of defence against an asset-seizing state. We pointed out in Chapter 2 that in the early 1990s Britain featured a dual state. On the one hand, moderate groups were accepted in passively inclusive fashion. On the other, radicals felt the force of the coercive state, intensified by the Criminal Justice and Public Order Act of 1994. But the radicals were not dissuaded; indeed, they were quite ingenious in developing means of political action that put them organizationally beyond the reach of the state (except as individuals on the front lines of protest subject to arrest). So in an odd way their tactics converted the actively exclusive arm of the state into a passively exclusive one, which allowed them space for political action. Protest was further criminalized by the Terrorism Act of 2000 (extremely elastic in its definition of terrorism) and the Criminal Justice and Police Act of 2001, though at the time of writing it remains to be seen how these will be implemented by the police and courts. If the experience of the 1994 Act is any guide, police and courts will be reluctant to use the full force of the law available to them against social movements.

It does takes a bit of this kind of procrustean stretching to render British history since 1979 into an illustration of the deleterious effects of active exclusion on democratization in civil society. The environmental movement was not destroyed by exclusion in the 1980s. A social movement did arise in the 1990s in response to a kind of passive exclusion that the major groups in conjunction with government now fostered. The movement then confronted the teeth of the actively exclusive face of the dual state. Still, when it comes to the state itself, the balance sheet for active exclusion is unremittingly negative: scope, franchise, and authenticity are all damaged. When it comes to civil society, some damage is observable, but resistance also has its successes. But there is one further negative associated with the impact of active exclusion on civil society that we have yet to address. This impact concerns the degree of diversity observable in the movement. We will now show that active exclusion damages diversity—though so does active inclusion.

Movement Diversity

The public sphere is a vital component of a functioning democracy (see e.g. Habermas, 1996*a*), as well as a source of democratic innovation. Its ability to perform these functions in contemporary complex societies depends crucially on the degree of political diversity that this sphere features. In the history of the development of the modern state, the bourgeois and working-class public spheres that we introduced in Chapter 1 may have been comparatively homogeneous, featuring as they did clear class interests. But even in those cases, unless there were differences of opinion stemming from diversity of interests and concerns there was nothing to talk about except strategy. (The development of Leninism illustrates the disastrous consequences for democracy of a complete subordination of difference to strategy.)

Difference in identities and interests is, as Iris Young (2000) points out at length, a resource for democratic communication because it provides the grist for dispute, debate, reflection, and renewal. The experience of the United States environmental justice movement that we discussed earlier in this chapter shows how the need for participants to negotiate across their very different backgrounds and ways of life itself stimulated the emergence of an innovative democratic form—a kind of discursive and critical pluralism.

Beyond the general importance of difference to democratic communication, environmentalism in particular constitutes, or can constitute, a multifaceted source of challenges to industrial society. To succeed in this critical task, the green public sphere needs to be able to foster the variety of challenges. Here as elsewhere, innovative thinking is most likely to occur at the intersection of different frameworks and worldviews. The idea of a multifaceted green public sphere in these terms is celebrated by Torgerson (1999). If environmentalism is to continue to be a source of ferment and new ideas, then such variety must be nurtured. Torgerson rightly exposes the danger of the monolithic visions pushed upon greens by thinkers such as Norton (1991) and Goodin (1992), who want to impose a single normative discipline on the movement. A public sphere disciplined in these terms would not necessarily succumb to environmental Leninism; but it would be a democratically impoverished place. Democratic authenticity, above all, flourishes to the extent of diversity in identities, interests, aims, and organizational forms. But another dimension of democratization, the scope of issues amenable to collective control, is also advanced to the degree of diversity in the movement. Obviously the more diverse the perspectives that are brought to bear, the greater the range of issues that is canvassed. (Any celebration of diversity does not mean the green public sphere has to be unbounded; it is united in a critique of unconstrained industrialism.)

Diversity is easy to celebrate in the abstract, but what does it mean in the particular? To recognize and measure diversity, we should begin by noting that diversity can come in the social background of participants, the organizational form taken by movement groups, the substantive area of concern, and the values and aims of groups.

To begin with social background, environmentalism has often been characterized as a movement of and for the relatively privileged, a concern that people can only come to once they have escaped poverty and income insecurity (Dalton, 1994, 1996; Inglehart, 1990; McCarthy and Zald, 1987). However, environmental risks and hazards fall disproportionately on low-income groups and, in the United States, members of racial and ethnic minorities. The experience of the environmental justice movement shows that such people can be mobilized into political action—or, rather, that they can mobilize themselves (Cole and Foster, 2001; Gould, Schnaiberg, and Weinberg, 1996). Normally this mobilization will occur only in response to a tangible local hazard, such as a waste incinerator or oil refinery over the fence. But it is hard to put this observation into comparative perspective because Norway and Germany in particular do not feature the extreme kind of income disparity or intensity of interracial and inter-ethnic inequality found in the United States.

The organizational form taken by the movement is easier to compare and assess across our four countries than is its social composition. The most prominent observable movement forms are political parties, interest groups, protest businesses, eco-consultancies, new social movements, and networks. Of our four countries, Germany comes closest to possessing all of these. Unsurprisingly given its electoral system, the United States is missing a green party of much significance (beyond the Nader presidential campaigns of 1996 and 2000, which hardly constituted a party in the normal sense; Nader himself never formally joined the party and there are actually two competing national Green Party organizations in the country). The United Kingdom until the 1990s and Norway with the exception of two anti-dam protests are missing new social movements and networks.

When it comes to diversity in identities, interests, values, and aims, environmentalism can of course cover a wide range of concerns. The movement can be home to moderates and radicals; ecocentric and anthropocentric value systems; wilderness defenders and public health advocates; groups with local, regional, national, and global foci; urban and rural interests; and substantive interests in animal liberation, environmental aesthetics, sustainable development, resource conservation, the distribution of risks, etc. At one level groups concerned with these different substantive aspects can simply go their own separate ways, such that it matters little whether or not they engage one another, and so in the larger democratic scheme of things none of them would be missed. But in practice the issue space of environmentalism is not like this; substantive concerns intersect, and often pull in somewhat different directions (for example, the conflict between animal liberationists and wilderness preservationists when it comes to the control of feral or introduced animal species). As Barry Commoner (1972) popularized it long ago, the first law of ecology is that 'everything is connected to everything else'.

In the terms we have now established for ascertaining variety in the movement, Norway is quite striking in terms of its relative uniformity. On the organizational front, Norway has no green party of any significance, despite its electoral system of proportional representation that ought to be conducive to the establishment and influence of such a party. Nor has Norway experienced any new social movement form of mobilization outside the Mardøla and Alta dam cases of the early and late 1970s respectively. Nor do we observe anything like the network form as seen in the United States environmental justice movement, and to a more limited degree in resurgent activism in Britain in the 1990s. Norway possesses only interest groups of a very moderate sort, and protest businesses such as Bellona. When it comes to substantive concerns, ecocentrism is surprisingly weak in this homeland of deep ecology, as symbolized by the tiny number of Greenpeace members in Norway, and the absence of any domestic opposition to the major blot on Norway's international environmental reputation: commercial whaling.

We can explain Norway's lack of movement diversity quite straightforwardly in terms of its actively inclusive state. Organization into the state has meant playing by a common set of rules and integration into a unified system. There has been no space in civil society for oppositional formations to develop their own rules of engagement—enabling, for example, the kind of pluralistic discursive democracy that the United States environmental justice movement invented.

Our other state that intervened actively to shape civil society, Britain in the 1979–90 Thatcher era, features a somewhat different story, but still uniformity looms large. Environmentalism in 1980s Britain featured a movement growing in size, though not in influence within the state. But this expansion meant more of the same in terms of a conventional and relatively moderate form of interest group organization. In our discussion of this era earlier in this chapter we noted that the 1980s saw improved co-ordination across the various groups as they confronted the common Thatcherite enemy. But this creation of linkages may even itself have acted to further enhance the movement's uniformity. Certainly there was no democratic innovation in the vicinity of the movement, despite the multiple causes for complaint and opposition that the unremittingly developmentalist Thatcherite programme generated.

Environmentalism in Britain in the 1980s saw no radical action of the new social movement variety, and no extension of the scope of movement activity to new issue areas. For example, when it came to opposition to the covering of huge areas of the remnant countryside of south-east England with housing estates, protest came only from the Tories of the shires, not from any self-consciously environmental movement. The 'great car economy' of which Thatcher herself spoke in glowing terms did not generate a counter-movement until the 1990s—beyond the appearances of established environmental groups at public inquiries about motorway construction with pre-ordained outcomes. Similar stories could be told when it came to the dismantling of planning controls, the destruction of the local governments to which environmentalists once had access, acid rain, and retreat from international environmental commitments. The lack of diversification in the movement is alleviated only by the sudden (and immediately reversed) transformation of the Green Party from a fringe group to a national player with its achievement of 15 per cent of the vote in the elections to the European parliament of 1989—though this itself came towards the end of the period of active exclusion.

Is the relative uniformity we observe in the British movement in the 1980s a consequence of the actively exclusive state? Certainly this highly prescriptive state set the terms for environmental action (along with just about everything else in British politics in this era). A causal connection can be established in terms of the reaction of the major groups to the suddenly cold climate. This reaction was largely defensive, and contributed to homogenization of the movement's profile. Overall, then, the proposition with which we began is corroborated. An interventionist state that seeks to prescribe the form taken by civil society is bad for diversity and so bad for democratization on the dimensions of both scope and authenticity. This proposition holds whether the state in question is actively inclusive, as in Norway, or actively exclusive, as in the United Kingdom.

Conclusion

We began this chapter with four propositions about democracy, the state, and social movements, three of which are counterintuitive and contradict the claims of democratic theorists who have contemplated these issues. These three are in fact the ones confirmed most strongly by the comparative analysis of this chapter. The proposition on which some doubt remains concerns the democratic destructiveness of the actively exclusive state in relation to civil society, which on the face of it is the most plausible of the four propositions.

The case of Norway shows that an inclusive state can undermine democracy in society as a whole. A narrow focus on the Norwegian state would identify it as the most effective in promoting democracy among our four countries, especially when it comes to expanding scope and franchise. A broader focus reveals the depletion of civil society and attenuation of democratic authenticity that has been a corollary of the Norwegian state's active inclusiveness. Passive inclusion in the United States has similar effects, though much less severe than in Norway. In the United States, these effects are ameliorated by a kind of exclusion felt by local activist groups that in the 1990s led to a reinvigorated public sphere (whose persistence hinges on heightened reflexivity in the movement).

The case of Germany shows that a passively exclusive state that has featured only modest democratization in its internal operations can prove surprisingly, if unintentionally, beneficial in fostering the democratization of the public sphere beyond the state. Germany features by far the most interesting set of democratic possibilities of our four states, because it is possible that this history means that its state may be able to accommodate the movement in a way that preserves democratic authenticity much better than in our other three countries.

Actively exclusive states of the British sort have proved less destructive than we expected in their effects on the public sphere—though some negative effects are apparent. And of course such states by definition are destructive when it comes to the degree of democracy prevailing in the state itself. Only when we broaden the focus to examine effects on the diversity of the movement is the full extent of the actively exclusive state's damage revealed: active exclusion has a homogenizing effect on the movement, though the effect is less severe than for actively inclusive Norway.

To summarize still more radically, our dynamic historical analysis reveals that within the category of relatively open societies, passively exclusive states can be more effective in facilitating the democratization of society as a whole than any kind of inclusive states. Conversely, the kind of state that is in the long run most problematic for democratization of society as a whole is the one that has so far done best when it comes to the state narrowly defined: actively inclusive Norway. However, this result might have to be reconsidered if an actively exclusive state more thoroughgoing and long-lasting than any we have seen to date were to be established.

These findings undermine not only popular assumptions about inclusion in the state necessarily being integral to the advance of democracy, but also the best efforts of most political theorists who have contemplated these questions. There are also some major implications for the strategic choices of social movements contemplating choices between action through conventional state-related means or in more oppositional public spheres. We address these implications in the next chapter.

6

Evaluating Movement Effectiveness
and Strategy

In the previous chapter we examined the implications of different kinds of states for the democratic well-being of civil society and the polity as a whole, with special reference to the role played by social movements. Movements are, however, concerned mainly with more instrumental questions of attainment of substantive ends—though even here we should enter two caveats. The first is that one defining characteristic of the *new* social movement form of organization is that it is often more concerned with identity than strategy, to use the terminology of Cohen (1985). The second is that democratic procedures and environmental ends are mutually reinforcing—or at least that is the consensus among green political theorists, especially in a context where the meaning of sustainability has to be negotiated (Barry, 1999: 205–6). But in this Chapter we narrow the focus to movement strategy.

There are three locations in which movement goals might be pursued: in the core of the state, in the periphery of the state, and in the public sphere of civil society beyond the state (setting aside international society, civil or otherwise). In this Chapter we evaluate the comparative effectiveness of environmental movements in these three locations, and the circumstances in which each makes most sense for the movement. That comparative effectiveness depends a great deal on the kind of state (inclusive or exclusive, active or passive) that the movement confronts. The most basic kind of choice that movements face is whether or not to take advantage of any kind of inclusion on offer. As we will see, some groups have quite consciously resisted inclusion, and we can learn from their experiences too. We will show that resisting the state's embrace does not have to mean powerlessness and lack of control over collective outcomes. At the end of the Chapter we examine the prospects for a 'dual strategy' that targets both the state and civil society. While popular among many advocates for and analysts of movements, we show that it makes sense at times, but not always.

In Chapter 3 we addressed the degree to which environmental concerns could be attached to core state imperatives. While we showed that there have been occasions where such attachment could occur (especially in the United States around 1970), the general conclusion of Chapter 3 was that environmental interests lose when they come into conflict with the core. In Chapter 7 we will show how recent developments related to ecological modernization and the salience of risk issues may enable more productive encounters with existing and newly developing state imperatives. The core being covered quite comprehensively in Chapters 3 and 7, in this chapter we will emphasize environmentalist activity in locations other than the state's core (though the core must always remain in view, for these locations only take shape in relation to it).

We begin by examining the variety of ways in which movements can be considered effective.

Defining Effectiveness: Policy and Beyond

Most obviously, social movements are effective to the extent their interests and demands are taken up and adopted by the state in the form of public policies. Claims to the effect that environmentalism was one of the most important and effective movements of the twentieth century are based on the proliferation of environmental policies worldwide, and we will touch on this measure of success briefly below. Goodin (1992), for one, believes that green movements and parties should properly aspire to no more than participation in policy making in conventional fashion. However, not all policy success comes from direct inclusion and so participation in the public policy making processes of the state. Movements may influence public policy from the outside, and we will demonstrate that this can happen even if a movement operates mostly as an oppositional public sphere in civil society.

Such influence 'from the outside' (most straightforwardly, upon public policy making in the periphery of the state) can occur in at least three ways. First, movements can change the terms of political discourse, which in turn can come to pervade the understandings of policy makers. Indeed, such change may be *the* enduring legacy of the first three or more decades of organized environmentalism—beginning with Rachel Carson's *Silent Spring* in 1962, questioning scientific domination of nature and the discourse of industrialism in which it was embedded. The very concept of 'the environment' is itself the result of a discursive shift, challenging a previously hegemonic discourse of industrialism (Dryzek, 1997). Associated concepts such as ecosystem, resource scarcity, pollution, and wilderness also made themselves felt in association with this shift. Other social movements that had similar success in changing public policy via the terms of discourse include the Civil Rights Movement in the United States, which successfully reframed the dominant liberal discourse in such a way as to secure social and political rights for

African-Americans; and the women's movement in a variety of countries, which reframed concepts of gender, family, public, and private affairs in ways that affected policy debates. Social movements, as Habermas (1996*a*) points out, do not just try to appropriate a share of 'administrative power;' they also embody diffuse and pervasive 'communicative power.' Part, but not all, of the causal mechanism here involves public opinion. As Torgerson (1999: 140) puts it, 'the public sphere does not directly govern, but influences government in an indirect fashion through the communicative power of opinion.' The power of the discourse of environmentalism, for example, was learned the hard way by Republicans in the US, first in their attempt to dismantle environmental standards when they took control of the Congress in 1994 and then in the 2001 development of George W. Bush's energy policy. On both occasions Republican leaders were hammered by public opinion polls and forced to back off high profile policy initiatives that contradicted environmental discourse.

A second way in which social movements can exercise influence on the state from afar occurs when they help constitute more tangible forums within civil society. Such forums are now a regular feature at high-profile international gatherings, beginning with the Global Forum at the 1992 United Nations Conference on Environment and Development in Rio. The Forum's movement activists influenced the official proceedings of the Conference, gaining media publicity and embarrassing official participants on key issues. Other examples can be found at regional and local levels, addressing issues such as renewable resources (Berger, 1985) and toxic wastes (Fischer, 1993).

Third, movement protest can draw a public policy response due to government's fear of political instability. Piven and Cloward (1971) point out that in the United States, welfare state programmes are generally only expanded at times of unruliness on the part of the poor.[1] In Germany, the anti-nuclear movement in the 1970s and 1980s caused changes in public policy (notably the cancellation of planned reactors) through creating fear of instability while being excluded from participation in policy making.

The collective outcomes that social movements can influence are not confined to public policies. Changes in the terms of political discourse can take effect not just in the state, but directly in society's political culture (Melluci, 1985; Torgerson, 1999; Iris Young, 2000). Movements can be educational, and change the distribution of power in society. The public understanding of the terms 'whaling,' or 'working woman,' or 'gay' now means something very different than it did before the growth of the relevant social movement, and these changed understandings and perceptions can change

---

[1] However, Piven and Cloward do not then conclude that movement action should be confined to protest. They recommend action through more conventional interest-group channels.

norms of social behaviour. The Aids Coalition to Unleash Power (ACT-UP), for example, was not just concerned to change governmental policy on AIDS in several countries, but also to change the public perception of gays, lesbians, bisexuals, and the transgendered (Gamson, 1989). Certainly those *opposed* to the goals of gay liberation see the battle as both political and cultural—and the same may be said for those opposing environmentalists (e.g. Sanera, 1996).[2]

An additional way that social movements can affect collective outcomes beyond the state is in terms of what Martin Jänicke (1996a) calls 'para-governmental' activity. Here, movement groups, perhaps acting in conjunction with economic actors such as corporations, can exercise something like governmental power that does not involve even ratification by government. Relationships might be adversarial (as in a consumer boycott) or co-operative (as in a dialogue).

Social movements are also effective to the degree they can impart a collective identity on participants who might otherwise be isolated and politically uninvolved (Melluci, 1989). The development of solidarity—the recognition of identities and common interests—and of what Mansbridge (1994) calls 'discursive communities' is important here. Feminism created solidarity among women. Earth First! developed an identity for radical environmentalists. Demands for multicultural education in the US constituted a discursive community of students of colour. Torgerson (1999) discusses the creation of the 'green public sphere' in which political lives can be lived as one of the biggest successes of environmentalism, irrespective of instrumental movement accomplishments.

In evaluating the effectiveness of the environmental movements in the states we are examining, we will take note of the changes in public policy that have been brought about. But we will also look at other arenas of effectiveness in order to understand and evaluate the larger impact of these movements. The intent is to address the circumstances in which movement organizations may effectively engage the state, and the circumstances in which movements may be effective in other ways. We start with a comparative analysis of success through engagement with the state.

---

[2] Further, as Tarrow (1994: 184–6) points out, even after a social movement's activist phase has passed, it can have long-lived impacts on political culture by establishing forms of collective action such as the sit-in and demonstration—the latter having been taken up even by conservative interests such as landed gentry fox-hunters in England and anti-tax protestors in Italy and elsewhere.

Environmental Policy Successes of Included Groups

The United States: Substantial Group Influence

In evaluating the impact of environmental movements on public policy over three decades or more, we need to do more than just recount the content of environmental policy in each country. We also need to ascertain the extent to which this policy was a result of the influence of included groups. As we argued in Chapter 3, the major burst of environmental policy legislation in the United States around 1970 can be explained in terms of an indirect connection between the state's legitimation imperative and environmental movement interests, in the context of a legitimation threat posed by the counter-culture. The context changed dramatically in 1973 with President's Nixon's growing crisis of personal legitimacy as the Watergate scandal unfolded, and the arrival of energy crisis with the OPEC oil embargo, but some momentum within the legitimation imperative was retained with the Endangered Species Act and the Safe Drinking Water Act in 1973 and 1974 respectively. Environmentalism clearly penetrated to the core of the state in this period.

Innovative environmental legislation continued in the early Carter Administration in 1976 and 1977 with the Resource Conservation and Recovery Act, the Toxic Substances Control Act, the Federal Land Policy and Management Act, the National Forest Management Act, the Clean Water Act, the Surface Mining and Reclamation Act, and amendments to the Clean Air Act. However, the main story after 1973 is the degree to which economic concerns highlighted by the energy crisis prevailed over environmental ones. Environmental policy victories continued—by now, we would argue, only in the periphery of the state—because the movement's lobbying organizations became firmly entrenched in Washington's power structure. And perhaps their efforts were facilitated by the continued need for positive action on the part of a federal government now reeling from the disgrace that Watergate brought to the presidency, and the public cynicism about government that this fed.

The last gasp of the era of United States leadership in environmental policy came in 1980 with the Comprehensive Environmental Response, Compensation, and Liability Act, better known as Superfund. This legislation was in large part a response to the events surrounding Love Canal and the associated anti-toxics movement, which called into question the government's ability to safeguard the health of its citizens, including its children. But while it would be an exaggeration to describe this situation as a legitimation crisis, the issue maintained some connection with that core imperative. The

Reagan era, however, confirmed the dominance of the economic imperative in federal policy making. Superfund faced an immediate implementation deficit in 1981, as the incoming Reagan administration perceived the law as a burden on business. (The first administrator of the program, Rita Lavelle, eventually served jail time for obstruction and perjury.) In keeping with its ideological commitment to reducing the burden of regulation on business, the Reagan administration immediately began to dismantle the institutional capacity of the state to manage and regulate environmental affairs (Andrews, 1997: 28). The US has been an environmental policy laggard ever since.

The most innovative environmental movement the United States saw in the next two decades was that associated with environmental justice. But as we saw in Chapter 3, when the movement's agenda extended beyond site-specific disputes and approached the core of the state, frustration ensued. Still, there was some response in the state's periphery. There is a sense that at least the issue has begun to take hold in various agencies, especially the EPA. One respondent notes that there are other more subtle ways that the environmental justice movement influences government: 'I think there are informal relationships that are developed, there is consciousness that is raised. There are problems that are brought to the attention of the appropriate people that otherwise wouldn't be brought to their attention' (Cole, interview, 1999). The EPA is more than a monolithic agency: 'within the institution, there are many, many good people who actually hear and understand what we're saying and would like to do something about it and then there are many people within the institution who have no interest in hearing what we have to say about it and then there are people who are in the institution who actively work against what we're saying' (ibid.). Still, former environmental justice activist Vernice Miller-Travis insists that 'EPA has really changed fundamentally in the way it interacts with the Environmental Justice community and . . . that's due mostly to external pressure on the agency [and] internal education within the agency from environmental justice advocates' (interview, 1999).

Similar changes in agency outlook and culture can be found elsewhere in the periphery of US environmental administration. After years of the agency's capture by the timber industry, the head of the Forest Service under President Clinton, Michael Dombeck, became a major supporter of a road-building ban, a key policy desire of the mainstream environmental movement. There was much talk about changing the nature of the Forest Service mission, and even a proposed policy shift toward preserving roadless areas. Though of great significance to environmentalists, such proposals remain in the periphery of the state. It has long been the case that Forest Service subsidy of logging, especially through construction of access roads, has made a net negative contribution to national income. Thus a road-building ban would actually be good for the economy, however bad it would be for the large timber corporations that are the major beneficiaries of this subsidy—and whose declining political weight helps to explain the proposed policy shift.

Also during the Clinton administration, Interior Secretary Bruce Babbitt became convinced by environmentalist arguments about the desirability of decommissioning ecologically harmful dams. Babbit even came to some news conferences with a sledgehammer, quoting Aldo Leopold. However, this success remained in the periphery—and ultimately only in the realm of rhetoric—as Babbitt knew that Congress would never allow the decommissioning of economically significant dams.

Yet what goes on at the top among figures such as Dombeck and Babbit is only part of the story when it comes to policy change. Equally important is what goes on in the day-to-day operations of government, under what is normally classified as 'administration' and 'implementation.' It is here that environmentalism's impact can be felt in the development of alternative forums for discussion, informal consultations with movement representatives regarded as legitimate participants, and the acceptance of alternative studies and information provided by environmental groups. The effects of such processes will not appear in legislation or executive orders, but rather in the details of local decisions (for example, the design of a road or an irrigation system; the kind of abatement technology a particular polluter may be required to install).

Obviously, three decades of United States environmental policy cover many cases of environmental policy success. It is not hard to ascribe these successes to the influence of movement groups—at least subsequent to the 'top down' burst of legislation in the early 1970s. For groups were very active in proposing policies that were subsequently taken up by administrators or legislators. Groups developed a professional policy capacity, acting as sources of expertise as well as pressure. And the crucial role played by the courts in US policy making only enters if somebody brings an action—that somebody is almost always an environmental group. If this conclusion seems a bit anodyne, we can put it into sharper perspective by looking at the United Kingdom, where policy advances are not easily ascribed to interest group activity.

The United Kingdom: Relatively Ineffectual Groups

The United Kingdom saw no counterpart to the dramatic burst of environmental policy innovation in the United States around 1970. The United Kingdom has never looked like anything other than a laggard when it comes to environmental policy (aside from air pollution regulation in response to 'killer fog' in

London in the 1950s). Weale (1997: 89–91) points out that indicators of key pollutants were over the period 1970–94 either unchanged or worse, with the single exception of sulphur dioxide. What was named the Ministry of the Environment in 1970 was in practice mainly a ministry of housing and local government, only secondarily concerned with land-use planning and nature conservation. More consequential matters with environmental ramifications continued to be dealt with by departments such as Transport, Trade and Industry, and Agriculture, Fisheries and Food—all of which had a developmentalist ethos with no environmental aspect or avenue for environmentalist influence. This situation began to change in 1997 with the Labour government's creation of a Department of the Environment, Transport and the Regions; the second Blair Labour government elected in 2001 added agriculture to what became the Department of Environment, Food, and Rural Affairs.

The first major environmental law in Britain was the 1974 Control of Pollution Act (COPA), but this did little more than bring together and formalize existing practice. There was no counterpart to the US EPA until the creation of the Environment Agency in 1996. Certainly the policy core has never been approached by British environmentalism. The traditional British approach to pollution control has been informal and co-operative, with compliance a matter of trust between regulator and polluter, and little prospect of any penalty for non-compliance (Connelly and Smith, 1999: 252–5). The overarching standard was a vague 'best practicable means' to achieve pollution reduction. While some pollution control did occur under this rubric (see Vogel, 1986 for a defence), this was an area of policy immune to the influence of environmental groups. With no explicit standards and guidelines for pollution control, everything turned on the content of the collaboration between industry and government regulators in specific cases. But environmentalists were excluded from this collaboration. Only in the 1990s did this informal approach to regulation come under serious scrutiny. Environmental groups also lacked the US alternative of action through the courts.

The 1980s were a blank spot in the history of British environmentalism, for reasons we have already discussed at length in Chapters 2 and 3. The environmental era looked as though it might make a belated entry into British politics with the famous conversion of Margaret Thatcher by Sir Crispin Tickell in 1988, based on the scientific validity of environmentalist claims concerning ozone depletion and climate change. The new opportunities for inclusion then revolved around the creation of sustainable development policies before and after the 1992 Rio Earth Summit (see Chapters 2 and 3). But a commitment to sustainable development in any form never got beyond the Department of the Environment. Other Departments, especially (and most importantly) Treasury, showed no interest in the 1994 White Paper *Sustainable*

Development: The United Kingdom Strategy—whose recommendations could not be implemented without their approval (Connelly and Smith, 1999: 269).

More significant in the mid-1990s was the degree to which Conservative Environment Minister John Gummer managed to curb the road-building mania of the Department of Transport and the powerful roads lobby. The Labour government elected in 1997 promised to emphasize public transport rather than road-building—but as of 2001 had delivered little on this front. Environmental lobby groups were active on the roads issue, but much of the running was in fact made by the more radical direct action anti-roads movement, which we discussed in earlier chapters.

While it is possible to point to sporadic advances in environmental policy in the United Kingdom, it is less easy to ascribe any of these to interest group influence. We have already noted how interest groups were long excluded from the collaborative regulatory relationship between government and industry. And as Connelly and Smith (1999: 249) point out, 'much of the content of recent UK environmental legislation—for instance the Wildlife and Countryside Act (1981) and the Environmental Protection Act (1990)—was the legally required national implementation of relevant EU directives.' The conclusion of a comparison of the United States and United Kingdom is that the more inclusive state in the US allowed more interest group influence in the development and implementation of environmental policies in the periphery of the state.

Norway: Policy Influence Organized by the State

In assessing the history of Norwegian environmental policy, the influence of included groups on policy must be analysed in terms different than the United States or United Kingdom. Because groups were from the outset tightly integrated into the policy process, it is hard to distinguish their positions from government policy. Indeed, they were brought into an expanded corporatist system specifically to help make policy. In Chapter 2 we saw how groups are organized into the system of government committees, helping to make policy even on issues that affect the core, such as green taxes. They do, however, occasionally run up against the core of the state; until the early 1980s, in the form of the hydro-power complex, thereafter in limits to the degree to which sustainable development is allowed to encroach upon the profitability of key industries, especially the oil industry (see Chapter 3).

The only other limit to group influence in Norway is a sectoral division of labour within government. Groups integrated into one sector (for example, fisheries) are not necessarily influential in another (for example, oil and gas) (see the discussion of fragmented government in Norway in Egeberg, Olsen, and Sætren, 1978). Sustainable development was supposed to change all this by being 'sector-encompassing', in the words of a 1988 White paper (Norwegian Ministry of the Environment, 1988–9). However, resistance from the ministries representing different sectors meant that little integration occurred (Langhelle, 2000: 200–2). Still, when it comes to policy in the periphery, we have to give environmental groups the benefit of any doubt, and ascribe real influence to them.

The consequences in terms of policy outcomes have been quite impressive in a comparative light, going back to the beginning of the environmental era, symbolized by the establishment of the Ministry of the Environment in 1972. A ten-year programme then both reduced pollution and led to some structural change in industry. The 'polluter pays' principle was introduced in the early 1970s, and work began that led to the Integrated Pollution Control Act approved in 1981 (Reitan, 1997)—putting Norway some fifteen years ahead of the United Kingdom on this issue. The Ministry of the Environment was also at the forefront of Norwegian initiatives in international environmental affairs, including acid rain that Norway imports from Britain and other European countries (Jansen and Mydske, 1998). Its UK counterpart has still not adopted any international role.

As Prime Minister, Gro Harlem Brundtland started the process of translating her United Nations report *Our Common Future* into Norwegian policy even before it was published in 1987. The idea was to make Norway an international pioneer in sustainable development by establishing sustainability as a general policy premise. Norway was also to take the lead on climate change, the dominant international environmental issue of the 1990s. Sustainable development was to be implemented across the whole of government; environmental issues were presented by the various ministries in a 'Green Book' as part of the state budget, which later became annual State of the Environment reporting. Specific quantitative targets were introduced for a number of goals, including carbon dioxide emissions. In keeping with *Our Common Future*'s prescription, sustainable development policy also involved an effort to increase public involvement, through both the established environmental groups and the citizen-consumer Environmental Home Guard, which we introduced in Chapter 2.

However, the course of sustainable development in Norway was not all plain sailing. As just mentioned, ministries disputed how sustainable development should be understood and how it would affect their sector. It became clear that Norway's forerunner position on climate change came at a cost to the competitiveness of industries traditionally central to the Norwegian economy, especially given the energy budget of transportation in a large and sparsely populated country. Thus momentum on this issue was interrupted as the core of the state was approached (though, as we argued in Chapter 3, in Norway environmentalists have often not been excluded from the core). Still, most other countries did not get to the point where this was even an issue. When it comes to the content of environmental policy, at least in the state's periphery, Norway has been at the front since the 1970s, and environmental groups have played an integral part as full participants in the policy process. It is not easy to answer the counterfactual question as to what matters would have looked like if they had not been present.

Germany: Limited Policy Influence

Turning to Germany, Jänicke and Weidner (1997) argue that during the first 1969–74 phase of environmental policy making, when a centre-left government (SPD/FDP) came into power for the first time and declared environmental problems one of the primary tasks of government, there was 'no noticeable public demand for this, nor was pressure being exerted by organized interest groups to which government would have to respond' (p. 136). The government's first programmes were modelled on the 1969 NEPA legislation in the US. Pollution control was key, and in 1972, the German constitution was amended to grant the federal government legislative power for statutory regulations on waste, air, noise, radiation, and environmental crimes; in these areas, federal law then superseded state law (p. 137). It is not surprising that in a passively exclusive state government leaders would take the initiative on new policy developments, especially those modelled on a country, the US, that had the respect of German leaders. The environmental movement had not yet organized to articulate its views.

True to the corporatist model, a German Council of Environmental Advisers, made up of university professors in the natural and social sciences, was set up in 1971. Representatives of industry were also brought to the table, and it is this institution, coupled with interest from the Chancellor, that spurred early German movement on environmental policy. A variety of new environmental laws, including those on air traffic noise, leaded fuel, waste disposal, DDT, and emission control was passed in the early 1970s.

Jänicke (1996*b*) points out that it is only in the 1974–82 period that environmental groups begin to try to press for enforcement and follow-through on promised further environmental policies. Initiatives were passed on wastewater and chemicals in 1976 and 1980. However, as we argued in Chapters 2 and 3, movement access remained limited and conditional. Even in Jänicke's third period of German environmental policy, 1982–7, the stage was dominated by co-operative measures involving the state and industry, but not environmental organizations. Matters then change with the arrival of ecological modernization, about which we will have more to say in Chapter 7. Initiatives focused on waste avoidance (1986), impact assessment (1990), environmental liability (1990), and packaging (1991). A focus on front-end waste management culminated in the Closed Substance Cycle and Waste Management Act of 1994 (Jänicke and Weidner, 1997*b*). By 1994, environmental protection officially became a goal of the state in the German constitution. Jänicke and Weidner claim the comprehensive environmental laws at both the state and federal level make the German environmental regulatory system one of the most complex in the world. As would be expected in a corporatist-structured nation, environmental advocacy organizations willing to support the project of ecological modernization of the economy have gained access to the state, though 'core' ministries such as transport and construction remain off-limits. But more radical groups, such as the BBU, still face exclusion.

As with our other corporatist system, Norway, it is not easy to disentangle the relative influence of state actors and included interest groups in policy making. However, through most of the era since the initial opening of the mid-1970s, access for interest groups has been limited and conditional, on terms set by state actors. These terms involve moderation and the need to demonstrate scientific expertise. In this context it is hard to see included interest groups as the driving force of policy. A more positive reading of German environmental history is that the movement developed a dual strategy involving both state-centred and civil-society based action. We will return to this issue later in this chapter.

To summarize radically: an 'insider' strategy has produced substantial payoffs in the periphery of the state in the United States, minimal results in the United Kingdom, considerable results in Norway that are however not easy to credit mainly to the groups themselves, and limited impact in Germany (until the 1990s).

Policy Influence Without Inclusion

Public policies can be adopted not just as a result of conventional interest group action within the halls of government, but also in response to action 'from afar' by social movements acting in civil society beyond the state. For Torgerson (1999), *The Promise of Green Politics* lies in the green public sphere, featuring discourse on environmental issues, public education, environmental media, public hearings and debates, and changes in environmental practice. Both Cohen and Arato (1992) and Habermas (1996*a*) point out that the public sphere can constitute a space in which people live their political lives, but it is also a source of influence over policy making. Habermas himself points to issues involving control of nuclear arms and power, genetic engineering, feminism, immigration, multiculturalism, and, of course, various ecological issues such as climate change and genetic engineering (p. 381).

Unfortunately, Habermas (especially 1996*b*) lapses into a rather mechanical model of influence via election campaigns and into legislation. We argue that there are many ways in which such influence can be generated and applied. In addition, Habermas and others ignore our central argument here that the conditions for both the existence, and the influence of, the green public sphere differ across state types. We now attempt to sort out the comparative degree to which observed policy changes in our four countries were influenced from afar by discourse in the public sphere.

This sort of influence is hardest to demonstrate for our inclusive states, because on any issue we might choose to examine there will also be action on the part of included groups. This is especially true of Norway. The major instances of mobilization outside expanded corporatist channels occur in Norway around 1970 and 1980 respectively on the Mardøla and Alta Dam issues. In both cases protests failed to stop construction of the dams. More recently the Bellona Foundation has adopted more confrontational tactics such as smokestack climbing, occupation of government offices, and demonstrations in shackles, all in the service of high-profile media coverage (Ambjørnsen, 1988). Bellona's leader, Fredric Hauge, became the highest-profile environmentalist in Norway. Bellona's campaigns have mostly been directed against specific polluters such as Titania, Falconbridge, and Norsk Hydro, and have led to more restrictive pollution permits for these companies. However, any more general impact on anti-pollution policy is hard to trace. By 2000 Bellona was in a strong position to influence policy because of the work it was doing in Russia in connection with the control of nuclear wastes in the region adjacent to Norway, for which it received both applause from politicians and project grants from the Ministry of Foreign Affairs.

But only rarely does the Norwegian environmental movement 'bark,' and even more rarely does the government heed that bark. Active inclusion, then, not only depleted civil society generally, but also depleted its ability to pressure the state from the outside.

One important avenue of pressure from the outside is public opinion. Public opinion mobilized to oppose policy proposals is rare in Norway, but pervasive in United States environmental history. This sort of mobilization dates back to the 1950s, when David Brower, head of the Sierra Club, organized a successful campaign against proposed dams at Echo Park in Dinosaur National Park, which included education, films, a letter-writing campaign, and the first full page newspaper advertisement from an environmental group. Many wilderness defence campaigns followed. In the ensuing decades, public opinion often acts as a kind of thermostat to curb anti-environmentalist zealotry of the sort that took hold of the early Reagan administration in the 1980s, the Republican Congress after 1994, and the George W. Bush administration in 2001. In each case public outcry forced the zealots to climb down. In 2001, public reaction to decreasing the arsenic standard in drinking water and drilling for oil in the Arctic Wildlife Refuge led the administration to change its approach.[3] Such episodes are also effective recruiting tools for movement groups.

Since 1980, some US environmental activists have consciously resisted inclusion, notably those in radical wilderness defence groups and the environmental justice movement (though as we have seen, the latter's position in regard to inclusion is more ambiguous). The policy impacts of such groups are hard to trace (we will return to this issue when we discuss dual strategies at the end of this chapter).

Public opinion has proven less of a constraint on government action in Britain, where (until the 1990s) direct action social movement activity has not had much of a policy impact, either. In some ways this is slightly odd because as long ago as the 1930s mass trespasses (notably at Kinder Scout in Derbyshire) forced the hand of government in opening public access to private landholdings. As we have seen, environmental groups in Britain have generally taken a moderate and accommodating approach to government, despite the rewards of that strategy proving meagre. Even in the 1980s when active exclusion left these groups out in the cold, they often appeared more concerned about regaining access than following an alternative civil-society based strategy. Dissent from groups in civil society was subdued through the strengthening of police powers and surveillance. Still, movement actions had an occasional, if limited, effect on government policy. Campaigns were targeted towards local communities and the media to mobilize opposition to government plans for nuclear power or road developments, with some success in curtailing plans for nuclear waste dumps on land and at sea. During the late 1980s anti-road development campaign groups organized local resistance to proposals in the London Assessment Scheme, forcing their abandonment (Wall, 1999: 35)—though this was just a small interruption to a massive national road-building programme. Local protests were also organized against threats to Sites of Special Scientific Interest, with occasional successes and media attention (Lamb, 1996: 110–16). Overall, in such an actively exclusive atmosphere, the only avenue open was public protest. Resistance in the Thatcher era was not futile, but it was quite limited and unable to influence the development of any new environmental policy. Arguably resistance was more productive in the 1990s, with the anti-roads movement now organized along new social movement lines (see Chapter 5), far more visible than previously.

It is in Germany that we can find graphic, significant, and persistent influence from oppositional civil society on public policy. The presence of

---

[3] The attacks of 11 September 2001 led the Administration to again call for Arctic Drilling, this time using the national security imperative to disarm environmental critics.

such an oppositional politics is of course one consequence of the passively exclusive German state, but exclusion did not mean lack of policy influence. Social movement pressure on policy is a broadly practised art. Mass protests like the opposition to nuclear power developments in Germany in the 1970s and early 1980s (attracting over 100,000 people) alerted state decision makers to public concerns and values not addressed through the conventional policy process. Protest against a nuclear reprocessing plant in Lower Saxony, for example, prompted an expert hearing on the safety of the development, which was subsequently abandoned after the German chancellor labelled it as 'politically unfeasible' (Wagner, 1994: 279).

An industrial park occupied by, among others, a BMW plant occupies the site of a proposed but abandoned nuclear fuel reprocessing facility in Wackersdorf, Bavaria, today. On the Mozartplatz in Salzburg, some 150 miles to the south across the Austrian border, stands a memorial to the Austrian citizens and 'unknown anarchists' who fought the German and Bavarian governments' plan to build the Wackersdorf facility in the 1980s. At the memorial's unveiling in July 2000, a Salzburg government official called the replica of a section of the construction site's perimeter fence—the location of several bloody skirmishes between protesters and police—a reminder of the strength of civil society. Wackersdorf is a textbook example of a social movement achieving its goals through action in civil society. As noted above, the federal government's first attempt to license a reprocessing facility in Gorleben in the 1970s failed due to opposition in Lower Saxony. In the early 1980s, Bavaria signaled its willingness to host such a facility and started to look for a suitable site. Once the federal government had made the reprocessing of used nuclear fuels the pillar of Germany's nuclear waste disposal policy in January 1985, the German Society for the Reprocessing of Nuclear Fuels applied for an initial construction permit at Wackersdorf. The Bavarian and German governments badly underestimated the level of public opposition to the project, which intensified in the wake of the Chernobyl disaster. In 1989, following several years of massive, occasionally violent protests and cost overruns (some of which resulted from court rulings forcing the authorities to take seriously issues of public health and environmental protection) the utilities abandoned the project in favour of sending spent fuel rods to existing British and French reprocessing facilities. Denied a formal (let alone equal) role in the decision making process, the movement relied on direct action to stop the project.

Wackersdorf is just one case, but it helped to move ecological issues back to the top of the public agenda, and is one of the most visible of a variety of actions, many of them successful, that took place in Germany in the 1970s and 1980s. The policy consequences came not just in terms of the cancellation or modification of environmentally destructive projects, but also in more positive actions such as the Kohl government's creation of the federal Ministry for Environment, Nature Conservation, and Nuclear Safety in 1986.

Among our four countries, movement influence over public policy 'from afar' in oppositional civil society is most vivid and effective in Germany. Such influence also occurs to a degree in the United States, despite the pull of passive inclusion, though often as just one movement tactic on an issue, often in conjunction with more conventional means. Effective oppositional action is very rare in actively exclusive Britain and actively inclusive Norway, really only gaining ground in Britain once active exclusion wanes in the 1990s. We turn now to influence over collective outcomes that does not involve public policy.

Paragovernmental Action

Aside from the influence they can exercise at a distance over public policy, groups operating in civil society outside the state can have an impact on collective outcomes in terms of paragovernmental action. For example, some environmentalists in the western US have turned to collaborative environmental planning, engaging directly with each other, land managers, and corporate users of resources in order to develop conservation plans bypassing governmental processes (Brick et al, 2000; Welsh, 2000). Sabel, Fung, and Karkkainen (2000) argue that 'communities across the country have organized to reclaim authority over their lived environment' through local co-operative problem-solving involving businesses and government officials as well as community activists on issues such as ecosystem management, land use planning, habitat conservation, and pollution regulation. On a national scale, the concern with organic foods in the US grew from a social movement to an industry with its own certification bodies over three decades with no national standards or policy forthcoming from the Department of Agriculture until the year 2000.

Movements can also convince economic actors to act in responsible ways where governments refuse or even resist action. The most famous of these examples (introduced in Chapter 3) was the ability of Greenpeace in Britain and Germany to convince Shell to ignore the British state's environmental standards and the expressed wishes of its government and dispose of the redundant Brent Spar oil storage platform on land, rather than at sea in 1995. International pressure on Nike and Gap with regard to sweatshops forced them to develop policies for production plants much stricter than local law. The shift of McDonalds from styrofoam to paper wrapping for its hamburgers in the US is one classic example where a company responded directly to consumer and movement demands without any governmental involvement. The tuna boycott of the 1980s, organized by Earth Island Institute, culminated in the 'dolphin safe' tuna programme, where the major canners of tuna insisted that their product be caught by means that would not endanger dolphins.

In Germany, a notable case of paragovernmental action was Greenpeace's campaign in the late 1980s and early 1990s to end the use of chlorine and chlorine dioxide bleach in paper production (http://www.greenpeace.de/GP_DOK_3P/HINTERGR/C13HI05.HTM). In 1985, Greenpeace began to highlight the risks to human and non-human health of chlorine bleach, staging protests at German paper companies and, subsequently, at Swedish and Finnish paper mills. As chlorine-free paper became commercially available in 1990, Greenpeace briefly took a less confrontational approach, seeking to persuade magazine publishers to use the new product. These efforts remained fruitless at first, however. The campaign's turning point came a year later when the organization had a plagiarized issue of *Der Spiegel* (Germany's leading newsweekly) printed on paper bleached without chlorine. Though marginally less white, the paper was otherwise of similar quality as the standard product. This publicity stunt disarmed paper companies' and publishers' claims that glossy magazines could not be printed on non-chlorine bleached paper without incurring an unacceptable loss of quality. At the end of 1992, *Der Spiegel* and several other German magazines pledged to use only chlorine-free paper, with virtually all of Germany's paper manufacturers switching to chlorine-free production in 1993. (The market share of chlorine-free paper sold in Germany has levelled off at about 50 per cent since the mid-1990s.) The expansion of availability of organic produce and meat in the UK is another example. A major shift in food production practices was brought about not by government, but by businesses responding to expanding environmental discourse and consumer demand in the wake of the BSE (mad cow disease) scandal and public concern about genetically modified foods. This may be a realm where the interests of business and consumers come together on environmental issues. We will further explore the possibilities for the coincidence of the environmental interests of business and consumers in Chapter 7.

Paragovernmental action ought to vary in direct proportion to the state's absence from environmental affairs. Conversely, it ought to be rare in inclusive states, though as our examples indicate it does exist in the passively inclusive United States. We do find that it is almost non-existent in Norway, where all environmental affairs are thoroughly organized into the state, thus making *para*governmental activity by included groups hard even to conceptualize. The reach of the Norwegian state is also long in terms of its penetration of the economy, as the majority or dominant shareholder in important large companies such as Statoil (oil), Norsk Hydro (industry), Telenor (phone, internet, cable TV), Den norske Bank (the biggest bank), and Statkraft (the main energy producer). This situation leaves very little room for environmental problem solving not involving state actors. The only very minor examples of paragovernmental activity in Norway occur in connection with the consultancy offshoots of the Bellona Foundation.

Cultural Change, Discourse Change

Social movements can also take effect in changing the terms of discourse and so the political culture of a society. To the extent this happens, such change can permeate the understandings of policy makers, and so change the content of policy. The very reason we have something called environmental policy is because a movement established the concept of 'the environment' in political discourse. But the effects of discursive shifts are also felt directly in changing individual action and social relationships, without necessary reference to public policy. 'Upon entering the public scene, environmentalism disturbed the established discourse of advanced industrial society' (Torgerson, 1999: 51). Environmentalism has taken effect in part by changing consumer behaviour, as well as reducing the acceptability of particular kinds of actions —for example, dumping recyclable materials, making campfires in old-growth forests, introducing exotic plants into gardens. Environmentalism's effects in these terms can be captured in terms of the emerging notion of ecological citizenship (Smith, 1998): we are citizens not just of states, but also of ecosystems, which like any kind of citizenship brings both privileges and responsibilities.

Surveys in all of the major countries have demonstrated a growth in environmental values. Environmentalism has changed the way people look at, and understand our relationship with, the world. Environmental awareness has certainly penetrated society more deeply than those who think of environmentalism as inextricably wedded to the protest culture of the 1970s and 1980s might think. In Germany, there has been a cultural sea change regarding environmental values (Kuckartz, 1998; Lehmann, 1999; Proferl *et al.*, 1997). In the US, as Phil Shabecoff (2000: 10) reflects, 'an esoteric enthusiasm for a small elite at the beginning of the century, environmentalism had been transformed into a planet-wide value by its end.' Riley Dunlap, the leading academic on public opinion on environmental issues in the US, argues that there is ample evidence to support the claim that 'environmentalism has brought about a fundamental shift in our beliefs and values' in the US (1989: 121).

Environmental discourse is in no way singular, as it ranges from reformist to radical to apocalyptic (Dryzek, 1997; Dryzek and Schlosberg, 1998), but its various manifestations have not simply shifted the terms of debate, they have also initiated changes in environmental practices. Iris Young (2000: 179) argues that the environmental movement offers an example of 'intrasociety change outside of state institutions,' changing practices in households, communities, and workplaces.[4]

This sort of effect has occurred in all four of our countries. The only real variation is that in Norway the process of cultural change has received a helping hand from the state—for example, in setting up the Environmental Home Guard in 1991 (though the original idea came from the Norwegian Society for the Conservation of Nature), and in pushing the idea of sustainable consumption. However, in all four countries environmental issues declined from the centrality in public consciousness that they achieved around 1990. In Germany and Norway this may be in part a result of the movement's policy successes. In the past in Germany, environmentalists had little difficulty mobilizing public opposition to visibly polluting smokestacks and foul-smelling rivers, but these obvious forms of environmental degradation have become rare. The complexity of most contemporary environmental problems and their solutions do not evoke the same visceral public response. Often some of the outrage they do provoke is directed at the environmentalists themselves. The Schröder government's ecological tax reform is a case in point (Dirschauer, interview, 1999).

Comparing Movement Effectiveness

Our discussion of movement effectiveness in four countries in terms of five sites—the state's core, its periphery, the public sphere influencing the state from afar, paragovernmental action, and cultural change—is summarized in Table 6.1. This table highlights substantial differences in both overall effectiveness and the effectiveness of particular sites. The short story for each country is as follows.

In actively inclusive Norway, we see substantial movement impact in both the core and periphery of the state, especially after defeats at the hands of the hydro-power complex in 1970 and 1980. The corollary is that action outside the state has been both rare and ineffective. Cultural change has occurred, but

---

[4] Given the extent of this shift, it is a bit surprising that opinion surveys in the United States and Germany at least reveal a widespread perception that little has changed. In a recent US poll, 55 per cent say that only a little progress has been made on environmental issues in the last thirty years, while only 18 per cent have a great deal of optimism that progress will be made in the next twenty (Gallup, 2000). A recent German study offers similar findings, with 55–61 per cent of respondents of the opinion that 'no substantial improvements' have been made in the past few years on most environmental issues; 86 per cent of those asked are confident that global pollution will 'definitely' or 'probably' increase in the future (Kuckartz, 2000).

TABLE 6.1 *Comparing Movement Effectiveness*

	USA	Germany	UK	Norway
Influence on Core	Substantial in early 1970s, none since then	Only with onset of ecological modernization in 1980s (see Chapter 7)	None	Substantial and persistent, especially after 1980
Influence in Periphery	Persistent and multifaceted	Relatively limited, beginning mid-1970s	Limited in 1970s and 1990s, almost none in 1980s	Substantial and persistent
Policy Influence at a Distance	Limited; hard to distinguish from interest group activity in periphery	Substantial, especially in 1970s and 1980s, smaller extent thereafter	Begins in 1990s	Very little
Paragovernmental Action	Frequent in 1980s and 1990s	Cooperative relationships between environmentalists and business beginning late 1980s	Begins in 1990s	Very little
Cultural Change	Substantial	Substantial	Substantial	Substantial and state-aided

even this has been state-aided. Norway illustrates both the successes and limits of statist environmentalism. After 1987 it 'carried the torch' on sustainable development (Langhelle, 2000), but—as we will argue in Chapter 7—the torch has now passed on, and there is little scope in Norway for environmental action that has to involve more dynamism in the political economy.

In the actively exclusive UK of the Thatcher era, environmentalism has no influence on the core of the state, a tiny amount of influence on the periphery, and no effect at a distance from the public sphere. As active exclusion wanes after 1989, there is a bit more influence in the periphery, and pressure from the public sphere has some effect on policy (especially on issues such as roads and food safety), but the impact remains comparatively small. Paragovernmental action too begins to take shape in the 1990s.

In the passively inclusive United States, movement influence at the core of the state is apparent in the early 1970s, as the need for legitimation temporarily displaced the economic imperative. Thereafter the majority of the action takes place in the state's periphery, including the implementation of environmental laws, as an institutionalized environmental movement led to a decline in oppositional civil society activity. Most movement influence on the state has been better at *stopping* things from happening than at creating any more positive policy developments. More recently, oppositional civil society activity has grown, despite the pull of passive inclusion, in large measure as a result of disillusion with the results of inclusion. Thus the green public sphere is in many ways in better shape in the 1990s than in Norway and the United Kingdom, second only to Germany.

In passively exclusive Germany, movement exclusion long meant that there was no environmentalist influence within the core or periphery of the state. However, there was substantial influence from the distance of a separate public sphere—whose conditions passive exclusion helped to foster. Unlike the United States, the green public sphere was instrumental in the development of policies, beyond being able to block anti-environmental government action. Matters become more complex beginning in the late 1980s; elements of passive exclusion remain, but enhanced opportunities for inclusion also open. This era also sees the development of substantial paragovernmental action involving the movement and business in relationships that are sometimes adversarial, sometimes co-operative. These circumstances present a novel and significant set of opportunities for environmentalism that we will explore in Chapter 7.

These comparative performance judgements require empirical corroboration. The problem is that there are no widely accepted summary indicators of environmental performance (of the sort we can use, for example, to measure welfare state development). Countries face different sorts of environmental problems, and some (for example, Japan) are adept at exporting environmental stress in a way that would not show up in summary indicators. That said, our identification of Norway and Germany as performance leaders and the UK and USA as laggards in the 1990s is corroborated by three recent summary assessments. Jahn (1998) computes an 'index of environmental performance' based on pollution levels (air, water, soil, and solid waste) and changes in these levels over a previous decade. For 1990, out of eighteen OECD countries, Germany ranks second, while Norway, the UK, and USA rank tenth, fourteenth, and fifteenth respectively. Scruggs (2001) computes a performance index based on rates of change in pollution levels between 1980 and 1995. Among seventeen OECD countries, Germany ranks first, while Norway, the US, and UK rank tenth, twelfth, and thirteenth.

Using more in-depth and nuanced comparison of government engagement with the idea of sustainable development over the 1987–98 period, Lafferty and Meadowcroft (2000: 412) classify Norway's response as 'enthusiastic' Germany and the UK as 'cautiously supportive', and the USA as 'disinterested' (they mean 'uninterested'). They recognize that in 1990 Germany was a pioneer, but that a rigid statist approach to policy and a preoccupation with the consequences of unification in the 1990s meant that it slipped back. However, they believe Germany was on the comeback trail in the late 1990s 'even before the formation of the SDP/Green coalition in the fall of 1998' (p. 419). We agree with Lafferty and Meadowcroft that the assessment of performance—and, we would add, potential—must be done in a way that goes beyond summary indices to look at policy commitments (and, we believe, problem solving beyond the state). The US was a pioneer in the 1970s because of the content of its policies, irrespective of immediate improvements in quantitative performance.

These comparisons are summarized in Table 6.2, along with the ranking of potential for environmental transformation that we will develop in this paper. For the sake of completeness, we also present a 2001 ranking of environmental sustainability done for the World Economic Forum by researchers at Yale and Columbia Universities in which we have little confidence.[5] The latter aside, these studies confirm our placement of the UK and USA in the laggard category in the 1990s, and Germany and Norway as leaders. But our case studies must dig beneath this surface, which is why we have looked at the variety of ways that movements can be considered effective, not all of which show up in summary performance measures.

The experiences and effects of movements as they have encountered the state can be drawn upon to draw lessons for movement strategy. State structures provide part of the context for strategy, but there are still choices to be made, and to these we now turn.

TABLE 6.2 *Comparative Environmental Performance Rankings, 1990s*

	Our ranking	Jahn index	Scruggs index	Lafferty and Meadowcroft	WEF index
Germany	1	1	1	2=	3
Norway	2	2	2	1	1
UK	3	3	4	2=	4
USA	4	4	3	4	2

[5] It is hard to know what to make of an index that rates Brazil and Russia as more sustainable than Italy and Belgium. Norway, the US, Germany, and the UK are ranked second, eleventh, fifteenth, and sixteenth among all the countries of the world. See http://www.ciesin.org/indicators/ESI/rank.html.

Choosing Inclusion vs. Opposition

When should movements opt for inclusion in state-based processes, and when should they opt for opposition in an active civil society? Four questions are relevant here. First, is inclusion an option—is the state structured so as to even allow entry? Second, can the defining interest of the group connect with any established or emerging state imperative? If the answer here is 'no', a third question enters: can an adequate payoff be expected in the periphery of the state, given that frustration is guaranteed once the core is approached? This is the toughest choice: movements ought to think long and hard before accepting inclusion on such limited terms. And fourth, does entry into the state leave behind a depleted capacity in civil society?

The clearest example of a positive answer to the second question remains the United States in the early 1970s, though in Chapter 7 we will show how changes related to ecological modernization and risk issues can now yield a positive answer for other countries. If the answer to both the second and third questions is no, then inclusion means co-option. As we saw in Chapter 4, inclusion generally means moderation on the part of the movement and the development of hierarchical and bureaucratic structures. If there is no connection to the core, then frustration is always a possibility, and the bargain of entry may well prove to be a bad one. In preceding chapters we have adduced several examples of activists regretting their commitment to state-based processes, ranging from Norwegian environmentalists who could not restrict offshore oil drilling in the far North to environmental justice advocates looking back on time wasted in EPA advisory committees in the United States. However, a lot still turns on just how much scope there is in the state's periphery for meaningful policy change. Such scope expands when governments find it expedient to reach out to green concerns—for example, in Margaret Thatcher's move in 1989 to head off green votes that might go to other parties, or in the Clinton–Gore courting of environmental votes in the 1990s, or in the major German parties' fear of the Green Party's electoral appeal.

In instrumental terms, the question of when movement groups should take an oppositional stance seems fairly straightforward: if they are excluded (in which case they have no choice), or if their interest cannot be attached to an imperative and the periphery of the state promises insufficient reward. It may be asking movements to be a bit heroic in considering in addition the effects of a strategy of inclusion on the democratic vitality of the civil society they leave behind. Civil society can be harmed by a group's departure for the state in two ways. First, group leadership may lose touch with its own grassroots, which are simply allowed to wither (as in Norway) or seen as a source of financial support and numbers to impress elected officials, not of ideas or criticism (as in the United States). The second is a drain on limited resources of time and energy: time spent working the corridors of power or participating in governmental advisory committees is time not spent on activism in the public sphere. This trade-off is especially important for smaller groups. Typically it will be the best and most energetic organizers who are picked for such roles, by the group itself or by government agencies. If these individuals come to think their state-based work has been a waste of time, burn-out may ensue and an organization may fold. German environmental groups are well aware of this risk. Greenpeace, for example, does not participate in 'consensus talks' involving state, business, and NGO representatives on the grounds that influencing public opinion to pressure government and industry to behave more responsibly toward the environment is a better use of its resources.

Contemporary social movements do not have central committees that could weigh up situations in terms of the criteria we have suggested and make a decision that then commits the movement. However, activists do occasionally reflect on such questions, if not quite in terms of the language we have developed here. Organizations as varied as Earth First! and the Center for Health, Environment, and Justice in the United States, ALARM-UK in the United Kingdom, and Bellona in Norway have developed oppositional strategies in self-conscious rejection of what they believe to be failed strategies of groups included in the state in more conventional interest group fashion. In allowing that choices can be made, our analysis becomes less deterministic—or, more accurately, it reflects real-world developments in which over time determinism gives way (if only partially) to reflection and choice.[6] Still, some choices may be poor ones—for example, the conventional strategies pursued by the established movement groups before and during the Thatcher era in Britain, the former time period producing access without much influence, the second just knocking politely on closed doors. Above all, movements must make sure that access also means influence. Often it does not—or produces rewards far less than appearances would suggest. The Clinton administration was much more welcoming of environmentalists than its two predecessors, but reality in terms of policy change fell short of the promise (which is not to deny some successes in the periphery).

The matter of choice is complicated further because the question may need revisiting as circumstances change. In the case of Germany, for example, the onset of ecological modernization makes inclusion—whose possibilities remain limited—a better bargain for groups than was previously the case. In

---

[6] Beyond the differences we highlighted in Chapter 4, this is another departure from those such as Kriesi et al. (1992) and Kitschelt (1986) who explain the form taken by social movements in terms of the political opportunity structures they face, but treat matters in terms that are both deterministic and static (Rucht, 1990 and Rootes, 1997 criticize this school of thought for oversimplifying interactions between states and movements).

the United States, it took the mainstream groups a long time to wake up to their diminished effectiveness after the waning of the connection to the legitimation imperative of the early 1970s.

Dual Strategies: Choosing Inclusion and Opposition

Among political theorists who have contemplated the question of inclusion versus opposition, most conclude that social movements should operate both inside and outside the state. Referring to the exemplary case of the women's movement, Cohen and Arato believe that 'The dual logic of feminist politics . . . involves a communicative, discursive politics of identity and influence that targets civil and political society and an organized, strategically rational politics of inclusion and reform that is aimed at political and economic institutions' (Cohen and Arato, 1992: 550). For Cohen and Arato, the justification of the dual strategy is largely the well-being of civil society itself: groups or their supporters influential within the state would help build a helpful constitutional, legal, and policy context for the movement outside. Hilary Wainwright (1994) reaches the same conclusion from a more instrumental perspective. Action within the state is needed to supply collective decisions with 'binding national and international authority' (p. 195), but without the movement outside, such policy action is unlikely (p. 197). As Fisk (1989: 178–9) puts it, 'Only if there is a continuation of politics by extra-parliamentary means will democracy be able to establish limits to the power of a dominant class,' because protest in civil society acts as a standing warning of what could happen if the state is unresponsive to demands. Like Cohen and Arato, Wainwright for her part hopes that included actors will continue to sustain the movement (p. 196). Iris Young, arguing against those who pin their hopes on civil society rather than the state,[7] concludes that 'social movements seeking greater justice and well-being should work on both these fronts, and aim to multiply the links between civil society and states' (Young, 2000: 156).

Political theorists generally pay little attention to constraints and possibilities within real-world states. However, a number of movement activists also advocate a dual strategy. David Brower, the leading American environmentalist of the twentieth century, was fond of saying that he was glad someone like Dave Foreman (founder of Earth First!) came along, because it made Brower's position seem more reasonable. Brower's own then-radical presence was once praised in identical terms by moderate environmentalist Russell Train. Mark Dowie (interview, 1999) argues that such a recognition is becoming more widespread in the US movement: 'I think wise people at both levels,

---

[7] Young mistakenly places Dryzek in this category (Young, 2000: 183).

grassroots and national, value the work of the other side and see ways of partnering and working together on some of these issues . . . I think there is a certain maturity coming now in the movement that has accepted the work of the different styles and different tactics of different people with the same objective.' In Britain, Duncan McLaren of Friends of the Earth believes that an initially difficult relationship between insiders and outsiders has evolved: 'From my perspective there is a great synergy between what the Direct Action people do—and the roads campaigns are a classic example of how that can work—them being in the trees and us being in the Treasury' (interview, 1999).

In the United States, the way this issue plays out is in terms of correcting the overemphasis of the mainstream groups on conventional interest group strategies. Roundly criticized by radical wilderness defence advocates, anti-toxics and environmental justice activists and others (see Dowie, 1995 for a critique, also our discussion in Chapter 4), in the 1990s these groups mostly recognized the need to broaden their range of activities. Such groups had long used tactics such as public education and media work as supplements to the main business of lobbying. However, in overemphasizing Washington corridors of power they had ignored the importance of local action, treated their grassroots as little more than a source of funds and numbers to impress members of Congress. This was a source of tension for many years. Katie McGinty, the head of the Council on Environmental Quality for most of the Clinton Administration, believes:

I do think that this shortcoming has been recognized, and it is in many ways being addressed by the environmental community, and I think the environmental groups are reactivating their grassroots in a much more vigorous way once again. (Interview, 1999)

However, McGinty notes only that the majors are reactivating 'their' grass-roots—which could translate into incorporating them more effectively into a conventional, insider politics—not the vast number of groups that have sprung up at the local level that regard the majors with suspicion. At least one of the leaders of the major US organizations seems not to have fully grasped the issue. When asked by us how the organization gives its grassroots members a say in the strategies and decision making of the organization, he simply claimed: 'we let people know what our issues are. They continue to support us.' The grassroots were also important because 'when you send a message to the Congress from the people back home, that's a big message'. To some leaders in the included environmental mainstream, civil society is only important as it props up the insider tactics of the group.

Luke Cole, Director of the California Rural Legal Assistance Foundation's Center on Race, Poverty, and the Environment, claims that he has not seen any evidence of the recognition on the part of the major groups of the problematic relationship between state-focused and civil-society centred groups. 'The DC-based organizations have not changed the way they do business in any way, shape, or form. They still come up with policy positions entirely on their own without consulting with any of the communities that will be affected by those policy decisions' (interview, 1999). Increasingly, groups emerging from these communities are more likely to try to balance localized action with their *own* attention to larger, national strategies. Passive exclusion of such groups from the accommodation of the majors and the state has led them to·constitute a public sphere, which with time develops a dual strategy of its own—consciously resisting the overemphasis on inclusion that characterizes the majors.

The United Kingdom too eventually saw something of a dual strategy evolve. Like the United States, this development was partly in reaction against the insider strategy of the majors. The 1980s experienced almost a 'nil strategy' as moderate groups were excluded and no significant oppositional social movement developed. Then, after 1989, moderate groups regained access (though, as we have argued, without much influence), while a wave of oppositional action began, the anti-roads movement being especially notable (see Chapter 5). The latter gained momentum as it became apparent that the mainstream groups were failing to have much success in curbing the developmentalist impetus of public policy. In Chapter 5 we did our best to relate the belated arrival of direct action in British environmentalism to the legacy of active exclusion, though the story was a complex one.

One of the elder statesmen of British environmentalism, Jonathon Porritt (1997: 66–7) disputes that these direct action campaigns are indicative of a 'new environmentalism', interpreting them as half of a dual strategy. He sees policy changes in the transport area (notably the shift in emphasis away from road-building toward public transport in the mid-1990s) as being 'as much the results of years of academic research and patient foot-slogging along the corridors of power as of high-profile direct actions, leading to an extraordinary level of interdependence between organizations for all that they are using highly divergent tactics'. Porritt is reluctant to grant too much to the radicals, and he misses the democratic benefits of revitalized oppositional civil society. However, it is clear that transport policy did not change direction until after the radical anti-roads movement made itself felt.

Germany's dual strategy begins more clearly in an oppositional public sphere, which developed in the 1970s and 1980s. Groups included in consultative relationships with the state were very moderate and quite inconsequential (see Chapter 2). However, the anti-nuclear movement's attempts to stop the construction of a nuclear reactor at Whyl beginning in 1975 involved direct action and occupation on the one hand, and action in the national courts on the other. The delay imposed by the legal strategy bought time for the movement's anti-nuclear values to spread and to change public opinion over a decade. While the environmentalists lost the court case in 1985, the government was by then unwilling to start construction.

Opportunities for inclusion increase with the establishment of the federal Environment Ministry in 1986, and the acceptance by all the major parties of ecological modernization (see Chapter 7). But as we pointed out in Chapter 3, this ministry functions as something of a co-optive device, given its lack of influence over more consequential parts of the federal government. Any dual strategy only really pays off with the rise of the Green Party, culminating in entry into a governing federal coalition as junior partner to the SPD in 1998. Looking at the relationship between the Green Party and groups in civil society since the 1998 election sheds light on the question of strategy. For environmental organizations, the existence of an SPD/Green government raises more troubling questions about the wisdom of pursuing a dual strategy than did the CDU/FDP coalition of 1983 to 1998. The danger is that the Greens may be too weak to get the SPD to enact aggressive environmental policies, while their participation in the coalition alienates their activist allies in civil society.

Our interviews show that Green politicians are acutely aware of how much the success, however limited, of their agenda depended on mass mobilization in civil society. They are not sure that institutionalized participation in parliamentary and administrative venues can replace this crucial resource. But they were also doubtful about environmental organizations' ability to reach out to an increasingly passive and indifferent public. Rekindling social movement mobilization in civil society from above is something of a contradiction in terms. The press release appears to have replaced the protest march as the most potent weapon in the arsenal of Germany's major environmental advocacy organizations.

Green MPs believe the decline of protests is the price they have had to pay for their success. On this view, organized representation in the political system, whether as political parties or advocacy groups, depresses mobilization in civil society by virtue of its existence. The growth of professional networks of environmental advocacy organizations may signal to people that their personal involvement and protest are no longer required. Their withdrawal from activism, however, reduces the effectiveness of these environmental policy networks. The paradox the Greens face is this: the better the environmental policy results politicians manage to negotiate, the more difficult it is to organize mass protests, even though further environmental policy progress actually requires further sustained public support (Hermann, interview, 1999). Green MPs have boosted the environmental expertise of parliament, but expertise without political power is not enough, and political power derives mostly from outside parliament. One Green MP summarizes the problem this way: 'Meaningful environmental protection encounters tremendous resistance in the wider society. Without outside support, we don't have any way of achieving our goals' (Fell, interview, 1999).

Until the election of the SPD/Green coalition, the prospect of unduly depleting civil society by entering policy making circles was negligible. Although CDU environment ministers, particularly Klaus Töpfer, maintained close ties to some environmental groups such as NABU and WWF, and were sometimes willing to meet them halfway, the force of the government's pro-economic growth agenda was never in doubt. In fact, Helmut Kohl fired Töpfer when business leaders objected to too much environmental zeal on his part, replacing him with Angela Merkel, who thus far was inexperienced in the field (von Weizsäcker, interview, 1999). Given the firm limits to inclusion under a conservative government, a dual strategy of action could less easily undermine the vitality of civil society. Few environmentalists were tempted to think of the CDU as their ideological ally. They were prepared to co-operate with the government where possible but had no trouble criticizing its actions where necessary. It is obviously less damaging to civil society to pursue a dual strategy that avoids co-optation when the government is controlled by your ideological foes rather than your friends.

Relations between Greens and environmental advocacy groups are close, but not as close as those who think of the Greens as an environmentalist party might expect. Some environmentalists' hopes of special treatment by the SPD/Green government have been disappointed. In the long run this should help them pursue a viable dual strategy vis-à-vis a left-of-centre/green government for whom the environment is not as central an issue as environmentalists would like. Environmentalists have better access to the SPD/Green coalition than ever before, but the activists we interviewed had no illusions about the imbalance between economic and environmental forces.

Early in the history of the German Greens, Petra Kelly advocated an uncomplicated division of labour between grassroots activists and Green MPs: activists and politicians would each do their part in civil society and in state institutions, respectively (Kelly, 1990). Matters did not work out this way originally, partly because the Greens were so powerless in parliament. Nonetheless, while outside of the government, the Greens developed a dual strategy based on influencing political discourse in civil society and on using parliament to influence public policy. The question now is if, after decades of exclusion that helped stoke the fire of civil society, that fire—and a thorough dual strategy—can remain burning in an era of inclusion in government. The Greens' parliamentary spokeswoman for environmental policy and BUND board member was not optimistic:

Our environmental associations have limited influence. They have fairly large numbers of members but little appeal beyond them. Even if you have 200,000 members but little pull beyond that you're not a heavy hitter. Unlike the unions, environmental associations haven't shown much of a public presence in various current debates. A press release every now and then is their sharpest weapon. They have to earn respect, and to earn respect they must show they have influence in the wider society. The influence of conventional environmental associations [i.e. BUND, NABU] is not very great. Greenpeace has greater influence because of its high name recognition and ethical integrity. But the environmental associations have a ways to go. (Hustedt, interview, 1999)

Examples or advocates of a dual strategy are harder to find in Norway, mainly because there is comparatively little action in civil society beyond the state. The main insider groups such as the Nature Conservation Society and Mountain Touring Association do not participate in, nor do they support, extra-legal strategies such as civil disobedience. However, Nature and Youth (the Nature Conservation Society's sub-group for youth) can sometimes be found engaging in this kind of activity, especially on energy issues. Nature and Youth members have been active in planning actions against proposals for gas-fuelled power plants in western Norway, though at the time of writing these proposals have not progressed very far due to technical problems and doubtful economic returns associated with the plants.

More prominent are groups organized to oppose particular site-specific projects, such as at Alta in 1980, when opponents of the Alta Dam took action in both mass protests and a (failed) court case.[8] In 2001 a minor waterfall project at Beiarn in northern Norway was cancelled after demonstrators from the Save Saltfjellet group (with connections to the Nature Conservation Society) stopped the first construction trucks. The Ministry for Oil and Energy withdrew construction permits for the dams after environmental groups, surprisingly supported by most political parties, decided that new impact assessments were necessary.

The American experience, where disillusion with the results of an insider strategy lead to a renewed emphasis on local, grassroots, and oppositional action, has no real parallel in Norway. In the 1990s new alternatives to the established system of expansive corporatism did develop—but these concerned an enhanced role for parliament, not oppositional civil society. It is not easy to trace the increased importance of parliament to any discontent with corporatism; rather it was a consequence of weak minority governments, and the rise of 'lobbyism' (Christiansen and Rommetvedt, 1999). The only other development that might be interpreted as part of a dual strategy occurs with the arrival after 1986 of the Bellona Foundation, often interpreted as the 'rebel' among green groups in Norway. However, 'the organization's political

---

[8] Unlike the United States, political issues rarely end up in court, for courts hardly ever rule against government. Since the adoption of its constitution in 1814, the Supreme Court has ruled against the state in less than five cases. In 1999 environmental groups tried to use the courts to change a wolf-killing policy, but again failed.

work is first and foremost ordinary bureaucratic work', according to a spokesman (Nilsen, 1996: 192), and Bellona is invited to present its opinions to government committees.

It is easy enough to conclude in the abstract that a dual strategy emphasizing both state and civil society is desirable for any social movement. But this is too easy a conclusion to reach. To put this conclusion into perspective, let us consider the times when it may not be appropriate.

First and most obviously, a movement will not be able to follow a dual strategy if it confronts a truly exclusive state; oppositional civil society may be the only option.

Second, if a movement's resources are scarce, it may not have enough to devote adequately to both the long march through the institutions *and* activism in civil society, both of which can be both demanding and frustrating. If inclusion promises meagre rewards for great effort (as in Britain prior to the Thatcher era), it is not a good use of scarce resources of time and energy.

Third, if a movement's defining interest can be attached to an established or emerging state imperative, then thoroughgoing entry into the state may be a good bargain. Historically, as we pointed out in Chapter 1, both the bourgeoisie and the organized working class have made such a choice.

Conversely, if some but not all of a movement's defining interest can be attached to an established or emerging state imperative, while other aspects of that interest challenge an imperative, a dual strategy is clearly desirable. This is the case with feminism, where a liberal feminist interest in equal opportunity resonates with the economic imperative of states, while more radical feminist demands for non-competitive human relationships contradict this imperative. Similarly, as we will see in Chapter 7, environmentalist interest in pollution control and conservation of material resources can be attached to the economic imperative via the idea of ecological modernization. Demands to protect the intrinsic value of natural systems cannot make this link. In such cases, it may even be desirable to think in terms of two movements pursuing very different kinds of strategies—not exactly a dual strategy at all. As one of us has argued previously (Dryzek, 1996a: 119), the 'happiest conceivable outcome may be a clear separation between two environmental movements: one within the state to take advantage of every bit of flexibility in the liberal democratic system, another outside, more democratic and vital'. However, not all situations feature this mix of compatibility and contradiction in the relationship between movement interest and state imperative. If much or most of what a movement seeks is attainable in the state's periphery, then the balance to be struck between insider and outsider action ought to be a matter of much more contextual judgement. Such judgements will turn on the resources available to a movement, the type of state it confronts, and the kinds of issues being dealt with. Some issues seem to be amenable to resolution within civil society—for example, Iris Young (2000: 179) describes the accomplishments of the environmental movement on the issue of recycling as 'intra-society change outside state institutions' (which later came to alter both private corporate behaviour and state laws). But, crucially, such success has *not* come about on issues such as energy policy in the US, or genetic engineering in the UK, or dams in Norway.

So while we endorse an engagement with dual strategies, we argue for a more reflective, situational understanding of such engagement. We are not arguing that everything can be accomplished in civil society, nor are we arguing that all movements should adopt a dual strategy.[9] We are simply noting that movements with limited resources should examine situations in order to identify where those resources are best spent, on which issues, and at which time. A blanket exhortation to engage in a dual strategy does not fit all situations equally.

Conclusion

There are many ways in which movements can be effective. Policy change resulting from participation in governmental structures is only one way, and as we have seen, the country that features the most complete emphasis on such inclusion—Norway—has, despite undeniable policy advances, featured an environmental movement that has been fairly anemic. Movements may also take effect through the pressure of oppositional civil society on the state from afar, though again, this effect differs across state types. It is likely to be more important in exclusive states, but *actively* exclusive states such as the UK in the 1980s resist this kind of influence at a distance too. Inclusion in Norway, as we have seen, weakens civil society, and there are few examples of environmental policy outcomes that can be traced to the influence of collective action in civil society. We do see such effects, though limited, in the UK after active exclusion softens in the 1990s, and a bit more in the US. However, the effects in the UK and USA are often negative—stopping proposed anti-environmental policies. Only in Germany do we see significant pro-active policy in response to environmental movement activity in civil society. But this activity is not just aimed directly at the state, and we can see changes in environmental discourse that take direct effect in the political culture in all of the states under study.

---

[9] Though it should be fairly obvious that we, along with Young, Habermas, Torgerson, and just about every other examiner of civil society, are arguing that a sole focus on the state is limited and problematic.

A close examination of movement successes within the state reveals that they generally do not interfere with core state imperatives; in our terms, they are confined to the state's periphery. This situation is common in the US since the early 1970s, occasional but more ineffectual in the UK in the 1990s. In Norway since 1980 the included movement has not always been confined to the periphery; in Germany, access even to the periphery came late.

We offer this analysis not only to explain the varied nature of effectiveness across the four nations under study, but also to assist movements in reflecting on when best to follow an insider strategy (when, obviously, that is an option), and when best to act from the public sphere. The bottom line is that inclusion (as a sole strategy) where there is no link to state imperatives is often going to be a bad bargain, because the included group must either remain tame (avoiding core imperatives), frustrated (as it runs up against the core), or be deflected (to more minor issues at the periphery). The good news is that imperatives—and so opportunities—can change with time and place, and are not completely immune to discursive reconstruction. We now turn to this question of the evolution of core state imperatives, in particular as suggested by notions of ecological modernization and the risk society. This evolution opens up new possibilities and choices for environmental movements. Indeed, the possibility of a more reflexive political economy in which determinisms of any sort wither comes into view, where dual strategies might come to make more sense.

7

Ecological Modernization, Risk Society, and the Green State

We have argued throughout that it matters a great deal to a social movement whether or not it can attach its defining interest to a core state imperative. If it can, then there are in principle no limits to the degree to which the movement can penetrate to the state's core once the movement has sought and achieved entry into the state. If it cannot, then the movement is likely to receive either symbolic or at best marginal rewards as a result of its engagement with the state. Whenever the movement's interest comes up against the core, the movement will lose; it is merely co-opted (see Chapter 3).

This situation long characterized environmentalism, which, locked in a zero-sum conflict with the economic imperative, with few exceptions lost whenever it approached the state's core. However, that situation may be changing. Proponents of ecological modernization now argue that economic and ecological concerns are potentially complementary; if so, environmentalism may for the first time be linked positively to the core economic imperative.[1] Ulrich Beck's risk society thesis suggests a different route for connecting movement goals and state imperatives. Beck posits a legitimation crisis in the context of risk that can be met by new forms of 'sub-politics' that effectively engage the citizenry in the selection, allocation, distribution, and amelioration of risks. If so, environmentalism may for the first time find effective linkage with the state's legitimation imperative.

These two developments could conceivably add up to a new state imperative: environmental conservation. The emergence of the economic imperative first democratized the modern state through inclusion of the bourgeoisie in the core, creating the capitalist state. The emergence of the legitimation imperative further democratized the state by including the organized working

---

[1] The basic literature on ecological modernization includes Weale (1992), Hajer (1995, 1996), Christoff (1996), and the special issue of *Environmental Politics* 9(1) (Spring 2000) on 'Ecological Modernisation Around the World'. Theorization of the concept can be traced to the works of German social scientists Joseph Huber and Martin Jänicke in the early 1980s (see Spaargaren, 2000: 46–50).

class in the core, creating the welfare state. The emergence of an environmental conservation imperative would democratize the state still further by including environmentalists in the core, creating the green state. The conservation imperative would entail rethinking both economic and legitimation imperatives—the economic with an eye towards synergy with natural processes, and legitimation with an eye towards the need for public reflection on continued technological modernization. It hardly need be said that as yet there is no green state in these terms. However, we will show in this chapter that elements of its development are being played out in our four countries.

A weak form of ecological modernization is tied only to the economic imperative in terms of 'pollution prevention pays'. Such is the case in Norway. We argue that what Peter Christoff (1996) calls strong ecological modernization is most conducive to the convergence of environmental interests and state imperatives, which can only be secured through a connection to issues of ecological legitimacy through public participation (Christoff himself is a statist who would disagree with this analysis). With this connection, strong ecological modernization demands an informed public that reflexively and democratically addresses environmental risks. It involves reshaping public policy and political-economic structures along ecologically sustainable lines, which in turn requires keeping movement politics alive (otherwise there will be a lapse to the weak form). Of the countries examined here, only Germany seems to be moving in the strong direction. The problem is that, historically, this sort of critical public sphere has been associated with passive exclusion, a condition that holds only for Germany of the countries considered here (and may not last there forever). Paradoxically, such states impose limits on the degree to which strong ecological modernization can penetrate state structures. However, we will show that the way history unfolds can overcome these limits—if not permanently. Also, reinforcing the sub-politics thesis, there can be more to strong ecological modernization than what is accommodated within the state.

We do not contend that environmentalists must be German to be successful. Although a green public sphere is most likely to arise and persist in passively exclusive states, variants of it exist in passively inclusive states, where its sustenance is harder work. The revitalization of the American grassroots in the 1990s and the re-emergence of radical environmental activism in the UK after the waning of active exclusion since 1989 suggests that no state abiding by liberal democratic principles is capable of permanently sidelining oppositional civil society. The grassroots US movements focus on the legitimation imperative that we associate with strong ecological modernization. The mainstream American groups target only the economic imperative and thus only weak ecological modernization (without using this language), so far with little policy response. The Blair Labour government in the United

Kingdom seems to recognize public demands and so the legitimation imperative, but gives mostly lip-service (and endless public inquiries) to these issues.

Passive states, inclusive or exclusive, willingly or not, permit enough movement diversity to sustain a radical programme consistent with the requirements of strong ecological modernization among a significant part of the
environmental *movement*—a necessary but not sufficient condition for
moving *society* in the direction of strong ecological modernization.

A critical public sphere and hence strong ecological modernization are least
likely to arise and hardest for environmentalists to sustain under conditions
of active inclusion. However, a weak version of ecological modernization and
so a pale green state *is* sustainable under active inclusion, as the case of
Norway will show. This sort of case is actually consistent with the bulk of
what Mol and Spaargaren (2000: 23) call 'the first generation studies in
Ecological Modernisation Theory' in the 1980s. (The literature, if not the policy practice, has now moved in a 'strong' direction.)

We pay close attention to two indicators of ecological modernization: public access to environmental information and ecological tax reform. The former is important because strong ecological modernization, linked to the
legitimation imperative, requires open debate on matters that affect environmental quality, which in turn depends on the public's access to information
that is analysed, interpreted, and presented in ways that non-professionals
can understand (World Bank, 1998: 11).[2] Confronted with an un-cooperative
state, agents in a green public sphere might organize to gather environmental
information themselves, or they might emphasize green discourses that
eschew the ecological sciences altogether. However, having access to information about the quality of the local water supply, soil toxicity, and the like can
strengthen the hand of environmental NGOs and citizens. This access is
significant because, all other things being equal, a state that tends towards
openness is more likely to accept strong ecological modernization than a state
that favours secrecy. Other things are not of course equal, as we will see.

Tax reform intended 'to shift from piecemeal environmental taxation to a
more thorough ecological tax reform where labour taxes are replaced by
environmental taxes' (European Environment Agency, 2000*b*: 397) is a
significant aspect of the sort of restructuring advocates of weak ecological
modernization have proposed. It is a central tenet of ecological modernization that pollution prevention pays, but green taxes are the other side of the
coin, reaffirming the principle that the 'polluter pays'. Weak ecological modernization addresses the economic imperative, and in so doing also attaches

---

[2] Our three European states are bound by the European Union's Directive 90/313 on freedom
of access to environmental information passed in 1990. Although Norway is not a member of the
EU, it does belong to the European Environmental Area and has agreed to incorporate existing
and future environmental directives in its national laws (Andersen and Liefferink, 1997: 31).

government revenue to environmental progress. A majority of EU member states has embarked on ecological tax reforms, with the Nordic Countries and the Netherlands leading the way (European Environment Agency, 2000*a*). Ecotaxes alone cannot effect 'a transition from incremental to radical innovations in which ecologically problematic procedures and products are substituted by unproblematic ones' (Kemp, 1997: 9). They make little sense when the risk is acute, requiring immediate action (Jänicke, 2000: 14). And evasive actions can sometimes undercut their effectiveness (Jänicke, 2000: 15). For these reasons we again need to look at green taxes in the context of other developments, rather than use them as a simple indicator of ecological modernization (in 1998, environmentally related taxes as a percentage of total government revenue were 5.8 per cent in Germany, 8.2 per cent in Norway, 8.3 per cent in the United Kingdom, 3.1 per cent in the United States[3]).

Ecological Modernization and the Risk Society Thesis

In its basic or weak form, ecological modernization involves solving environmental problems by making capitalism less wasteful within the existing framework of production and consumption. The technical fix looms large (Street, 1992). 'Pollution prevention pays'; low pollution indicates productive efficiency in the use of resources. A clean and pleasant environment means happy healthy workers; environmental problems are solved in the present (informed by the precautionary principle—action need not await scientific proof) rather than postponed to a future where their resolution will be more expensive. The price of the broad acceptability of such a programme is that ecology is conceptualized in thin terms. Radical green critiques of technology and capitalism are muted by the claim that economic growth and environmental protection can be mutually supportive (Dryzek, 1997: 137–52).

What Hajer (1995) calls 'techno-corporatist' (weak) ecological modernization is based on the idea that 'dominant institutions indeed *can* learn and that their learning can produce meaningful change' (Hajer, 1996: 251).[4] Biologists, economists, and engineers are responsible for drawing up environmental quality standards and technologies that meet these standards. Social scientists can identify ways of modifying 'anti-ecological' cultural patterns and behaviors. Weak ecological modernization is a moderate social project (Hajer, 1996: 253; for a defence see Mol, 1996). It is attractive to state officials

---

[3] Source: OECD Database on Environmentally Related Taxes, www.oecd.org/env/policies/taxes/index.htm.

[4] From our point of view, Hajer's terminology is unfortunate (as well as unnecessary), because, as we will show for Germany, corporatism can actually be instrumental to strong ecological modernization.

because it promises to meet their need to promote economic growth and improve environmental conditions with minimal disruption. It implies the progressive inclusion of mature groups that have discarded radical critique, informal organization, and protest politics in favour of pragmatic advice, professional organizational hierarchy, and interest-group activity. While radical environmentalism may have been important in getting environmental issues on the agenda, its confrontational politics and rejection of economic growth become liabilities. Here there is a comfortable fit with life-cycle theories of social movements, wherein the movement begins in inchoate radicalism and ends in the corridors of power (see Chapter 1).

We will argue that weak ecological modernization ultimately fails to deliver on its promise of securely connecting ecological aims to core state imperatives. In the words of Christoff (1996: 490) it offers little hope for 'promoting enduring ecologically sustainable transformations and outcomes across a range of issues and institutions'. The risk of co-optation is high because only modest goals can be linked to the economic imperative in the absence of a credible movement threat to destabilize existing political and economic institutions. Weak ecological modernization, linked only to the economic imperative, never challenges the legitimacy of the state's complicity in practices that generate environmental risks. A weak ecological modernity defined by managerial solutions to environmental problems (Luke, 1999) downplays the critique of industrialism by emphasizing policy learning and institutional adjustment rather than fundamental social change (Hajer and Fischer, 1999).

A particularly graphic illustration of weak ecological modernization and its limits is provided by Gonzalez (2001) in an analysis of automobile pollution control policy in California. California policy emphasizes technological changes to car engines that will reduce emissions, and is driven by powerful economic interests rather than environmentalists. However, despite the success of this policy, total emissions continue to grow as the number of cars on the road and the average per-car distance travelled per year both increase faster than technical change can reduce emissions. Land use planning that would reduce reliance on the car—the kind of structural change that strong ecological modernization implies—is simply not on the anti-pollution agenda.

In technocratic form, 'Ecological modernisation is much more the repressive answer to radical environmental discourse than its product' (Hajer, 1996: 254). The question that motivates many social movements—what kind of society do we want—is difficult to pose in pure efficiency terms. Ecological modernization thus poses a serious challenge to environmentalists wishing to keep radical critique alive. Noting the environmental movement's crucial role in bringing about industrial society's critical self-examination, Hajer wonders what will happen to the movement's 'history of reflexivity':

The question that looms large is the extent to which the environmental movement has been able to perpetuate this reflexivity once it decided to argue its case in the appealing terms of ecological modernization. (Hajer, 1995: 102)

The answer, we suggest, depends on whether and to what effect environmental groups can show an oppositional and discursive face, and so move ecological modernization in the strong direction, problematizing norms and values driving modernization processes (Hajer, 1995: 280–1). Strong ecological modernization resists subordinating ecology to economics, is attentive to interactions among a broad array of political, economic, and social institutions, favours communicative rationality and participatory public deliberation, accepts and indeed requires movement activism, and recognizes the transnational aspects of issues. What Hajer (1996) terms 'ecological modernization as cultural politics' goes beyond encouraging public participation in order to 'explore how new perspectives on society can be created' through open public debate (Hajer, 1996: 260) concerning the actors and practices implicated in environmental degradation. Ecological modernization in its strong form requires a vibrant civil society.

Be it weak or strong, ecological modernization is attractive to many environmentalists because it provides a way for their concerns to be taken seriously in a world where economics is the first concern of governments. In other words, it facilitates a link to the economic imperative of states. Beck's theory of the risk society (1992: 1994) can be deployed to make a link to the legitimation imperative. The risk society thesis is that politics in developed societies is increasingly about the production, selection, distribution, and amelioration of risks. Such risks can relate to nuclear power, genetically modified organisms, food safety (as in the Mad Cow Disease/BSE issue in Europe), and toxic chemicals in the environment.

To Beck, the degree to which this new politics supplants the class politics of industrial society heralds a 'reflexive modernity' in which society confronts the unintended consequences generated by the combination of science, technology, and economics that has driven 'progress' since the early nineteenth century. The idea of technological progress itself is called into question, along with faith in economic growth and scientific rationality. The result is a crisis in the legitimacy of the political economy. Reflexive modernization is society's resultant self-confrontation. Although the transition from industrial to risk society is rooted in the developmental logic of industrial society, social movements play a crucial role in initiating industrial society's process of self-confrontation with its own foundations. Risk society is reflexive not only in so far as the consequences of industrial society undermine these foundations; it is also reflexive in the sense of being self-critical. As a result of environmental activism and the public awareness of risks it generates, citizens start questioning the prospects for managing environmental crises by further reliance on economic growth and technological rationality. New possibilities for social and political transformation arise from people's growing awareness that they are living in a society whose habits of production and consumption may be undermining the conditions for its future existence. Thus Beck believes that reflexive modernization is accompanied by waning influence of state structures compared to diverse 'sub-political' spaces of civil society, of the sort we discussed at length in previous chapters.

Sub-politics is consistent with the politics of ecological modernization in its strong sense.[5] The politics of ecological modernization can turn out to be contentious because 'the invasion of ecology into the economy opens it to politics' (Beck, 1999: 100). Industry and business are forced to respond to this invasion of the economic sphere with strategies that observe 'the standards of politics requiring legitimation' (Beck, 1999: 101). This politicization of the economic sphere can be interpreted as a battle over the terms of ecological modernization: environmentalists aim to ecologize economics, bringing recognition to the reality of the economic system as a subsystem of nature (Daly, 1996), while government and industry stress those aspects of ecological modernization that are most consistent with existing economic priorities. Ecologizing economics entails a more thorough local focus, in both understanding the consequences of economic action and in decision making processes. From our point of view it therefore becomes crucial to ascertain the degree to which the state (and its imperatives) are declining in importance as a site of political action in comparison with these sub-political spaces.

Both strong ecological modernization and sub-politics emphasize the role of public deliberation in democratizing and legitimating science and technology. Beck's ecological democracy would democratize the politics of expertise by rolling back the industrial coalition's colonization of politics, law, and the public sphere:

My suggestion contains two interlocking principles: first, carrying out a division of powers and, second, the creation of a public sphere. Only a strong, competent public debate, 'armed' with scientific arguments, is capable of separating the scientific wheat from the chaff and allowing the institutions for directing technology—politics and law—to reconquer the power of their own judgement. (Beck, 1999: 70)

The result would be public science wherein 'research will fundamentally take account of the public's questions and be addressed to them' (Beck 1999: 70). Public science, Beck hopes, would help lay citizens win back the competence to make their own judgement, independently of experts, by making hazards that are not really visible or otherwise directly perceivable culturally

---

[5] From the ecological modernization theory side, this connection is accepted by Spaargaren, 2000: 62–4.

perceptible. (It is ironic that Beck's nemesis, Aaron Wildavsky, issues an identical call for 'citizen risk detectives', except that Wildavsky expects citizens to debunk alleged risks. See Wildavsky, 1995.)

Thus we can envisage two paths towards the green state, each with its own set of movement strategies. In one scenario, professional environmental NGOs pursue technocratic or weak ecological modernization within the state's decision making apparatus. In the other scenario, environmental NGOs do not limit their activities in this way, but instead follow the dual strategy of action in the state and civil society. While intrinsically attractive for all the reasons set out at the end of Chapter 6, the dual strategy presents movements with two problems. First, states are likely to prefer weak to strong ecological modernization. Second, some state configurations are not very conducive to the kind of public sphere and its relationship to the state that strong ecological modernization requires (as we will show in this chapter). We are more likely to find strong ecological modernization in states whose structures promote (if by accident rather than design) a flourishing civil society—though there are times when the odds in this respect can be beaten. Still, movement strategies will have to vary across different national contexts. The politics of strong ecological modernization is not available to all states equally, as we will now show.

Norway: Weak Ecological Modernization and Little Sub-politics

Strong ecological modernization is unlikely where civil society has been depleted, either through the state's actively inclusive or actively exclusive stance towards social movements. The more problematic case is actually that of active inclusion, as liberal democratic regimes appear incapable of sustaining actively exclusive strategies for very long. States such as Norway cultivate groups that moderate their demands in exchange for state funding and guaranteed participation in policy making, to the extent they can hardly be called NGOs. Their moderation means that included groups embrace any weak ecological modernization on offer. Groups outside the state-funded sector are few and far between. Conventional and routinized forms of engagement dominate environmental politics, so ecological modernization is initiated and controlled by the state.

Contrary to conventional wisdom, we expect that Norwegian environmentalists may in the long run be little more likely to connect environmental values to state imperatives than their counterparts elsewhere. Norwegian environmental policy in the 1980s and 1990s does however fit a trajectory of weak ecological modernization. The achievements are undeniable, and Norway is rightly regarded as a leader among European countries (Sverdrup,

1997: 74). Pollution levels in Norway are relatively low, and integrated pollution control was introduced as early as 1981. Momentum intensified with the Brundtland-associated sustainable development push in the late 1980s. As Langhelle (2000) puts it, Norway then 'carried the torch' on sustainable development. The sector-encompassing ambitions of this programme and associated state of the environment reporting further promoted ecological modernization, as did the subsequent policy emphasis on sustainable consumption. In addition, Norway does very well on the informational aspects of ecological modernization. Norway's Freedom of Information Act predates the 1990 EU directive on access to environmental information by twenty years and covers all of the latter's provisions (Killingland, 1996: 309).

Perhaps the most significant accomplishment in ecological modernization came with the victory of environmentalists and research institute representatives over recalcitrant industry participants on the green tax issue in 1989–92, which led to the implementation of green taxes beginning in 1991. The argument that these taxes reconcile environmental and economic values carried the day. The Nordic countries have pioneered the use of eco-taxes, and by the end of the 1990s in Norway they accounted for 9 per cent of tax revenues. However, their popularity in Norway may be for fiscal as much as environmental reasons: income from taxes related to oil has enabled Norway to avoid deep cuts in social services of the sort common in the rest of Western Europe. Still, as we concluded in Chapter 3, there have been times when Norwegian environmentalists have succeeded in attaching their interests to the state's economic imperative. However, there are limits to this assimilation—indicating perhaps the limits of weak ecological modernization.

In the 1990s Norway consciously took the lead in an effort to curb greenhouse gas emissions. But this policy ran up against 'the most long-standing principle of Norwegian environmental policy: that is, the principle that Norwegian policy should not put Norwegian industry and commerce in a disadvantageous position compared with foreign competitors' (Langhelle, 2000: 208, citing Jansen and Osland, 1996). The centrality to Norway's economy of energy-intensive industry, notably aluminium (relying on cheap hydro-electricity) and oil and gas production, also imposes limits. In contrast to other Nordic countries, energy and environment remain in separate ministries, and old energy-related political networks can resist the encroachment of ecological modernization (Midttun and Kamfjord, 1999). Hydropower and then North Sea oil have been at the heart of Norway's economic policy (especially after the energy shocks of the 1970s). Green taxes too had their reach limited when their implementation continued to be opposed by companies in key industrial and energy sectors (Kasa, 2000), preventing energy taxes from contributing to ecological restructuring. The opposition of industry to a carbon tax in the 1990s revealed the limits to consensual policy action of the sort that weak ecological modernization requires (Reitan, 1998).

In light of its undeniable accomplishments, why do we remain sceptical about Norway's capacity to pursue strong ecological modernization? The answer is that when limits are encountered, such as those imposed by the international position of industry and commerce or the centrality of hydro-power and oil, there is no countervailing pressure from civil society that might inspire a search for creative solutions. Episodes in the politics of hydro-power (and pollution) suggest that sub-politics has existed in Norway. Opposition to hydro-power was a focal point for Norway's movement until the early 1980s, but since then the issue has been dormant and depoliticized. Environmental activism has declined since inclusion reached its zenith around the issue of sustainable development in the late 1980s and early 1990s, when groups such as the Nature Conservation Society experienced a short-lived increase in membership. Although public access to environmental information has been very good by international standards, it remains something of an empty gesture in the absence of an autonomous green public sphere. Further, 'in actual practice the authorities do not always respond fully and in proper form to all information requests' (Killingland, 1996: 310).

Waning public involvement in Norway's established environmental NGOs in the 1990s has coincided with only a limited increase in direct action. The resurgence of grassroots environmentalism in the UK and the US in the 1990s, let alone the anti-statist environmentalism of Germany in the 1970s and 1980s, has no parallel here. The Bellona Foundation, established in 1986, became in the 1990s Norway's highest-profile environmental group. Bellona is not tied to the state after the fashion of the mainstream groups, and its style is occasionally confrontational. Another sub-politics aspect appears in its consultancy activities. But like Greenpeace, Bellona operates more like a company than a charity, still less a movement. A portion of the group's revenue has come from business interests, and as we pointed out in Chapter 6 by the end of the 1990s it was accepting project grants from the government. This type of 'environmental enterprise' is not unique to Norway, but this organizational form may be the only viable environmentalist response to the co-optation and decline of older groups in an actively inclusive state.

Norway also offers little scope for connecting environmental concerns to the legitimation imperative via any risk society scenario. In our other three countries, chemical pollution, biotechnology, and nuclear power have raised the need for legitimation in the context of risk, opening the door to oppositional action and sub-politics. In Norway, these issues are largely absent, and legitimation plays out in more old-fashioned terms, tied to a popular but expensive welfare state. Norway's export-oriented oil industry supports that welfare state, so legitimation actually points in an anti-environmental direction.

Perhaps the muted quality of Norwegian environmental politics in the 1990s simply reflects the reality that environmental degradation is less severe in Norway than in more heavily industrialized countries. But it also reveals, we argue, the analgesic and even anti-democratic face of the actively inclusive state. Ecological modernization in Norway is weak and set to remain a moderate, top-down project. There are no significant actors raising critical questions about the basic structure of the political economy or about the basic direction of public policy, no social movements to constitute an autonomous public sphere that can act as both a source of ideas and a reminder to policy makers of the seriousness of concerns that need to be addressed.

The United States: Some Sub-politics, No Ecological Modernization

The days when the United States was an environmental pioneer (enabled, as we argued in Chapter 3, by a link between environmentalism and the legitimacy imperative in the early 1970s) are a distant memory. Of course, there has remained plenty of activity in the periphery of the state, where movement access remained. But the term ecological modernization is not part of US policy discourse, nor is there much in policy practice to suggest pursuit under any other name (beyond the California emissions case we mentioned earlier). And although there are sporadic initiatives that join business and environmentalists, such as those associated with Amory Lovins and his *Factor Four* (the idea that prosperity can be doubled while halving resource use; see also Lovins and Lovins, 1999), these do not find their way into government.

The terms of debate in Washington in the 1990s were set by a conservative Congressional majority that saw environmental regulation as a drag on the economy, with economics and ecology remaining cast in old-fashioned zero-sum terms. 'Rather than asking more fundamental questions about how to balance and integrate economic growth and ecological sustainability, policy makers are mired in efforts to defend or attack the regulatory system that has been in place since the 1970s' (Bryner, 2000: 277). The approach to pollution regulation remains very much 'end of pipe'. And with few exceptions the politics of land management and wilderness protection still pits old adversaries against one another (loggers, miners, and ranchers on one side, environmentalists on the other). The environmental justice movement may in Lois Gibbs's words have succeeded in 'plugging the toilet' on toxic wastes, but this has not led to the creative redesign of production processes to minimize waste generation as sought even by weak ecological modernization. In short, if we seek ecological modernization in the United States we find very little, certainly when it comes to the national state and the mainstream of US business. As Andrews (1997: 41) puts it, when it comes to pollution control, 'The basic structure of

U.S. environmental policy . . . has remained entrenched in the paradigm of detailed federal standards and technology-based permits, rather than evolving further towards pollution prevention and ecological modernisation principles.'

Green taxes have not been widely applied in the United States, where *any* new taxes are extremely unpopular. An energy tax proposed by the Clinton administration failed by two votes in Congress, although several hundred eco-taxes exist at the state and local levels (Beck et al., 1998: 31). The economic logic associated with environmental initiatives appears under the heading of 'free market environmentalism' in the United States (for example, Anderson and Leal, 2001), not ecological modernization. This may explain the greater popularity of tradable permit schemes, such as the SO_2 trading scheme introduced by the 1990 Clean Air Act Amendments to deal with regional acid rain pollution (Lovei and Weiss, 1998: ix). The absence of so much as a public *debate* on ecological tax reform underscores our point concerning the irrelevance of ecological modernization in the United States. Significantly, presidential candidate Al Gore renounced his earlier commitment to eco-taxes during the 2000 election campaign.

Gore once believed in something like weak ecological modernization, as indicated by his 1992 book, *Earth in the Balance*. President George W. Bush thinks of the economy and the environment in inflexible zero-sum terms, and so never got close to that. In an exchange during the second presidential debate in October 2000, Gore supported tax incentives to encourage the development of renewable energy production technologies while asserting the mutual compatibility of environmental conservation and economic growth; though he retreated from his earlier support for energy taxes. Gore called Bush's plan to promote the domestic production of fossil fuels and his preference for voluntary agreements with industry to regulate pollution outdated ways of thinking about the environment/economy relationship. Bush, in turn, questioned the scientific merit of global warming projections, foreshadowing his decision as president to take the United States out of the Kyoto Treaty. Defending this decision to a European audience in July 2001, the president said: 'My job is to represent my country. We want to reduce greenhouse gases. . . . But first things first, as far as I'm concerned. Our strategy must make sure working people in America aren't thrown out of work' (Hutcheson, 2001). It is hard to imagine a clearer refutation of the central tenet of ecological modernization. The George W. Bush administration's position on global warming received strong political support from resource-intensive industries. The response from industries that operate in multinational political and regulatory regimes and are thus wary of an international backlash against US unilateral action was somewhat less enthusiastic.

Presidential administrations and congressional majorities come and go. But if we look at the underlying capacity for ecological modernization, we find a number of deficiencies. Jänicke and Weidner (1997*a*) and their collaborators explain comparative environmental policy performance in terms of such a capacity. Aside from the strength and competence of actors inside and outside government committed to environmental values, this capacity refers to the framework of political institutions and the structure of the economy. On the positive side, the United States does very well when it comes to scientific and technical aspects of capacity, mainly because agencies must justify regulatory proposals to the courts and to the public (Andrews, 1997: 35). But overall, Andrews (1997: 25) interprets the history of environmental policy in the United States in terms of 'swings of the pendulum . . . between initiatives to create and initiatives to destroy such a capacity'. These swings are themselves indicative of both the zero-sum framing of environmental issues and a lack of underlying capacity—one aspect of which is the capability for consensual action. Co-operative action of the sort weak ecological modernization requires is problematic in a system where business is hostile to labour and to the idea of government (while lapping up government contracts and subsidies), resource-intensive businesses attack environmentalists (often sponsoring anti-environmental groups and campaigns), and environmentalists distrust business. There is no government agency in a position to promote policy integration and consensual action. The EPA has little budgetary discretion, and its hands are tied by congressional direction to implement single-medium statutes. This situation is indicative of a more general lack of environmental policy integration in government (Andrews, 1997: 38–9).

The way passive inclusion plays out helps to explain the lack of ecological modernization in the United States. Once included, groups engage in adversarial politics—be it in lobbying or in court actions. To an outsider, the range of acceptable positions within the pluralist system may look narrow, but within this range adversarial politics is still the norm. The traditional picture of American pluralism is in terms of public policy as the resultant of competing groups pulling in different directions. It is difficult to frame matters in the positive-sum terms required by weak ecological modernization in such a situation. Citing a long list of precursors, Jänicke (1997: 13) sees the ability to undertake consensual or co-operative action as a key aspect of state environmental policy capacity. (For quantitative cross-national evidence of a positive association between degree of corporatism—the main form of consensual policy making—and environmental policy performance, see Scruggs, 1999, 2001.) Co-operative exercises do exist in the United States, and designs such as environmental mediation, policy dialogues, and regulatory negotiation have been pioneered here (Dryzek, 1990). However, such forums are normally billed as forms of conflict resolution: typically, they come into play only after the various parties to a conflict have fought each other to a standstill in more adversarial institutions, especially the court system (Weber, 1998). More truly co-operative structures exist—but only at the local level. Examples include the Resource Advisory Councils for the management of Western grazing lands that involve ranchers, government officials, and environmentalists (Welsh, 2000); collaborative management processes in the same region (Brick, *et al.*, 2000); and the kind of 'backyard' structures celebrated by Sabel, Fung, and Karkkainen, 2000).

In previous chapters we pointed to the diversity of the US environmental movement, and the resurgence of activism in the 1980s and 1990s among those who felt themselves excluded from the kind of relationships that insider groups had established in government. Thus the United States may well have sufficient vitality in the green public sphere to help turn weak ecological modernization into the strong form, especially as the focus is so often on legitimacy, reflexivity, and democratic participation. The only minor difficulty here would come with the historically difficult relationships between the leadership of the major groups and grassroots activists. The sort of mutual hostility and contempt in such relations in the United States is largely absent from say the German movement, where mainstream and grassroots groups still share a sense of tilling different sections of the same field.[6] Still, as we pointed out in Chapter 6, mutual hostility has given way to more productive relationships between insiders and radical activists in the United States. The mainstream's inclusion in the state has brought many disappointments, but it has not robbed the movement as a whole of its ability to 'preserve its reflexivity'—even though specific organizations may have lost theirs. Such a dynamic follows the developmental logic of the passively inclusive state, which absorbs interests faster than exclusive states, but more slowly than actively inclusive states such as Norway. As older groups are absorbed, newer, more radical ones can emerge to take their place in the public sphere.

But these positive features of the contemporary American movement turn out to be beside the point when it comes to ecological modernization. The real difficulty in the United States comes not with any deficiencies in the character of its civil society that would preclude *strong* ecological modernization (the Norwegian problem), but much earlier, with the system's inability to turn zero-sum conflicts between economic and environmental interests into *weak* ecological modernization. Here, movement vitality is no help. The same might be said of the country's strong freedom of information and right-to-know toxics laws (the Freedom of Information Act was first passed in 1966

---

[6] Sociologically, this is because today's leaders of German mainstream groups were themselves anti-statist activists in the 1970s and early 1980s—unlike many of their US counterparts most of them have not been shaped by the calculating professional ethic imparted by elite law, business, and public policy schools. But the divide is less sharply defined in Germany also because passive exclusion has given Germany's mainstream environmental NGOs far fewer opportunities for inclusion in the state, thus preserving a sense of opposition and exclusion among all environmental activists—at least until the 1998 election.

and substantially revised in 1974; Adler, 1997). They would help turn weak into strong ecological modernization, but are no help in the absence of the weak form.

Issues of risk are more salient in the United States than in Norway, and they do produce some sub-politics, though they have not occasioned quite the crises that have been observable in the United Kingdom and Germany. The simple fact that the United States is a big place means that many risks are localized, so it is no surprise that the major risk-related movements, anti-toxics and environmental justice, begin as series of local actions. These move-ments are risk society phenomena in Beck's terms. They call economic and technological progress into question, and refuse to accept that hazards can be managed through established policy making structures deploying scientific expertise. There are numerous critiques of the technocentric process of risk assessment, and of the lack of democratic participation in both the direction of scientific inquiry and the application of science to policy-making (see e.g. Fischer, 1995; O'Brien, 2001). Moreover, the environmental justice, anti-toxics, and public-interest science movements engage a kind of sub-politics that involves co-operation with activists in other localities, direct action protests and campaigns against polluters and government, shading into more conventional action such as lobbying, consultation, and court challenges.

In the United States, science actually lacks the authority it possesses in environmental policy in Germany and the United Kingdom. Science often holds itself apart from the public and its desires, and communication is seen as only unidirectional, from the experts to the public. The scientific commun-ity has not accepted that its own legitimation and effectiveness could depend on the information and support it receives from the public (Sarewitz, 1996). Further, the science carried out by government agencies is influenced by powerful political actors. For example, the first EPA study on dioxin was completed in 1985; it was a review of the available literature on animal studies and cancer. A risk assessment was done based on this available evidence, and the EPA developed a recommended exposure level. But this level was the low-est ever recommended by any scientific or policy body in the world, and was immediately challenged by industry. So the EPA began a 're-evaluation' of dioxin exposure, which ultimately raised the acceptable risk level. Challenged by both grassroots groups and the scientific community, the EPA tried again. When the final report (or set of reports) came out in 1995, members of Congress attacked the conclusions because they were not peer reviewed. There are still no updated exposure guidelines from the EPA; in the mean-time, not only the victims of dioxin exposure, but also the scientific process and the public's opinion of it have taken a beating.

A related reason for the loss of scientific authority is the adversarial nature of most rule making. Each side presents its own scientists, making it hard to maintain the appearance of scientific neutrality (Weiland, 2001: 14). Science loses its neutrality and become another commodity for sale. Adversarial policy making also forces science into a peculiar position in environmental impact assessment. According to the courts' interpretation of NEPA, impact assessments can be challenged only on the basis of the adequacy of the document, not its integration into policymaking. This forces government agencies preparing the documents to employ scientists to overstate the negative environmental impacts of the developments they are proposing.

Mistrust of science and experts has led to sub-political practices, such as 'popular epidemiology' (Fischer, 2000). In the most cited case (the basis for the popular film *A Civil Action* starring John Travolta), citizens in the vicinity of toxic waste sites in Woburn, Massachusetts, carried out their own study of the incidence of leukemia and birth defects after refusing to accept government reassurances. Despite the rejection of the results by state and government agencies, they were used in a lawsuit against one of the companies, which was settled out of court (Brown and Mikkelsen, 1990). Another example of this public science is the 'Bucket Brigades' organized by the California environmental group Communities for a Better Environment (CBE). Communities located near oil refineries have a common problem: accidental or deliberate 'toxic release events' or 'airborne toxic events'. Most states just require industry to self-report such events, or send inspectors out (usually after the smoke has cleared). Citizens may use video cameras to show releases, but those can only show smoke, not whether or not regulated pollutants are involved. So CBE developed an easy-to-use air sampling kit; citizens take the sample and send it to an independent laboratory. CBE then sends the documentation to the community organizations and local, state, and federal monitoring agencies. This system uses public involvement in the scientific process to put some serious pressure on industry that has, in the past, avoided scrutiny. CBE now makes available its 'Bucket Brigade' kits to any interested communities, so they can do the scientific monitoring of toxic events. There is a growing 'public interest' science in the US as well. 'Science shops', where communities bring scientific questions to researchers willing to focus on public concerns, have expanded (see Sclove, 1995, or the Loka Institute at www.loka.org).

The localized character of most risk issues in the United States does not preclude a more pervasive sub-politics that transcends the local level, but retains local roots. The vehicle here is the network, as we discussed in Chapter 5. It is noteworthy that environmental justice as a movement is quite successful when it sticks to local actions and network associations. It runs into major difficulties as soon as it renounces sub-politics and adopts more conventional trappings. In Chapter 3 we reported on the disappointments of environmental justice activists who had made the transition into government, and the meagre impact of the Office of Environmental Justice and National Environmental Justice Advisory Committee within the EPA. In a passively inclusive state, the lure of this sort of inclusion may therefore need resisting if sub-politics and reflexivity are to be protected.

The United States does, then, feature some sub-politics in the presence of risk issues. However, the ecological transformation of its state and political economy remains unlikely so long as the structural and political-economic obstacles to even weak ecological modernization that we have identified persist.

The United Kingdom: Sub-politics by Default and Belated Ecological Modernization

We are interested in the United Kingdom primarily because it is the best approximation we can find to an actively exclusive state, though as we have pointed out, active exclusion began to wane in 1989. The extreme form of market liberalism that defined the 1979–89 era had little time for environmental values under any rubric, and stressed the need for deregulation in order to promote economic growth (even the 1995 Environment Act had a deregulatory impetus in requiring cost–benefit analysis for regulatory proposals). It is no surprise that ecological modernization failed to make any inroads. In a way, this contingent anti-environmental feature makes it hard to discern the impact on the prospects for ecological modernization of active exclusion *per se*, though there are good reasons to suppose that active exclusion is detrimental. In particular, it destroys any potential for consensual environmental policy making of the sort that is key to capacity building. The conflictual terms in which the main axes of politics are cast by active exclusion precludes any co-operative search for positive sum measures that would involve environmentalists and business.

By the 1990s, environmental groups could re-enter the corridors of power as the excesses of market liberalism eased and the British state reverted towards a more passive orientation, mixing inclusion and exclusion. But the government did not adopt ecological modernization's components as policy. As Weale (1997: 105) puts it:

there is little policy development on what might be regarded as the central tenets of ecological modernization. There is: little use of pollution charges in accordance with the polluter pays principle; only haphazard encouragement of research and development for cleaner technologies; virtually no work on reconceptualising measures of economic well-being to net out from national income accounts defensive environmental expenditures; and a poor record on energy conservation.

Moreover, there was no policy integration across central government departments. Policy making continued to be dominated by a requirement to demonstrate scientific proof of a hazard prior to policy response—the antithesis of the precautionary principle (Hajer, 1995). Environmental regulation that did exist was very much an end-of-pipe affair. Road-building continued to be the focus of transportation policy, lip service to alternatives by the Blair Labour government after 1997 notwithstanding.

Proclaimed commitments to sustainable development in the wake of the 1992 Earth Summit generated several White Papers in the 1990s, but little of policy substance. In 1997 a Sustainable Development Unit was established in the new Environment Agency, and it began pushing a cross-sector approach, but it faced an uphill struggle against other departments (S. Young, 2000: 254–5). These developments did open doors to government for the environmental movement, but as we saw in previous chapters, inclusion often acted as a burden upon environmental groups. Jacobs (1997: 5) casts doubt on the value of sustainable development in the United Kingdom:

on occasion the urge of environmentalists to join the political mainstream has threatened to give utopianism a good name. But for all its success in uniting former opponents on a more or less common environmental platform, sustainable development has not succeeded in making the environment into a central political issue.

As opportunities for consultation became more plentiful in the areas of sustainable development and biodiversity in particular, sections of the movement appeared to be settling into an increasingly moderate, institutionalized relationship with government. Following Jänicke, this development ought to have increased the potential for consensual action and so environmental policy capacity—itself instrumental to the pursuit of ecological modernization. Yet this did not happen. For the relationship with government often involved consultation without influence, with a large element of co-optation of environmentalists (see Chapter 3). Pollution control policy in the United Kingdom has traditionally been a matter of co-operation—a far cry indeed from the legalistic, politicized, and adversarial character of regulation in the United States. But the co-operation in question is between government regulators and corporations at the micro level of implementation; it is done in secret with no possibility for environmentalist participation or public scrutiny. In the absence of any commitment to ecological modernization on the part of regulators or polluters, there is no structural facilitation of ecological modernization resulting from such co-operation.

Aside from having to escape the legacy of active exclusion, ecological modernization (especially its stronger version) is impeded by the British tradition of secrecy in government. The UK's response to the EU's 1990 environmental right-to-know directive has been contradictory. Hallo (1996: 6) assigns the UK to a middle group of countries situated between those with good general access to information prior to the adoption of the directive and those that lacked such laws and have progressed most slowly. While today's Britons have better access to environmental information than their parents, one observer cautions that the 'concept and language of rights have always found acceptance with rhetoricians in the UK more easily than they have been accommodated within its legal systems' (Roderick, 1996: 274). The Official Secrets Act of 1911, which prevented officials from releasing information to the public unless specifically permitted to do so, remains part of the ethos of government. Prior to the Environmental Protection Act of 1990 and the Environmental Information Regulations Act of 1992, most information held by regulatory agencies about pollution and the state of the environment was kept secret (Davis, 1996). Today acceptance in principle of greater openness clashes with officials' hostility to, or at least unfamiliarity with, public participation in environmental policy making.

The United Kingdom did however see two significant developments at the end of the decade that indicated a belated arrival of some elements of ecological modernization. Until 2000 there was little in the way of green taxation, though revenue from these taxes appeared high because of the traditionally high taxes on fuel and transportation, in place for purely fiscal reasons, not environmental ones. But in 2001 a Climate Change Levy came into operation, imposing a per-kilowatt charge on energy generated by fossil fuels used by business and government bodies. The charge was opposed by the Conservative Party (which promised to abolish it in its manifesto for the 2001 general election) and the Confederation of British Industry, and its implementation was accompanied by the negotiation of a complex system of discounts and exemptions for many industries. Still, this tax broke one major barrier to ecological modernization in the United Kingdom—the resistance of Treasury to any such use of the taxation system (on the strength of which see Voisey and O'Riordan, 1997: 49; Weale, 1997: 106).

More radical still was a report issued in 1998 by the Royal Commission on Environmental Pollution entitled *Setting Environmental Standards*, which recommended abandoning the traditional British secretive and informal approach to regulation. The report recommended 'that the whole process of analysis, deliberation and synthesis should take place in a context in which the articulation of public values should be included at all stages of the policy process' (Weale, 2001: 362–3). Democratization would go further than mere consultation of stakeholders, but instead seek to involve *citizens* in the process (Weale, 2001: 368). In its discursive democratic prescriptions, the report is actually consistent with strong ecological modernization. The report met with a belated and lukewarm response from the government, and at the time of writing it remains unclear whether any of its recommendations will be adopted, especially in light of what Voisey and O'Riordan (1997: 49) identify as a major barrier to sustainable development in the United Kingdom: 'the role of citizen is seen as a rhetorical focus, but a practical nightmare.'

The early 1990s also saw a growing dialogue between NGOs and business. Borrowing from Beck, Rose (1993: 294) describes this as 'a sort of unpolitics,' though a better description is 'paragovernmental activity', in the terms we established in Chapter 6. In 1996 Greenpeace organized a conference for business groups to emphasize the opportunities for strategic alliances with environmental interests and the market opportunities for environmentally benign technologies. Of the mainstream environmental organizations, Greenpeace has often stood out as the least willing to take part in formal governmental processes. Greenpeace had challenged Thatcher's claims of international leadership on ozone and climate change issues, dubbing Britain the 'Dirty Man of Europe' (Lowe, interview, 1999). In the early 1990s Greenpeace dealt quite closely with government over climate change issues, but then strategically shifted its position, electing to remain outside of the Sustainable Development Roundtable. Both Greenpeace and the World Wide Fund for Nature have worked directly with major companies on issues such as CFC production and industrial fishing (Grove-White, 1997: 18). Friends of the Earth has moved into environmental consultancy with private companies and engaged in a 'green consumerism' campaign (Byrne, 1997: 134). New environmental groups have emerged to facilitate relationships with the business community, such as the Environment Council and the Forum for the Future.[7] Unlike the Norwegian Environmental Home Guard campaign, however, these initiatives occurred without state involvement let alone state funding. These developments can be described as weak paragovernmental ecological modernization.

We have seen that belated moves in the direction of ecological modernization can be discerned in the United Kingdom, beginning in the late 1990s. The United Kingdom is still behind Germany and Norway in this respect, but in advance of the United States. But any movement from weak to strong ecological modernization requires an active oppositional civil society, capable of engaging sub-politics in Beck's terms. As pointed out in earlier chapters, the 1990s did see oppositional movement politics arise for the first time in the United Kingdom. While we have emphasized the importance of anti-roads protests, Greenpeace, alone of the more organized and established groups, has also played a role. The organization maintained media-based campaigns and reasserted its role as 'environmental policeman' through highly symbolic protests, the most dramatic and influential of these being the 1995 occupation of Shell's Brent Spar platform, discussed in Chapter 3. Grove-White (1997:

---

[7] The Environment Council's origins in the conservation movement can be traced much earlier, although in its new form it focuses on liaison and education between the movement, business community and government. Forum for the Future, led by former Green Party figures Jonathon Porritt and Sarah Parkin, seeks to develop constructive policy solutions as a consultancy to business and government.

17) believes that the Brent Spar controversy essentially 'rewrote the rules' in British environmental politics, bypassing the government through an effective consumer campaign and illustrating 'the mounting significance of public opinion for emerging new concerns about corporate social responsibility.' An editorial in the *Independent* (21 June 1995, p. 20) similarly concluded from the campaign's success: 'It is now clear that neither governments nor big business are strong enough to withstand a new phenomenon: an alliance of direct action with public opinion.' In Beck's terms, the Brent Spar issue was resolved through sub-politics within civil society (see also Wapner, 1996). It is an example of paragovernmental action (though not of ecological modernization).

The British environmental movement has had some success in recasting the relationship between certain development initiatives and the state's economic imperative. In both the nuclear and transport inquiries of the 1970s environmental groups presented economic arguments. The cost of nuclear power development was subsequently—and quite ironically—highlighted through the Conservatives' privatization programme. The reluctance of the corporate world to acquire nuclear power resources emphasized their true cost, and it is this that has led to the demise of nuclear development. With road development too, government policy in the late 1990s began to shift as the economic burden of road construction upon the state became increasingly evident (and exacerbated by the costs of dealing with increasing direct action protest). Organizations such as FoE and CPRE have consequently developed a much stronger relationship with members of Treasury.

Paragovernmental activity and recent developments in taxation and Royal Commission proposals notwithstanding, the United Kingdom lingers well behind Germany and Norway in the ecological modernization stakes. It remains to be seen whether effective inclusion in the state's core via that route is possible. However, these developments do suggest that ecological modernization is possible in a context that has become passively inclusive—not just in actively inclusive Norway and passively exclusive Germany. Moreover, the arrival of social movement activism in the 1990s suggests that the kind of oppositional politics necessary for a strong version of ecological modernization to gain ground is present. However, so far the movement activism is mostly in the anti-roads area, where the state still shows its actively exclusive face. The ecological modernization policy momentum is entirely in the area of pollution control, where there is no oppositional movement activity. Without that activity, radical proposals such as the 1998 report of the Royal Commission on Environmental Pollution are unlikely to be implemented. That social movement activity is possible on pollution issues is illustrated by the anti-toxics and environmental justice movements in the United States, which have no British counterpart. This absence in the United Kingdom is puzzling in light of the risk-society thesis—according to which one would expect movement mobilization in the vicinity of risks imposed by pollution. The risk that attained greatest prominence in the 1990s came with BSE/Mad Cow disease, but this became framed as a health and food supply issue, not an environmental one, and it inspired little movement activity. Risks associated with genetically modified organisms and their release into the environment saw more in the way of movement action (e.g., destruction of crops), and the 2001 Foot and Mouth disease outbreak brought loud criticisms from both environmentalists and farmers. Again, all of these issues are distant from the anti-pollution policy area where ecological modernization has been stirring, but the broad issue of industrialized food production—where both the government and science have taken a beating in public opinion—may offer a unique route to ecological modernization policies.

Still, the continuing influence of the partial and ineffective inclusion that long characterized the United Kingdom remains detrimental when it comes to anything like strong ecological modernization. The shock of active exclusion that characterized the 1980s was perhaps unfortunate in that it demonstrated to environmental groups that a return to this traditional alternative was not so bad after all. At any rate, our conclusion about the destructive impact of active exclusion on the prospects for ecological modernization remains a firm one. It remains to be seen whether the United Kingdom can escape this destructive legacy.

Germany: Stronger Ecological Modernization and the Professionalization of Sub-politics?

We have argued in previous chapters that a passively exclusive state is conducive to a vibrant civil society. Confronted with this situation, a passively exclusive state will, we argue, be the most likely of our four kinds of states to move from weak towards strong ecological modernization, a move that looks improbable in actively inclusive Norway. This very development may in turn change the character of the state, softening its exclusive aspect. However, because even mainstream groups are less likely to suffer co-optation than their counterparts in more inclusive settings, the movement as a whole is likely to retain resistance alongside engagement—the kind of dual strategy we discussed in Chapter 6.

With the 1998 election of an SPD/Green coalition government, German environmental NGOs had to revise upwards their assessment of the prospects for pursuing their ends through policy initiatives based on ecological modernization. Environmental NGOs enjoy better access to public officials as a result of the Greens' participation in parliament and government, although activists say that opportunities for access to and influence in the SPD/Green federal government have remained far behind expectations (Musiol, interview, 1999). Moreover, social movement activity had by 1998 declined from its peak a decade or so earlier. As the Green Party's parliamentary spokeswoman for the environment explains:

Sixty-eighters—members of the peace and anti-nuclear movements—are getting older. These people no longer attend protest marches. Young people today tend to be apolitical and have a different relationship to the state. And the state itself has changed for the better so that radical opposition is no longer necessary. Politically motivated young people are more likely to seek change through conventional political channels such as interest groups and parties. (Hustedt, interview, 1999)

More than in most countries, the discourses of sustainable development and ecological modernization have come to dominate environmental politics in Germany. At issue is an 'ecological transformation of industrial society' not its abolition. In a comparative light, Germany's environmental policy record in the 1980s and 1990s looks positive. Stricter government regulations have dramatically reduced acute water, air, and soil pollution (Jänicke and Weidner, 1997*b*), though green taxes have so far made a smaller impact than might be expected. Nuclear energy—once the chief cause of environmental mobilization—has suffered serious setbacks, culminating in the SPD/Green government's plan for gradual phase-out.[8] This plan, which envisions that few if any plants will be taken off the grid immediately, is a compromise that aims to balance the state's economic and legitimation needs, but it is hard to see how even this could have happened without the prior new social movement activity (Hunold, 2001). The nuclear issue is the most graphic and significant kind of risk society issue that Germany has confronted. However, issues of environmental risk have been especially salient since the 1970s, perhaps having much to do with the fact that Germany is a heavily industrialized, densely populated country in the heart of Europe, subject to risks generated beyond its borders as well as within them. Beck's work on the risk society, though presented in generally applicable terms, owes much to his German location.

The environmental movement's confrontational strategies of the late 1970s and 1980s had their successes, as we showed in Chapter 6. Not least of these was inducing the state to adopt ecological modernization as both discourse and policy practice in the mid 1980s, when environmentalists were still excluded. Still, confrontation has now receded, along with acceptance of environmental policy tools that rely on market-based ecological incentives

---

[8] The SPD called for ending the country's reliance on nuclear energy as early as 1988, but the environmentalist wing of the party is in the minority. Prior to Chernobyl, the SPD was closely allied with nuclear industry unions and sharply critical of the anti-nuclear movement.

(Zittel, 1996). The pragmatists who control the Green Party today reject eco-radical goals and embrace the aim of ecologically modernizing the country's social-market economy. Environmental advocacy organizations willing to support the ecological modernization project have, after a long struggle, gained access to the state, whose passively exclusive character they have diluted. But radical groups such as BBU still face passive exclusion. Their role in sub-political activity has been largely supplanted by a burgeoning sector of for-profit environmental consultancies. Public agencies and firms interested in ecologically sustainable development increasingly bypass traditional environmental NGOs altogether in favour of these for-profit consultancies for information and advice.

The pattern of movement history, then, is one of radical beginnings followed by the formation of a political party that has become a permanent presence on the German electoral landscape, together with the creation of environmental advocacy groups, some of which have close ties to the Greens but all of which have kept an independent organizational and political identity. These environmental NGOs do not have quite the discursive and democratic vitality of the social movements of the 1970s and 1980s. Given that the Greens were in opposition until 1998 (and lacked an effective parliamentary presence 1990–4) and there were limited opportunities for environmental NGO inclusion in environmental policymaking, professionalized sub-politics became a mainstay of environmental NGO activity alongside the state's modest ecological modernization program.

Unlike some among the US environmental justice movement and radical wilderness defenders, German environmental NGOs active in oppositional civil society do not reject the country's consensus-seeking, rationalist discourse and policy style. The discourse of German environmental politics, state-centred or not, fits the give-and-take between expertise and counter-expertise described in Beck's model of ecological democracy. As noted above, some environmentalists' hopes of special treatment by the SPD/Green government have been disappointed. But in the long run this could actually help them pursue a viable dual strategy vis-à-vis a left-of-centre/green government for whom the environment is not as central an issue as environmentalists would like. Few activists we interviewed believed that co-optation was going to be a serious problem for environmental NGOs.

Mainstream environmental NGOs too regard ecological modernization as the best means of securing the role of environmental values in politics and economy even though environmental issues no longer occupy the top of the political agenda, taking a back seat to economic policy. Environmental NGOs believe their ability to shape public policy against the wishes of business associations and labour unions waxes and wanes in direct proportion to public concern for environmental issues. The dominance of business in environmental policy debates derives from the fact that individual firms must implement many of the policies demanded by environmental NGOs and enacted by state officials. In that context, it makes sense for environmental NGOs wishing to be seen as 'reasonable' partners in policy making to embrace conceptions of environmentalism that seek to bridge the gap between business and environmental protection. A veteran environmental scientist and Social Democrat MP summarizes the challenge as follows:

> The situation is completely different today: local environmental calamities and protests and the spirit of unruliness are gone. But environmental calamities reach all areas of life. Keeping them politically alive requires scientific proof that there is no necessary contradiction between ecology and the economy. If you can piggyback the issue of the environment onto the dominant issue of the economy, the environment will have a chance again. For all intents and purposes, it is no longer possible to argue for the environment against the opposition of business. (von Weizsäcker, interview, 1999)

Business too has changed. Even industrial managers, particularly younger ones who work outside major corporations, include sustainable development and climate protection among their top ethical priorities, albeit subject to the constraints of capitalist growth (Hustedt, interview, 1999). Consequently, the movement's earlier battle with industry in some sectors has turned into a 'critical dialogue' rooted in the shared discourse of sustainable development. Yet Germany's big businesses, particularly utilities and chemical companies, have not budged very much from their negative view of environmentalists, and vice versa. Although both NABU and the Institute for Applied Ecology have accepted eco-sponsoring agreements, and the Institute for Applied Ecology has signed eco-auditing contracts with large firms (Musiol, interview, 1999), many environmentalists believe the greatest potential for making an impact lies with medium-sized firms, where managers have greater freedom over setting company policy than do managers in publicly held corporations beholden to the stock market as well as politically conservative managers and supervisory boards. This is not to say that environmentalists and managers share the same conception of sustainable development. In fact, acceptance of sustainable development by major industrial associations is seldom more than superficial (Streese, interview, 1999). However, that some corporations are willing to discuss environmental measures and have accepted sustainability as their guiding principle indicates a cultural shift in power relations in favour of environmentalists and gives further credence to the ecological modernization thesis.

The kind of programme accepted by Green politicians and NGOs alike is a far cry from that championed by the citizens' initiatives of the 1970s. Still, pragmatically inclined environmental NGOs claim the state and certain sectors of the economy have become less resistant to environmental change.

Nuclear power is a dramatic case in point. The anti-nuclear movement and the economic imperative long conflicted. But following forty years of federal support for nuclear energy, after the 1998 election environmentalists suddenly had the federal government on their side on this issue—up to a point. The SPD/Green government's commitment to end the nuclear energy programme signalled the persistent political influence of the antinuclear movement. However, it is economics ministry officials and nuclear industry representatives who have negotiated the terms of ending the programme, with environmentalists and the environment ministry apparently sidelined. Thus passive exclusion persisted, and so did protest. Radicals such as the BBU still operate outside policy making. As discussed in Chapter 5, the anti-nuclear movement has shown that it can still mobilize large numbers of activists in a separate public sphere, even after the elevation of the Greens in 1998. When numerous environmental groups rejected the Greens' acquiescence on the shipment of reprocessed nuclear wastes, non-violent protests continued.

Though now restricted mostly to the anti-nuclear movement, the oppositional sphere remains comparatively large and vital. The 'strong' aspect of ecological modernization in Germany is confirmed by the fact that sub-political activities have not been killed off, although they have been thoroughly professionalized. One of the movement's responses to the state's exclusionary strategy of the 1970s and early 1980s was to establish environmental policy institutions outside the state. The Working Group of Ecological Research Institutes alone comprises approximately eighty institutes (Hey and Brendle, 1994: 133). The Institute for Applied Ecology, founded in 1977, sought to meet the demand for scientific and technical data that could be used to support plaintiffs challenging environmentally questionable industrial facilities in the courts. Additional independent ecological research institutes were established in subsequent decades. Examples include the Wuppertal Institute for Climate, Environment, and Energy and the Potsdam Institute for Climate Research. These two research organizations receive part of their funding from the federal government. While they do not share the movement origins of the Institute for Applied Ecology, they contribute information and proposals to environmental policy debates. Politically, they counterbalance the various state agencies charged with gathering and interpreting environmental data for the public bureaucracy.

The greatest potential for assuming paragovernmental powers lies in technical areas of environmental policy that require expertise rather than mass mobilization (Brendle, interview, 1999). Eco-auditing is a good example. Advising companies on retooling their operations according to ecological criteria is one of the bread-and-butter issues of the Institute for Applied Ecology. In keeping with the theme of ecological modernization, moreover, Germany's independent ecological research institutes have pioneered market-based environmental policy tools that would shift more regulatory tasks to the private sector. Setting industrial norms and standards—a task historically left to private-sector associations—is a further case in point. Here government has been more than happy to outsource highly technical deliberations and decisions to nongovernmental experts, including environmental NGO representatives.

There remain obstacles to stronger ecological modernization, prominent among which is the German tradition of administrative secrecy in government, which has been slow to bow to European pressure to improve public access. The Federal Freedom of Access to Environmental Information Act of 1994 came into force eighteen months after the deadline set by the 1990 EU directive had passed (Gebers, 1996: 97). The Act empowered citizens to obtain environmental information held by administrative agencies at all levels of government. Previously citizens without a legally valid claim based on property rights could not obtain such data.

The Act, however, has failed to dislodge an entrenched pattern of administrative secrecy. Most of the country's 445 municipal and county environmental agencies remained less than forthcoming with information concerning the quality of drinking water and the existence of industrial soil contamination. Many also charged steep fees for information (Ahrens and Stoller, 1995). In a 1999 ruling, the European Court of Justice struck down most of the Act's provisions, although it found no grounds for the EU Commission's complaint that German fees for access to environmental information effectively discouraged freedom-of-information requests. However, the Court ruled that German citizens' access to environmental data remained inadequate by EU standards.

This situation may be about to change. The SPD/Green coalition signed the 1998 Aarhus UN Convention, which seeks to narrow the grounds on which administrators may withhold environmental data. Some environmental activists believe the new convention will help to eliminate the worst elements of what Thomas Lenius (BUND) calls Germany's 'Prussian administrative tradition' (Pötter, interview, 1998).

Germany has, then, experienced stronger ecological modernization than the other three countries in this study, however short it may fall of Christoff's ideal type. Along with the salience of risk issues, this experience in turn has enabled more effective connection of environmental movement interests to core state imperatives than in the UK, USA, and even Norway. These developments were facilitated by the passively exclusive character of the German state, which provided the space and impetus for the development of a green public sphere. Ironically, strong ecological modernization is advanced as exclusion diminishes with the entry of environmental NGOs into the state and the Greens into government. How long will this combination of circumstances persist? Our structural and historical analysis could be deployed to suggest that this state of affairs is unstable, because it is conditional on the recent experience and memory of an autonomous green public sphere. If so, Germany may lapse into passive inclusion of the American sort, with an associated weakening of ecological modernization. Alternatively, it could develop a kind of environmental corporatism that includes a green elite, but passively excludes others. The latter would not necessarily be a bad outcome, possibly constituting a further turn of the historical spiral in which passive exclusion means a revitalized public sphere—which in turn might go the way of the social movements of the 1970s and 1980s. But that is to look too far into the future.

Conclusion

If we array our four countries according to the degree they have achieved strong ecological modernization and associated sub-politics, and by implication the degree of connection this reveals between environmental movement interests and core state imperatives, then Germany is in front. Germany has reaped the benefits of a history of passive exclusion, though how long it can continue to do so remains unclear. Norway may be ranked second, but only on the dimension of ecological modernization, which it is pursuing in weak form. But nothing stronger can be envisaged for Norway, and no sub-politics is apparent. Ecological modernization now plays some role in public policy making in the UK, which together with some paragovernmental activity would place the UK behind Germany and Norway but in front of the USA. In the USA, national politics still exhibits an old-fashioned stand-off between economy and environment. The USA featured by far the strongest connection between environmental values and core state imperatives around 1970, but that peak has not been attained since, nor does it look to return in the near future.

At first sight it might seem paradoxical, but on reflection understandable, that in the 1990s we see a resurgence of environmental activism in the ecological modernization laggards, the USA and UK. This resurgence occurs despite the passively inclusive character of the US state that ought to absorb and neutralize radicalism, and despite the recovery of the UK from the active exclusion of the Thatcher era. These developments themselves indicate the waning of structural determinism: state structure may be less important than it once was in determining the form taken by social movements. This in turn indicates heightened reflexivity. That is, activists can look to the history of inclusion and see what it has and, more to point, has not accomplished, and draw lessons for their own orientation to the state.

8

States and Social Movements: Conclusions

States and social movements cannot escape one another. The outcomes of their interaction give shape to the political world. This is true historically, and remains true in this age of globalization. Part of this dynamic entails reshaping of the state as it incorporates movements, but that is only part of the story. The 'life-cycle' of movements as they relate to states is much more than a one-way drive to inclusion.

Inclusion and its Consequences

The history of states and social movements does reveal several examples of the eventual inclusion of previously confrontational movements in the state. However, we have argued that effective inclusion can only occur when a movement can attach its interest to one or more of the imperatives that constitute the state's core. In the deeper past, this was most clearly true for the inclusions of the bourgeoisie and the working class. When it comes to environmentalism, the first such attachment, to the state's legitimation imperative, was made in the United States around 1970, explaining why the US could become the environmental policy pioneer in this period. The subsequent history of environmentalism in all our countries is one of failure when the state's economic core is approached, at least until the advent of ecological modernization and the eventually enhanced salience of environmental risk. In the mid-1980s, environmentalists in Norway could be welcomed into the core of a state that embraced weak ecological modernization. Matters played out somewhat differently in Germany, where passive exclusion meant that environmentalists could not receive the sort of state embrace experienced by their Norwegian cousins, even though public policy moved in the direction of ecological modernization.

When a connection between movement interests and state imperatives cannot be made, inclusion is largely co-optive, dissipating movement energies to little effect—aside from restricted influence in the state's periphery. The result is often regrets and second thoughts on the part of activists. When policy influence is limited, inclusion is costly not just in terms of scarce movement resources, but because its price is moderation and bureaucratization for included groups, meaning alienation of the grassroots from the leadership. Professionalization and hierarchy for environmental groups arrived early and thoroughly in the inclusive states of the US and Norway, though the sorts of skills and organization required were very different in the two countries, eventually becoming controversial and challenged in the US but not in Norway. Similar developments came later and partially in the UK and Germany, receiving impetus whenever exclusion from the state was softened or lifted.

The implication here is not that movements should always shun the state. Rather, it is a matter of weighing the advantages and disadvantages of insider action and more confrontational strategies. The balance will vary with the historical context, which can sometimes undergo dramatic shifts of the sort we have charted in Chapter 7. But if inclusion leads only to modest policy reforms, movements should think long and hard about whether the loss in civil society is worth it—especially if that loss reduces the possibilities for effective policy reforms in the future.

The simplest response to these difficulties is a 'dual strategy' involving action in the state along with continued confrontation from the public sphere. But as we pointed out in Chapter 6, such a strategy itself is optimal only in particular historical circumstances—notably when the movement does not confront a thoroughly exclusive state, and when there is a mix of compatibility and contradiction between movement aims and state imperatives.

The Green State and the Green Public Sphere

Whatever the historical context, we have shown that when it comes to environmentalism a thoroughgoing ambition for comprehensive movement inclusion in the state is never desirable. In Chapter 7 we argued that an emerging connection of environmental values to both economic and legitimation imperatives could help establish a green state with a conservation imperative. There are, however, two paths to ecological modernization, likely to attract different sorts of environmental groups. Moderate mainstream groups seek the connection of environmental concerns only to the economic imperative of the state. More radical groups in the public sphere, such as the environmental justice movement in the United States, the anti-roads and anti-GMO movements in the United Kingdom, and the anti-nuclear movement in Germany raise legitimation questions. Such groups both highlight issues of environmental risk and promote the more participatory aspects of modernization.

Any development of a green state would be on a par with two prior transformations of the modern state. These earlier transformations were the alignment of the defining interest of the bourgeoisie in profit with the emerging economic growth imperative to constitute the liberal capitalist state, and the linkage of the defining interest of the working class in redistribution with an emerging legitimation imperative to constitute the welfare state. Both of these earlier transformations led to the wholesale inclusion of the relevant social movement in the state (though in the case of the working class, that assimilation was never quite complete). But the green transformation of the state would be different. We showed in Chapter 7 that both strong ecological modernization and an effective state-related politics of environmental risk require a vital green public sphere.

The environmentalist connection to the state remains insecure inasmuch as it is contingent on the presence of an active oppositional public sphere—as in Germany.[1] Ecological modernization in its weak form does not require such an oppositional sphere, as the case of Norway shows. Yet we would hesitate to describe a state pursuing weak ecological modernization as a green state. Anything stronger and more secure requires an effective and autonomous public sphere as both a memory and a presence. The United States and United Kingdom eventually saw more progress in this direction than Norway, though these two states remain behind Norway when it comes to the (weak) ecological modernization of their political economies. They also lag well behind Germany in their capacities for strong ecological modernization. The reason for this backwardness in the United States is the lack of any weak version of ecological modernization embraced by moderate groups and government that could then be extended in a stronger direction—economy and environment are still perceived to point in opposite policy directions. The reason in the United Kingdom is that the policy areas that have seen the beginnings of ecological modernization (energy and pollution control) are not the areas where radical movement activism is found.

New social movements as they flourished in the 1970s and 1980s may now be more of a memory than a presence. However, they do have successors. These include the persistent anti-nuclear movement in Germany, activist networks (such as environmental justice) both within and across countries, the unstructured radicalism of movements against roads and genetically modified organisms in the UK, the transnational anti-globalization movement, and even protest businesses such as Greenpeace.

---

[1] American and British observers might point out that this situation is not so different from a welfare state that continuously has to be fought over and for, and has been eroded when its corresponding public sphere has been depleted or co-opted. But countries such as Germany and Norway show that a welfare state can be sustained without an oppositional public sphere.

Any emphasis on the public sphere as opposed to the state does not mean that a movement is powerless. The state can be pressured from a distance even where there is little or no access; in Germany, the public policy retreat from nuclear energy and embrace of ecological modernization began while greens were still excluded. However, it remains the case that actively exclusive states cannot be shifted so easily. But whatever the character of the state, movements can affect social outcomes by changing the terms of discourse and so political culture, and contribute to the production of paragovernmental solutions to problems.

Consequences for Democracy

The public sphere constituted in part by social movements is, then, crucial to any green transformation of the state and the prospects for environmental change more generally. But it also matters enormously when it comes to democracy. Democracy and environmentalism are analytically distinct but practically reinforcing values, as we argued in Chapter 5. In assessing a country's democratization trajectory, we need to look beyond the state into civil society.

Once we look this far, we see that Norway, whose actively inclusive state is internationally admired for its democratizing qualities, has a public sphere sufficiently attenuated to create worries about the totality of Norwegian democracy. Similar problems are present but less serious in the United States, where movements often spend some time mobilizing in civil society before finding acceptance in the state, and where eventually some movements recognized and resisted the perils of ineffective inclusion. The more recent development of a green public sphere in the United Kingdom is just as significant from the point of view of democracy as the limited inclusions in the British state that began in the 1990s, though both involved escapes from active exclusion. The British state of the 1980s was not as destructive of civil society as we initially hypothesized (though were more thoroughgoing active exclusion ever achieved by any state, we might have to revise this judgement about the limited damage active exclusion can cause). Our examination of Germany shows that a state only thinly democratic in its own structure and operations can, even if by default rather than design, foster democratization in the public sphere. In the long run, this means that any accommodation between movement and state that does occur is less likely to be at substantial cost to democratic authenticity than in our other cases.

Against Naïve Anti-Statism and Naïve Statism

Within green political thinking there are two sorts of orientation to the state. The most long-lived and ubiquitous is unremittingly hostile, anticipating the demise of the state in favour of either confederations of self-sufficient communities (e.g. Bookchin, 1982) or bioregional authorities imbued with localist ecological consciousness (McGinnis, 1998) or grassroots participatory democracy. Another orientation simply takes the state for granted, and develops a list of green actions for the state to take. For example, Goodin (1992) argues that if greens can participate in governing coalitions then better environmental policy ought to follow, provided that they are armed with his green theory of value.

Both of these orientations are wrong because oversimplified. Against green enthusiasts for decentralization and grassroots democracy, we recognize that the state is likely to be a dominant political force for the foreseeable future— and that the state can sometimes be transformed in a greener direction. Against normative green statists, we recognize the major constraints that often systematically prevent states acting in accord with environmental values, irrespective of the presence of greens in government. The German Greens followed Goodin's advice and brought their green theory of value into the federal governing coalition—to modest effect, and with successes that can be explained largely in terms of the continued presence of an oppositional public sphere that has kept conservation issues on the political agenda by pressuring Green and non-Green politicians and public officials alike. Al Gore brought his green theory of value to the number two spot in the United States government, and was thoroughly frustrated by the power of the economic imperative. Naïve anti-statism and naïve statism both fail because they lack any sense of context and historical dynamics in the political economy. The same can be said for naïve democratic exhortation on behalf of a more inclusive state.

Contextualizing Analysis—Including Our Own

Analysts whose concerns are more empirical can also be tripped up as a result of inattention to the dynamics we have just outlined. For example, scholars who explain social movements in terms of political opportunity structures have an essentially static viewpoint (see Chapter 4). Even those whose analysis is more dynamic in describing the life-cycle character of movement activity interpret the cycle solely in terms of movement aging. They offer no analysis of the changing context in which movements arise, and which they can also help constitute (for example, by changing the character of the state). In contrast, our historical view can explain how different sorts of inclusion can develop and be resisted, and trace their influence on the form taken by both the state and movements.

A contextual, historical viewpoint also enables us to identify the historical specificity of our own analysis. The idea and reality of reflexive action undermines any deterministic vestiges in our account of the causal force of state structures. Subpolitics that involves the citizenry in the selection, allocation, distribution, and amelioration of environmental risks is in part a response to widespread recognition of state failure in this area. Paragovernmental action can render the state irrelevant on particular issues—though we have pointed out that the conditions for both subpolitics and paragovernmental action vary considerably depending on the context provided by state structure.

Contemporary shifts in both movement activity and political authority away from the state further complicate our account. Movements such as those concerned with genetically modified food, biopiracy, and the environmental effects of globalization and free trade bring green public spheres into the international system. The European Union plays an increasing role in the formulation of environmental policy, while the North American Free Trade Agreement and World Trade Organization have massive environmental effects. At the beginning of the modern environmental era in the 1960s such agreements and organizations were insignificant in their environmental impact. By the 1990s the EU was a major influence on national environmental legislation in the member states, which often had to respond to EU directives—though substantial cross-national differences within the EU remained. We could analyze bodies such as the EU and NAFTA in the terms we have developed. For the most part the EU is a passively exclusive polity, committed to a weak form of ecological modernization but with a widely recognized democratic deficit, which has saddled it with a legitimation problem. NAFTA, in contrast, is actively exclusive as a result of its market liberalism, and completely uninterested in ecological modernization. Both the EU and NAFTA confront transnational public spheres.

Conclusion

The ease with which the idea and actuality of the public sphere can be applied to the transnational level contrasts with the difficulty entailed in creating institutional analogues to the state in the international system, the EU experience notwithstanding. This contrast underscores our emphasis on the public sphere—not as an alternative to the state, but as a partner and opponent in historical interaction. The latest phases of that interaction point to forms of politics in which the state's role is less dominant than before. But this development does not gainsay the continuing importance of the state in providing (sometimes inadvertently) a large part of the structural context for this interaction, and the important possibility of transforming the state itself in a greener direction. Yet whether we care about the substantive ends sought by social movements, the transformation of the state, or the continued democratic well-being of society, or all three, we conclude that civil society is not just a resting place for social movements on their way to the state. It is meaningful and sometimes crucial as a site of political action in its own right.

REFERENCES

Aardal, Bernt. 1990. 'Green Politics: A Norwegian Experience.' *Scandinavian Political Studies*, 13: 147–64.

Adler, Allan R. (ed.). 1997. *Litigation Under the Federal Open Government Laws*, 20th edn. Washington, DC: American Civil Liberties Union.

Ahrens, Ralf, and Detlef Stoller. 1995. 'Geheimniskrämer in Amtsstuben.' *Tageszeitung*, 28 July, p. 7.

Almond, Gabriel A. 1988. 'The Return to the State.' *American Political Science Review*, 82: 850–74.

Ambjørnse, Ingvar. 1988. *Bellona: Gudinnen som ble vaktbikkje*. Oslo: J. W. Cappelens Forlag AS.

Andersen, Mikael Skou, and Duncan Liefferink (eds.). 1997. *European Environmental Policy: The Pioneers*. Manchester: Manchester University Press.

Andersen, Svein S., and Atle Midttun. 1994. 'Environmental Opposition in Norwegian Energy Policy: Structural Determinants and Strategic Mobilisation.' 232–63 in Helena Flam (ed.), *States and Anti-Nuclear Movements*. Edinburgh: Edinburgh University Press.

Anderson, Terry L., and Donald R. Leal. 2001. *Free Market Environmentalism*. New York: Palgrave.

Andrews, Richard N. L. 1997. 'United States.' 25–44 in Martin Jänicke and Helmut Weidner (eds.), *National Environmental Policies: A Comparative Study of Capacity-Building*. Berlin: Springer.

——1999. *Managing the Environment, Managing Ourselves: A History of American Environmental Policy*. New Haven: Yale.

Arato, Andrew. 1993. 'Interpreting 1989.' *Social Research*, 60: 609–46.

Arendt, Hannah. 1958. *The Human Condition*. Chicago: University of Chicago Press.

Balistier, Thomas. 1996. *Straßenprotest. Formen oppositioneller Politik in der Bundesrepublik Deutschland*. Münster: Westfälisches Dampfboot.

Barry, John. 1999. *Rethinking Green Politics: Nature, Virtue, and Progress*. London: Sage.

Beck, Hanno, Brian Dunkel, and Gawain Kripke. 1998. *Citizens' Guide to Environmental Tax Shifting*. Washington, DC: Friends of the Earth.

Beck, Ulrich. 1992. *Risk Society: Towards a New Modernity*. London: Sage.

——1994. 'The Reinvention of Politics: Towards a Theory of Reflexive Modernization.' 1–55 in Ulrich Beck, Anthony Giddens, and Scott Lash (eds.), *Reflexive Modernization: Politics, Tradition and Aesthetics in the Modern Social Order*. Cambridge: Polity.

——1999. *World Risk Society*. Cambridge: Polity.

Bennet, Colin. 1992. *Regulating Privacy: Data Protection in Europe and the United States*. Ithaca, NY: Cornell University Press.

Berger, Thomas R. 1985. *Village Journey: The Report of the Alaska Native Review Commission.* New York: Hill and Wang.

Berntsen, Bredo. 1994. *Grønne linjer. Natur og miljøvernets historie i Norge.* Oslo: Grøndahl Dreyer.

Berry, Jeffrey M. 1977. *Lobbying for the People: The Political Behavior of Public Interest Groups.* Princeton: Princeton University Press.

Blowers, Andrew. 1987. 'Transition of Transformation? Environmental Policy Under Thatcher.' *Public Administration,* 65: 277–94.

Bluhdorn, Ingolfur. 1995. 'Campaigning for Nature: Environmental Pressure Groups in Germany and Generational Change in the Ecology Movement.' 167–220 in Ingolfur Bluhdorn, Frank Krause, and Thomas Scharf (eds.), *The Green Agenda.* Keele: Keele University Press.

Boanes-Dewas, Katie. 1993. 'Participatory Democracy in Peace and Security Decision Making: The Aotearoa/New Zealand Experience.' *Interdisciplinary Peace Research,* 5 (2): 80–108.

Bookchin, Murray. 1982. *The Ecology of Freedom.* Palo Alto, Calif.: Cheshire

Brand, Karl-Werner. 1999. 'Dialectics of Institutionalisation: The Transformation of the Environmental Movement in Germany.' *Environmental Politics,* 8: 35–58.

Brick, Philip, Donald Snow, and Sarah Van De Wetering (eds.). 2000. *Across the Great Divide: Explorations in Collaborative Conservation and the American West.* Washington, DC: Island Press.

Brown, Phil, and Edwin J. Mikkelsen. 1990. *No Safe Place: Toxic Waste, Leukemia, and Community Action.* Berkeley: University of California Press.

Brulle, Robert. 2000. *Agency, Democracy, and Nature: The U.S. Environmental Movement from a Critical Theory Perspective.* Cambridge, MA: MIT Press.

Bryner, Gary C. 2000. 'The United States: "Sorry-Not Our Problem".' 273–302 in William M. Lafferty and James Meadowcroft (eds.), *Implementing Sustainable Development: Strategies and Initiatives in High Consumption Societies.* Oxford: Oxford University Press.

Buhrs, Ton, and Robert V. Bartlett. 1993. *Environmental Policy in New Zealand: The Politics of Clean and Green.* Auckland: Oxford University Press.

Bullard, Robert D. 1993. *Confronting Environmental Racism: Voices from the Grassroots.* Boston: South End Press.

Bunce, Valerie. 1992. 'Two-Tiered Stalinism: A Case of Self-Destruction.' 25–46 in K. Z. Poznanski (ed.), *Constructing Capitalism: The Re-Emergence of Civil Society and Liberal Economy in the Post-Communist World.* Boulder, Colo.: Westview.

Byrne, Paul. 1997. *Social Movements in Britain.* London: Routledge.

Carter, Jimmy. 1982. *Keeping the Faith: Memoirs of a President.* New York: Bantam.

Center for Responsive Politics. 2000. *Influence Inc.* Washington, DC: Center for Responsive Politics. Online at http://www.opensecrets.org/pubs/lobby00/index.asp.

Christiansen, Peter Munk, and Hilmar Rommetvedt. 1999. 'From Corporatism to Lobbyism? Parliaments, Executives, and Organized Interests in Denmark and Norway.' *Scandinavian Political Studies,* 22: 195–220.

Christoff, Peter. 1996. 'Ecological Modernisation, Ecological Modernities.' *Environmental Politics,* 5: 476–500.

Cohen, Jean. 1985. 'Strategy or Identity? New Theoretical Paradigms and Contemporary Social Movements.' *Social Research,* 52: 663–716.

——and Andrew Arato. 1992. *Civil Society and Political Theory.* Cambridge, Mass.: MIT Press.

Cohen, Joshua, and Joel Rogers. 1992. 'Secondary Associations and Democratic Governance.' *Politics and Society,* 20: 393–472.

Cole, Luke, and Sheila Foster. 2001. *From the Ground Up: Environmental Racism and the Rise of the Environmental Justice Movement.* New York: New York University Press.

Commoner, Barry. 1972. *The Closing Circle.* New York: Bantam.

Connelly, James, and Graham Smith. 1999. *Politics and the Environment: From Theory to Practice.* London: Routledge.

Connolly, William (ed.). 1969. *The Bias of Pluralism.* New York: Atherton.

Cornelsen, Dirk. 1991. *Anwälte der Natur: Umweltschutzverbände in Deutschland.* Munich: Beck.

Crozier, Michel, Samuel P. Huntington, and Joji Watanuki. 1975. *The Crisis of Democracy: Report on the Governability of Democracies to the Trilateral Commission.* New York: New York University Press.

Cunningham, Frank. 1987. *Democratic Theory and Socialism.* Cambridge: Cambridge University Press.

Dalton, Russell. 1994. *The Green Rainbow: Environmental Groups in Western Europe.* New Haven: Yale University Press.

——1996. Citizen Politics: Public Opinion and Political Parties in Advanced Industrial Democracies. 2nd edn. Chatham, NJ: Chatham House.

——and Manfred Kuechler (eds.). 1990. *Challenging the Political Order: New Social Movements in Western Democracies.* Cambridge: Polity.

Daly, Herman E. 1996. *Beyond Growth: The Economics of Sustainable Development.* Boston: Beacon.

Davis, S. H. 1996. *Public Involvement in Environmental Decision-Making: Some Reflections on the Western European Experience.* Washington, DC: World Bank.

Department of the Environment, United Kingdom, 1988. *Our Common Future: A Perspective by the United Kingdom on the Report of the World Commission on Environment and Development.* London: HMSO.

Diani, Mario. 1992. The Concept of Social Movement. *Sociological Review,* 40:. 1–25.

——1995. *Green Networks: a Structural Analysis of the Italian Environmental Movement.* Edinburgh: Edinburgh University Press.

Dobson, Andrew. 1990. *Green Political Thought.* London: Unwin Hyman.

Doherty, Brian. 1999. 'Paving the Way: The Rise of Direct Action Against Road-Building and the Changing Character of British Environmentalism.' *Political Studies,* 47: 275–91.

——and Marius de Geus. 1996. *Democracy and Green Political Thought.* London: Routledge.

——and Peter Rawcliffe. 1995. British Exceptionalism? Comparing the Environmental Movement in Britain and Germany. 131–42 in Ingolfur Bluhdorn, Frank Krause, and Thomas Scharf (eds.), *The Green Agenda.* Keele: Keele University Press.

Domhoff, G. William. 1967. *Who Rules America?* Englewood Cliffs, NJ: Prentice-Hall.

Dowie, Mark. 1995. *Losing Ground: American Environmentalism at the Close of the Twentieth Century.* Cambridge, Mass.: MIT Press.

Downes, David. 1998. 'To Dance with Wolves? Environmental Organisation Involvement in the Ecologically Sustainable Development Process.' Ph.D. Thesis, Department of Politics, Monash University, Melbourne.

——2000. 'The New Zealand Environmental Movement and the Politics of Inclusion.' *Australian Journal of Political Science*, 35: 471–91.

Dryzek, John S. 1990. 'Designs for Environmental Discourse: The Greening of the Administrative State?' 97–111 in Robert Paehlke and Douglas Torgerson (eds.), *Managing Leviathan: Environmental Politics and the Administrative State.* Peterborough, Ont.: Broadview.

——1996a. *Democracy in Capitalist Times: Ideals, Limits, and Struggles.* Oxford: Oxford University Press.

——1996b. 'Political Inclusion and the Dynamics of Democratization.' *American Political Science Review*, 90: 475–87.

——1997. *The Politics of the Earth: Environmental Discourses.* Oxford: Oxford University Press.

——and David Schlosberg (eds.). 1998. *Debating the Earth: The Environmental Politics Reader.* Oxford: Oxford University Press.

Dunlap, Riley. 1989. 'Public Opinion and Environmental Policy.' 87–134 in James P. Lester (ed.), *Environmental Politics and Policy: Theories and Evidence.* Durham, NC: Duke University Press.

Dyson, Kenneth H. F. 1980. *The State Tradition in Western Europe: A Study of an Idea and Institution.* Oxford: Oxford University Press.

——1982. 'West Germany: The Search for a Rationalist Consensus.' 17–46 in Jeremy Richardson (ed.), *Policy Styles in Western Europe.* London: Allen and Unwin.

Easton, David. 1953. *The Political System.* New York: Knopf.

Eckersley, Robyn. 1996. 'Environmental Security Dilemmas.' *Environmental Politics,* 5: 140–6.

Egeberg, Morten, Johan P. Olsen, and Harald Sætren. 1978. 'Organisasjonssamfunnet og den segmenterte stat.' 115–42 in Johan P. Olsen (ed.), *Politisk Organisering: Organisasjonsteoretiske synspunkt på folkestyre og politisk ulikhet.* Bergen: Universitetsforlaget.

European Environment Agency. 2000a. *Environment in the European Union at the Turn of the Century.* Copenhagen: European Environment Agency.

——2000b. *Environmental Taxes: Recent Developments in Tools for Integration.* Copenhagen: European Environment Agency.

Evans, Peter B., Dietrich Rueschemeyer, and Theda Skocpol (eds.). 1985. *Bringing the State Back In.* Cambridge: Cambridge University Press.

Evans, Sarah M., and Harry C. Boyte. 1986. *Free Spaces: The Sources of Democratic Change in America.* New York: Harper and Row.

Fischer, Frank. 1993. 'Citizen Participation and the Democratization of Policy Experise: From Theoretical Inquiry to Practical Cases.' *Policy Sciences*, 26: 165–87.

——1995. 'Hazardous Waste Policy, Community Movements and the Politics of Nimby: Participatory Risk Assessment in the USA and Canada.' 165–82 in Frank Fischer and Michael Black (eds.), *Greening Environmental Policy: The Politics of a Sustainable Future*. London: Paul Chapman.

——2000. *Citizens, Experts, and the Environment: The Politics of Local Knowledge*. Durham, NC: Duke University Press.

——and Maarten A. Hajer (eds.). 1999. *Living with Nature: Environmental Politics as Cultural Discourse*. Oxford: Oxford University Press.

Fisk, Milton. 1989. *The State and Justice: An Essay in Political Theory*. Cambridge: Cambridge University Press.

Flam, Helena. 1994*a*. 'Political Responses to the Anti-Nuclear Challenge: (1) Standard Deliberative and Decision-making Settings.' 299–328 in Helena Flam (ed.), *States and Anti-Nuclear Movements*. Edinburgh: Edinburgh University Press.

——1994*b*. 'Political Responses to the Anti-Nuclear Challenge: (2) Democratic Experiments and the Use of Force.' 329–54 in Helena Flam, ed., *States and Anti-Nuclear Movements*. Edinburgh: Edinburgh University Press.

Flynn, Andrew, and Philip Lowe. 1992. 'The Greening of the Tories: the Conservative Party and the Environment.' 9–36 in Wolfgang Rüdig (ed.), *Green Politics Two*. Edinburgh: Edinburgh University Press.

Foreman, Dave. 1998. 'Putting the Earth First.' 358–64 in John S. Dryzek and David Schlosberg (eds.), *Debating the Earth: The Environmental Politics Reader*. Oxford: Oxford University Press.

Freedom House. 2000. *Democracy's Century: A Survey of Global Political Change in the 20th Century*. New York: Freedom House.

Freeman, Jo. 1975. *The Politics of Women's Liberation*. New York: McKay.

Fyfe, Nicholas R. 1995. 'Law and Order Policy and the Spaces of Citizenship in Contemporary Britain.' *Political Geography*, 14: 177–89.

Gallie, W. B. 1968. *Philosophy and the Historical Understanding*. Rev. edn. New York: Shocken.

Gallup. 2000. 'Poll Topics and Trends: Environment.' http://www.gallup.com/poll/topics/environment.asp.

Gamble, Andrew. 1988. *The Free Economy and the Strong State*. Basingstoke: Macmillan.

Gamson, Josh. 1989. 'Silence, Death, and the Invisible Enemy: AIDS Activism and Social Movement Newness.' *Social Problems*, 36: 351–67.

Gebers, Betty. 1996. 'Germany.' 95–110 in Ralph E. Hallo (ed.), *Access to Environmental Information in Europe*. Dordrecht: Kluwer.

Goodin, Robert E. 1992. *Green Political Theory*. Cambridge: Polity Press.

——1996. 'Enfranchising the Earth, and its Alternatives.' *Political Studies*, 44: 835–49.

Gonzalez, George A. 2001. 'Democratic Ethics and Ecological Modernization: The Formulation of California's Automobile Emission Standards.' *Public Integrity*, 3: 325–44.

Gore, Albert. 1992. *Earth in the Balance*. Boston: Houghton Mifflin.

Gottlieb, Robert. 1993. *Forcing the Spring: The Transformation of the American Environmental Movement*. Washington, DC: Island Press.

Gould, Kenneth, Allan Schnaiberg, and Adam Weinberg. 1996. *Local Environmental Struggles: Citizen Activism in the Treadmill of Production.* Cambridge: Cambridge University Press.

Grant, Wyn. 1995. *Pressure Groups, Politics and Democracy in Britain.* Hemel Hempstead: Harvester Wheatsheaf.

Greider, William. 1992. *Who Will Tell the People? The Betrayal of American Democracy.* New York: Simon and Schuster.

Grove-White, Robin. 1991. 'The UK's Environmental Movement and UK Political Culture.' Lancaster: Centre for the Study of Environmental Change, University of Lancaster.

——1997. 'Brent Spar Rewrote the Rules.' *New Statesman,* 20 June: 17–19.

Guggenberger, Bernd. 1980. *Bürgerinitiativen in der Parteiendemokratie.* Stuttgart: Kohlhammer.

Gundersen, Frode. 1996. 'Framveksten av den Norske Miljøebevegelsen.' 37–81 in Kristin Strømsnes and Per Selle (eds.), *Miljøvernpolitikk og Miljøvernorganisering mot år 2000.* Oslo: Tano Aschehoug.

Habermas, Jürgen. 1989. *Structural Transformation of the Public Sphere: An Inquiry into a Category of Bourgeois Society.* Cambridge, Mass.: MIT Press.

——1996a. *Between Facts and Norms: Contributions to a Discourse Theory of Law and Democracy.* Cambridge, Mass.: MIT Press.

——1996b. 'Three Normative Models of Democracy.' 22–30 in Seyla Benhabib, (ed.), *Democracy and Difference: Contesting the Boundaries of the Political.* Princeton: Princeton University Press.

Hager, Carol. 1995. *Technological Democracy: Citizenry and Bureaucracy in the German Energy Debate.* Ann Arbor: Michigan University Press.

Hajer, Maarten A. 1995. *The Politics of Environmental Discourse: Ecological Modernization and the Policy Process.* Oxford: Oxford University Press.

——1996. 'Ecological Modernisation as Cultural Politics.' 246–68 in Scott Lash, Bron Szerszynski, and Brian Wynne (eds.), *Risk, Environment, and Modernity: Towards a New Ecology.* London: Sage.

——and Frank Fischer. 1999. 'Beyond Global Discourse: The Rediscovery of Culture in Environmental Politics.' 1–20 in Frank Fischer and Maarten A. Hajer (eds.), *Living with Nature: Environmental Politics as Cultural Discourse.* Oxford: Oxford University Press.

Hall, Stuart, and Martin Jacques. 1983. *The Politics of Thatcherism.* London: Lawrence and Wishart.

Hallo, Ralph E. (ed.). 1996. *Access to Environmental Information in Europe: The Implementation and Implications of Directive 90/313/EEC.* London: Kluwer Law International.

Hannigan, J. A. 1985. 'Alain Touraine, Manuel Castells and Social Movement Theory: A Critical Appraisal.' *Sociological Quarterly,* 26: 435–54.

Heilbroner, Robert. 1974. *An Inquiry Into the Human Prospect.* New York: W. W. Norton.

Hengsbach, Friedhelm, Ralf Bammerlin, Christoph Diringer, Bernhard Emunds, and Matthias Möhring-Hesse. 1996. *Die Rolle der Umweltverbände in den demokratischen Lernprozessen der Gesellschaft.* Stuttgart: Metzler-Poeschel.

Hernes, Hans-Kristian, and Knut H. Mikalsen. 1999. 'From Protest to Participation? Environmental Groups and the Management of Marine Fisheries.' Paper presented at the Joint Sessions of the European Consortium for Political Research, Mannheim, April.

Hey, Christian, and Uwe Brendle. 1994. *Umweltverbände und EG. Strategien, politische Kulturen und Organisationsformen*. Opladen: Westdeutscher Verlag.

Hillyard, Paddy, and Janie Percy-Smith. 1988. *The Coercive State*. London: Fontana.

Holliday, Ian. 1993. 'Organised Interests After Thatcher.' 307–19 in Patrick Dunleavy, Andrew Gamble, Ian Holliday, and Gillian Peele (eds.), *Developments in British Politics 4*. Basingstoke: Macmillan.

Hulsberg, Werner. 1988. *The German Greens*. Translated by Gus Fagan. London: Verso.

Hulse, Carl. 1999. 'Group Puts Disaster Data on Internet.' *New York Times*, 12 Sept., section 1, p. 32.

Hunold, Christian. 2001. 'Corporatism, Pluralism, and Democracy: Toward a Deliberative Theory of Bureaucratic Accountability.' *Governance* 14: 151–68.

——2002. 'Environmentalists, Nuclear Waste, and the Politics of Passive Exclusion in Germany.' *German Politics and Society* 19: 44–64.

Hutcheson, Ron. 2001. 'Bush Stands Firm on Missile Defense.' *Philadelphia Inquirer*, 20 July.

Hyland, James L. 1995. *Democratic Theory: The Philosophical Foundations*. Manchester: Manchester University Press.

Inglehart, Ronald. 1990. *Culture Shift in Advanced Industrial Societies*. Princeton: Princeton University Press.

Inkeles, Alex (ed.). 1991. *On Measuring Democracy: Its Consequences and Concomitants*. New Brunswick, NJ: Transaction.

Isaac, Jeffrey C. 1993. 'Civil Society and the Spirit of Revolt.' *Dissent*, 40: 356–61.

Jacobs, Michael. 1997. 'Introduction: The New Politics of the Environment.' 1–17 in Michael Jacobs (ed.), *Greening the Millennium? The New Politics of the Environment*. Oxford: Blackwell.

Jahn, Detlef. 1998. 'Environmental Performance and Policy Regimes: Explaining Variations in 18 OECD Countries.' *Policy Sciences*, 31: 107–31.

Jänicke, Martin. 1996a. 'Democracy as a Condition for Environmental Policy Success: The Importance of Non-Institutional Factors.' 71–85 in William M. Lafferty and James Meadowcroft (eds.), *Democracy and the Environment: Problems and Prospects*. Cheltenham: Edward Elgar.

——1996b. 'Jenseits des additiven Ansatzes.' *Politische Ökologie*, 14 (May/June): 39–41.

——1997. 'The Political System's Capacity for Environmental Policy.' 1–14 in Martin Jänicke and Helmut Weidner (eds.), *National Environmental Policies: A Comparative Study of Capacity-Building*. Berlin: Springer.

——2000. *Ecological Modernization: Innovation and Diffusion of Policy and Technology*. Berlin: Forschungsstelle für Umweltpolitik.

——and Helmut Weidner (eds.). 1997a. *National Environmental Policies: A Comparative Study of Capacity-Building*. Berlin: Springer.

Jänicke, Martin and Helmut Weidner. 1997*b*. 'Germany.' 133–55 in Martin Jänicke and Helmut Weidner (eds.), *National Environmental Policies: A Comparative Study of Capacity-Building*. Berlin: Springer.

Jansen, Alf-Inge, and Per Kristen Mydske. 1998. 'Norway: Balancing Environmental Quality and Interest in Oil.' 181–207 in Kenneth Hanf and Alf-Inge Jansen (eds.), *Governance and Environment in Western Europe: Politics, Policy and Administration*. London: Longman.

——and Oddgeir Osland. 1996. 'Norway.' 179–256 in Peter Munk Christiansen (ed.), *Governing the Environment: Politics, Policy and Organization in the Nordic Countries*. Copenhagen: Nordic Council of Ministers.

Jessop, Bob, Kevin Bonnett, Simon Bromley, and Tom Ling. 1988. *Thatcherism*. Oxford: Polity Press.

Joppke, Christian. 1993. *Mobilizing Against Nuclear Energy: A Comparison of Germany and the United States*. Berkeley: University of California Press.

——and Andy Markovits. 1994. 'Green Politics in the New Germany: The Future of an Anti-Party.' *Dissent* (Spring): 235–40.

Jordan, A. G. and J. J. Richardson. 1987. *Government and Pressure Groups in Britain*. Oxford: Clarendon Press.

Jordan, Grant, and William A. Maloney. 1997. *The Protest Business: Mobilizing Campaign Groups*. Manchester: Manchester University Press.

Kaase, Max. 1984. 'The Challenge of the "Participatory Revolution" in Pluralist Democracies.' *International Political Science Review*, 5: 299–318.

Kasa, Sjur. 2000. 'Policy Networks as a Barrier to Green Tax Reform: The Case of CO2-Taxes in Norway.' *Environmental Politics*, 9 (4): 104–22.

Katzenstein, Peter J. 1987. *Policy and Politics in West Germany: The Growth of a Semisovereign State*. Philadelphia: Temple University Press.

Kelly, Petra. 1984. *Fighting for Hope*. Translated by Marianne Howarth. Boston: South End Press.

——1990. *Mit dem Herzen denken. Texte für eine glaubwürdige Politik*. Munich: Beck.

Kemp, René. 1997. *Environmental Policy and Technical Change: A Comparison of the Technological Impact of Policy Instruments*. Cheltenham: Edward Elgar.

Kerwin, Cornelius M. 1999. *Rulemaking: How Government Agencies Write Law and Make Policy*, 2nd edn. Washington, DC: CQ Press.

Killingland, Tore. 1996. 'Norway.' 309–16 in Ralph E. Hallo (ed.), *Access to Environmental Information in Europe*. Dordrecht: Kluwer.

King, Gary, Robert O. Keohane, and Sidney Verba. 1994. *Designing Social Inquiry: Scientific Inference in Qualitative Research*. Princeton: Princeton University Press.

Kitschelt, Herbert P. 1986. 'Political Opportunity Structures and Political Protest: Anti-Nuclear Movements in Four Democracies.' *British Journal of Political Science*, 16: 57–85.

——1988. 'Left-Libertarian Parties: Explaining Innovation in Competitive Party Systems.' *World Politics*, 40: 194–234.

——1989. *Logics of Party Formation: The Structure and Strategy of Belgian and West German Ecology Parties*. Ithaca, NY: Cornell University Press.

Klausen, Jan Erling, and Staale Opedal. 1998. 'The "Ifs" and "Hows" of Participation: NGOs and Sectoral Environmental Politics in Norway.' In Marco Joas and Ann-Sofie Hermanson (eds.), *The Nordic Environments: Comparing Political, Administrative and Policy Aspects.* Finland: Aabo University.

——and Hilmar Rommetvedt. 1994. *Miljøpolitikk: Organisasjonene, Stortinget og forvaltningen.* Oslo: Tano Aschehoug.

Klein, Ansgar. 1996. 'Die Legitimität von Greenpeace und die Risiken symbolischer Politik: Konturen und Probleme einer medialen Stellvertreterpolitik im Bewegungssektor.' *Forschungsjournal Neue Soziale Bewegungen*, 8: 11–14.

Kolb, Felix. 1997. 'Der Castor-Konflikt: Das Comback der Anti-AKW-Bewegung.' *Forschungsjournal Neue Soziale Bewegungen*, 10 (3): 16–29.

Kraak, Michael, and Heinrich Pehle. 2001. 'The Europeanisation of Environmental Policy: The German Perspective.' Paper prepared for *The Europeanisation of Environmental Policy Workshop*, Cambridge, 29 June–1 July.

Kriesi, Hanspeter. 1995. 'The Political Opportunity Structure of New Social Movements: Its Impact on their Mobilization.' 167–98 in J. Craig Jenkins and Bert Klandemans (eds.), *The Politics of Social Protest: Comparative Perspectives on States and Social Movements.* Minneapolis: University of Minnesota Press.

——1996. 'New Social Movements in a Political Context.' 152–84 in Doug McAdam, John D. McCarthy, and Mayer N. Zald (eds.), *Comparative Perspectives on Social Movements.* Cambridge: Cambridge University Press.

——Ruud Koopmans, Jan Willem Duyvendek, and Marco G. Giugni. 1992. 'New Social Movements and Political Opportunities in Western Europe.' *European Journal of Political Research*, 22: 219–44.

——Ruud Koopmans, Jan Willem Duyvendek, and Marco G. Giugni. 1995. *New Social Movements in Western Europe: A Comparative Analysis.* Minneapolis: University of Minnesota Press.

Kuckartz, Udo. 1998. *Umweltbewußtsein und Umweltverhalten.* Berlin: Springer-Verlag.

——2000. *Umweltbewusstsein 2000 in Deutschland: Ergebnisse einer repräsentativen Bevölkerungsumfrage.* Online at http://staff-www.uni-marburg.de/~kuckartz/

Kuechler, Manfred, and Russell J. Dalton. 1990. 'New Social Movements and the Political Order: Inducing Change for Long-Term Stability.' 277–300 in Russell J. Dalton and Manfred Kuechler (eds.), *Challenging the Political Order: New Social Movements in Western Democracies.* Cambridge: Polity.

Lafferty, William M., and James Meadowcroft (eds.). 1996. *Democracy and the Environment: Problems and Prospects.* Cheltenham: Edward Elgar.

—— ——2000. 'Patterns of Governmental Engagement.' 337–421 in William M. Lafferty and James Meadowcroft (eds.), *Implementing Sustainable Development.* Oxford: Oxford University Press.

Lahusen, Christian. 1996. *The Rhetoric of Moral Protest: Public Campaigns, Celebrity Endorsement and Political Motivation.* Berlin: Walter de Gruyter.

Lamb, Robert. 1996. *Promising the Earth.* London: Routledge.

Langguth, Gerald. 1986. *The Green Factor in German Politics.* Translated by Richard Straus. Boulder, Colo.: Westview.

Langhelle, Oluf. 2000. 'Norway: Reluctantly Carrying the Torch.' 174–208 in William M. Lafferty and James Meadowcroft (eds.), *Implementing Sustainable Development: Strategies and Initiatives in High Consumption Societies*. Oxford: Oxford University Press.

Lavelle, Marianne. 1991. 'Talking about Air.' *National Law Journal*, 10 June: 30.

Lehmann, Jürgen. 1999. *Befunde empirischer Forschung zu Umweltbildung und Umweltbewußtsein*. Opladen: Leske and Budrich.

Lehmbruch, Gerhard. 1984. 'Concertation and the Structure of Corporatist Networks.' 60–80 in John H. Goldthorpe (ed.), *Order and Conflict in Contemporary Capitalism*. Oxford: Clarendon Press.

——and Philippe Schmittter (eds.). 1982. *Patterns of Corporatist Policy-Making*. London: Sage.

Lijphart, Arend. 1977. *Democracy in Plural Societies: A Comparative Exploration*. New Haven: Yale University Press.

Lindblom, Charles E. 1977. *Politics and Markets: The World's Political-Economic Systems*. New York: Basic Books.

——1982. 'The Market as Prison.' *Journal of Politics*, 44: 324–36.

Lippman, Walter. 1922. *Public Opinion*. New York: Harcourt Brace.

Long, Tony. 1998. 'The Environment Lobby.' 105–18 in Philip Lowe and Stephen Ward (eds.), *British Environmental Policy and Europe*. London: Routledge.

Loughlin, John, and B. Guy Peters. 1994. 'If Administrative Reform Is the Answer, What Are the Questions?' Unpublished manuscript.

Lovei, Magda, and Charles Weiss, Jr. 1998. *Environmental Management and Institutions in OECD Countries: Lessons from Experience*. Washington, DC: World Bank.

Lovins, Amory B., and L. Hunter Lovins. 1999. *Natural Capitalism: Creating the Next Industrial Revolution*. Boston: Little, Brown.

Lowe, Philip, and Andrew Flynn. 1989. 'Environmental Politics and Policy in the 1980s.' 255–79 in John Mohan (ed.), *The Political Geography of Contemporary Britain*. Basingstoke: Macmillan.

——and Jane Goyder. 1983. *Environmental Groups in Politics*. London: George Allen and Unwin.

——and Stephen Ward. 1998. 'Domestic Winners and Losers.' 87–104 in Philip Lowe and Stephen Ward (eds.), *British Environmental Policy and Europe*. London: Routledge.

Luke, Timothy. 1999. 'Eco-managerialism: Environmental Studies as Power/Knowledge Formation.' 103–20 in Frank Fischer and Maarten A. Hajer (eds.), *Living with Nature: Environmental Politics as Cultural Discourse*. Oxford: Oxford University Press.

McCarthy, John D., and Mayer N. Zald. 1977. 'Resource Mobilization and Social Movements: A Partial Theory.' *American Journal of Sociology*, 82: 1212–39.

——1987. *Social Movements in an Organizational Society*. New Brunswick, NJ: Transaction.

McCormick, John. 1991. *British Politics and the Environment*. London: Earthscan.

——1993. 'Environmental Politics.' 267–83 in Patrick Dunleavy, Andrew Gamble, Ian Holliday, and Gillian Peele (eds.), *Developments in British Politics 4*. Basingstoke: Macmillan.

McGinnis, Michael Vincent. (ed.), 1998. *Bioregionalism*. New York: Routledge.

Mansbridge, Jane. 1992. 'A Deliberative Theory of Interest Representation.' 32–57 in Mark P. Petracca (ed.), *The Politics of Interests: Interest Groups Transformed*. Boulder, Colo.: Westview.

——1994. 'What is the Feminist Movement?' 27–34 in Myra Marx Ferree and Patricia Yancey Martin (eds.), *Feminist Organization: Harvest of the New Women's Movement*. Philadelphia: Temple University Press.

Mathews, Freya (ed.). 1996. *Ecology and Democracy*. London: Frank Cass.

Mayer, Margit and John Ely (eds.). 1998. *The German Greens: Paradox Between Party and Movement*. Philadelphia: Temple University Press.

Meadows, Donella H., Dennis L. Meadows, Jørgen Randers, and William H. Behrens III. 1972. *The Limits to Growth*. New York: Universe Books.

Melucci, Alberto. 1985. 'The Symbolic Challenge of Contemporary Movements.' *Social Research*, 52: 789–816.

——1989. *Nomads of the Present: Social Movements and Individual Needs in Contemporary Society*. Philadelphia: Temple University Press.

Mendelsohn, Harold A., and Irving Crespi. 1970. *Polls, Television and the New Politics*. Scranton, Pa.: Chandler.

Midttun, Atle. 1988. 'The Negotiated Political Economy of a Heavy Industrial Sector: The Norwegian Hydropower Complex in the 1970s and 1980s.' *Scandinavian Political Studies*, 11 (2): 115–43.

——and Svein Kamfjord. 1999. 'Energy and Environmental Governance under Ecological Modernization: A Comparative Analysis of Nordic Countries.' *Public Administration*, 77: 873–95.

Miljøverndepartementet. 1999–2000. *St. prp. Nr. 1*. Oslo. (Norway Ministry of the Environment annual budget proposal).

Mol, Arthur P. J. 1996. 'Ecological Modernisation and Institutional Reflexivity: Environmental Reform in the Late Modern Age.' *Environmental Politics*, 5: 302–23.

——and Gert Spaarargen. 2000. 'Ecological Modernisation Theory in Debate: A Review.' *Environmental Politics*, 9: 17–49.

Myers, Norman. 1993. *Ultimate Security: The Environmental Basis of Political Stability*. New York: Norton.

Nilsen, Knut-Erik.1996. Miljøstiftelsen Bellona. Døgnflua som overlevde. 185–98 in Kristin Strømsnes and Per Selle (eds.), *Miljøvernpolitikk og miljøvernorganisering mot år 2000*. Oslo: Tano-Ascheoug.

Nollert, Michael. 1995. 'Neocorporatism and Political Protest in the Western Democracies: A Cross-National Analysis.' 138–64 in J. Craig Jenkins and Bert Klandemans (eds.), *The Politics of Social Protest: Comparative Perspectives on States and Social Movements*. Minneapolis: University of Minnesota Press.

Nordby, Trond. 1994. *Korporatisme på norsk 1920–1990*. Oslo: Universitetsforlaget.

——1996. 'Hvem Styrer Hvem? Statlige Utvalg som Maktorganer.' *Nytt Norsk Tidsskrift*, 13: 281–94.

Norton, Bryan G. 1991. *Toward Unity Among Environmentalists*. Oxford: Oxford University Press.

Norwegian Ministry of the Environment. 1988–9. *Miljø og utvikling: Norges oppføl-ging av Verdenskommisjonenes rapport.* Oslo: Miljøverndepartementet.

NOU. 1996. *1996: 9 Grønne skatter—en Politikk for Bedre Miljø og høy Sysselsetting.* Oslo: Statens Forvaltningstjeneste. (Official Committee Recommendation.)

O'Brien, Mary. 2001. *Making Better Environmental Decisions.* Cambridge, Mass.: MIT Press.

OECD. 1979. *Technology on Trial.* Paris: OECD.

——1999. *Economic Instruments for Pollution Control and Natural Resources Management in OECD Countries: A Survey.* Paris: OECD.

Offe, Claus. 1981. 'The Attribution of Public Status to Interest Groups: Observations on the West German Case.' 123–58 in Suzanne Berger (ed.), *Organizing Interests in Western Europe.* Cambridge, Mass.: MIT Press.

——1984. *Contradictions of the Welfare State.* Cambridge, Mass.: MIT Press.

——1985. 'New Social Movements: Challenging the Boundaries of Institutional Politics.' *Social Research*, 52: 817–68.

——1990. 'Reflections on the Institutional Self-Transformation of Movement Politics: A Tentative Stage Model.' 232–50 in Russell J. Dalton and Manfred Kuechler (eds.), *Challenging the Political Order: New Social Movements in Western Democracies.* Cambridge: Polity.

——1998. 'From Youth to Maturity: The Challenge of Party Politics.' 165–79 in Margit Mayer and John Ely (eds.), *The German Greens: Paradox Between Party and Movement.* Philadelphia: Temple University Press.

O'Neill, Michael. 1997. *Green Parties and Political Change in Contemporary Europe: New Politics, Old Predicaments.* Brookfield, Vt.: Ashgate.

O'Riordan, Timothy. 1985. 'Culture and the Environment in Britain.' *Environmental Management*, 9 (2): 113–20.

——Ray Kemp, and Michael Purdue. 1988. *Sizewell B.* Basingstoke: Macmillan.

Paehlke, Robert. 1988. 'Democracy, Bureaucracy, and Environmentalism.' *Environmental Ethics*, 10: 291–308.

Pakulski, Jan, and Stephen Crook 1998. 'Ebbing the Green Tide? Environmentalism, Public Opinion and the Media in Australia.' Hobart: School of Sociology and Social Work, University of Tasmania.

Papadakis, Elim. 1984. *The Green Movement in West Germany.* London: Croom Helm.

Paterson, Matthew. 2000. *Understanding Global Environmental Politics: Domination, Accumulation, Resistance.* New York: St Martin's Press.

Pehle, Heinrich. 1998. *Das Bundesministerium für Umwelt, Naturschutz und Reaktorsicherheit: Ausgegrenzt Statt Integriert? Das Institutionelle Fundament der Deutschen Umweltpolitik.* Wiesbaden: Deutscher Universitäts-verlag.

Peters, B. Guy, and Christian Hunold. 1999. *European Politics Reconsidered.* New York: Holmes and Meier.

Phillips, Anne. 1995. *The Politics of Presence: The Political Representation of Gender, Ethnicity, and Race.* Oxford: Oxford University Press.

Pierson, Paul (ed.) 2001. *The New Politics of the Welfare State.* New York: Oxford University Press.

Piven, Frances Fox, and Richard A. Cloward. 1971. *Regulating the Poor: The Functions of Public Welfare.* New York: Random House.

Poguntke, Thomas. 1999. 'Die Bündnisgrünen in der babylonischen Gefangenschaft der SPD?' 83–102 in Oskar Niedermayer (ed.), *Die Parteien nach der Bundestagswahl 1998.* Opladen: Leske & Budrich.

Porritt, Jonathan. 1997. 'Environmental Politics: The Old and the New.' 62–73 in Michael Jacobs (ed.), *Greening the Millenium? The New Politics of the Environment.* Oxford: Blackwell.

Pötter, Bernhard. 1998. 'In den Amtsstuben soll Öko-Glasnost aufkommen.' *Tageszeitung,* 12 Nov., p. 9.

President's Council on Sustainable Development (PCSD). 1999. Archived at http://clinton4.nara.gov/PCSD/Publications/index.html.

Proferl, Angelika, Karin Schilling, and Karl-Werner Brand. 1997. *Umweltbewußtsein und Alltagshandeln.* Opladen: Leske & Budrich.

Pulzer, Peter. 1992. 'Political Ideology.' 303–26 in Gordon Smith, William E. Patterson, Peter H. Merkl, and Stephen Padgett (eds.), *Developments in German Politics.* Durham, NC: Duke University Press.

Raschke, Joachim. 1993. *Die Grünen. Wie sie wurden, was sie sind.* Cologne: Bund-Verlag.

Rawcliffe, Peter. 1998. *Environmental Pressure Groups in Transition.* Manchester: Manchester University Press.

Reitan, Marit. 1997. 'Norway: A Case of Splendid Isolation.' 287–330 in Mikael Skou Andersen and Duncan Liefferink (eds.), *European Environmental Policy: The Pioneers.* Manchester: Manchester University Press.

——1998. 'Ecological Modernisation and "Realpolitik": Ideas, Interests and Institutions.' *Environmental Politics,* 7: 1–26.

Riddell, Peter. 1989. *The Thatcher Decade.* Oxford: Basil Blackwell.

Robinson, Mike. 1992. *The Greening of British Party Politics.* Manchester: Manchester University Press.

Robinson, Nick. 2000. 'The Politics of the Car: The Limits of Actor-Centred Models of Agenda-Setting.' 199–217 in Benjamin Seel, Matthew Paterson, and Brian Doherty (eds.), *Direct Action in British Environmentalism.* London: Routledge.

Rochon, Thomas R. 1990. 'The West European Peace Movement and the Theory of New Social Movements.' 105–21 in Russell J. Dalton and Manfred Kuechler (eds.), *Challenging the Political Order: New Social and Political Movements in Western Democracies.* New York: Oxford University Press.

Roderick, Peter. 1996. 'United Kingdom.' 249–76 in Ralph E. Hallo (ed.), *Access to Environmental Information in Europe.* Dordrecht: Kluwer.

Rokkan, Stein. 1966. 'Norway: Numerical Democracy and Corporate Pluralism.' 70–115 in Robert A. Dahl (ed.), *Political Oppositions in Western Democracies.* New Haven: Yale University Press.

Rommetvedt, Hilmar, Arild Aurvag Farsund, and Kjersti Melberg. 1998. 'Corporatism and Lobbyism in Norwegian Environmental Policy-Making.' Paper presented at the meeting of International Political Science Association, Research Committee 36: Political Power, 15–18 May, University of Nijmegen.

Rootes, Christopher A. 1992. 'The New Politics and the New Social Movements: Accounting for British Exceptionalism.' *European Journal of Political Research*, 22: 171–92.

——1995. 'Britain: Greens in a Cold Climate.' 66–90 in Dick Richardson and Chris Rootes (eds.), *The Green Challenge*. London: Routledge.

——1997. 'Shaping Collective Action: Structure, Contingency and Knowledge.' 81–104 in Rica Edmondson (ed.), *The Political Context of Collective Action: Power, Argumentation and Democracy*. London: Routledge.

——1999. 'Reaction, Rejection or Renewal? Reflections on the Resurgence of Environmental Protest in Britain.' Paper presented at the Joint Sessions of the European Consortium for Political Research, Mannhein, 26–31 March.

——2000. 'The Revival of Social Movements? The Environmental Movement in Britain in Comparative Context.' Paper presented at the Conference of the International Sociological Association, Research Committee 48, Social Movements, Social Change, and Collective Action, Manchester, 3–5 Nov.

Rose, Chris. 1993. 'Beyond the Struggle for Proof: Factors Changing the Environment Movement.' *Environmental Values*, 2: 285–98.

Rose-Ackerman, Susan. 1995. *Controlling Environmental Policy: The Limits of Public Law in Germany and the United States*. New Haven: Yale University Press.

Rosenbaum, Walter. 1989. 'The Bureaucracy and Environmental Policy.' 212–37 in James P. Lester (ed.), *Environmental Politics and Policy: Theories and Evidence*. Durham, NC: Duke University Press.

Rosenblum, Nancy L. 1998. *Membership and Morals: The Personal Uses of Pluralism in America*. Princeton: Princeton University Press.

Rucht, Dieter. 1990. 'Campaigns, Skirmishes and Battles: Anti-Nuclear Movements in the USA, France and West Germany.' *Industrial Crisis Quarterly*, 4: 193–222.

——and Jochen Roose. 1999. 'The German Environmental Movement at a Crossroads?' *Environmental Politics*, 8: 59–80.

Rudig, Wolfgang. 1994. 'Maintaining a Low Profile: The Anti-Nuclear Movement and the British State.' 70–100 in Helena Flam (ed.), *States and Anti-Nuclear Movements*. Edinburgh: Edinburgh University Press.

Sabel, Charles, Archon Fung, and Bradley Karkkainen. 2000. 'Beyond Backyard Environmentalism.' *Boston Review*, online http://bostonreview.mit.edu/BR24.5/sabel.html

St. Clair, Jeffrey. 1995. 'Cashing Out Corporate Environmentalism in the Age of Newt.' Paper Presented to the Public Interest Law Conference, Eugene, Ore.

Sanera, Michael. 1996. *Facts, Not Fear*. Washington, DC: Regnery Publishing.

Sarewitz, Daniel. 1996. *Frontiers of Illusion: Science, Technology, and the Politics of Progress*. Philadelphia: Temple University Press.

Saward, Michael. 1992. *Co-optive Politics and State Legitimacy*. Aldershot: Dartmouth.

Schlosberg, David. 1999. *Environmental Justice and the New Pluralism: The Challenge of Difference for Environmentalism*. Oxford: Oxford University Press.

Schmitter, Philippe C. 1981. 'Interest Intermediation and Regime Governability in Contemporary Western Europe and North America.' 287–327 in Suzanne Berger (ed.), *Organizing Interests in Western Europe*. Cambridge: Cambridge University Press.

——1992. 'The Irony of Modern Democracy and Efforts to Improve its Practice.' *Politics and Society*, 20: 505–12.

——and Gerhard Lehmbruch (eds.). 1979. *Trends Toward Corporatist Intermediation*. Beverly Hills, Calif.: Sage.

Sclove, Richard. 1995. *Democracy and Technology*. New York: Guilford.

Scruggs, Lyle. 1999. 'Institutions and Environmental Performance in Seventeen Western Democracies.' *British Journal of Political Science*, 29: 1–31.

——2001. 'Is There Really a Link Between Neo-Corporatism and Environmental Performance? Updated Evidence and New Data for the 1980s and 1990s.' *British Journal of Political Science*, 31: 686–92.

Sebaldt, Martin. 1997. *Organisierter Pluralismus: Kräftfeld, Selbstverständnis und Politische Arbeit Deutscher Interessengruppen*. Opladen: Westdeutscher Verlag.

Seippel, Ørnuf. 1999. 'Environmentalism, Democracy, and Political Opportunity Structures: The Case of Norwegian Environmental Movements.' *Environmental Politics*, 8: 49–76.

Selle, Per, and Kristin Strømsnes. 1998a. 'Membership and Democracy: Should we Take Passive Support Seriously?' Unpublished paper, Department of Comparative Politics, University of Bergen.

—— ——1998b. 'Organised Environmentalism? Democracy as a Key Value.' *Voluntas*, 9: 319–44.

Shabecoff, Philip. 2000. *Earth Rising: American Environmentalism in the 21st Century*. Washington, DC: Island Press.

Shulman, Stuart. 2000. 'Citizen Agenda-Setting, Digital Government, and the National Organic Program.' Paper presented at the Annual Meeting of the American Political Science Association, Washington, DC.

Skocpol, Theda. 1979. *States and Social Revolutions*. Cambridge: Cambridge University Press.

——1985. 'Bringing the State Back In: Strategies of Analysis in Current Research.' 3–37 in Peter B. Evans, Dietrich Rueschemeyer, and Theda Skocpol (eds.), *Bringing the State Back In*. Cambridge: Cambridge University Press.

Slaton, Christa Daryl. 1992. 'The Failure of the United States Greens to Root in Fertile Soil.' 83–118 in Matthias Finger and Louis Kriesberg (eds.), *Research in Social Movements, Conflict and Change: The Green Movement Worldwide*. Greenwich, Conn.: JAI Press.

Smillie, Ian, and Ian Filewod. 1993. 'Norway.' 215–32 in Ian Smillie and Henry Helmich (eds.), *Non Governmental Organisations and Governments: Stakeholders for Development*. Paris: OECD.

Smith, A. T. H. 1995. 'The Public Order Elements.' *Criminal Law Review*, 19–37.

Smith, Mark. 1998. *Ecologism: Towards Ecological Citizenship*. Buckingham: Open University Press.

Spaargaren, Gert. 2000. 'Ecological Modernization Theory and the Changing Discourse on Environment and Modernity.' 41–73 in Gert Spaargaren, Arthur P. J. Mol, and Frederick Buttel (eds.), *Environment and Global Modernity*. London: Sage.

Street, John. 1992. *Politics and Technology*. New York: Guilford.

Sverdrup, Liv Astrid. 1997. 'Norway's Institutional Response to Sustainable Development.' *Comparative Politics*, 6: 54–82.

Switzer, Jacqueline Vaughn. 1998. *Environmental Politics: Domestic and Global Dimensions*. 2nd edn. New York: St Martin's.

Tarrow, Sidney. 1994. *Power in Movement: Social Movements, Collective Action and Politics*. Cambridge: Cambridge University Press.

Taylor, Bob Pepperman. 1992. *Our Limits Transgressed*. Lawrence, Kan.: University Press of Kansas.

Thiele, Leslie Paul. 1999. *Environmentalism for a New Millennium: The Challenge of Coevolution*. Oxford: Oxford University Press.

Thuen, Trond. 1995. *Quest for Equity: Norway and the Saami Challenge*. St. John's, Newfoundland: ISER Books.

Tiefenbach, Paul. 1998. *Die Grünen: Verstaatlichung einer Partei*. Cologne: PapyRossa.

Tilly, Charles, Louise Tilly, and Richard Tilly. 1975. *The Rebellious Century, 1830–1930*. Cambridge, Mass.: Harvard University Press.

Torgerson, Douglas. 1999. *The Promise of Green Politics: Environmentalism and the Public Sphere*. Durham, NC: Duke University Press.

Tyme, John. 1978. *Motorways Versus Democracy*. London: Macmillan.

Van der Heijden, Hein-Anton. 1997. 'Political Opportunity Structure and the Institutionalisation of the Environmental Movement.' *Environmental Politics*, 6: 25–50.

——, Ruud Koopmans, and Marco Giugni. 1992. 'The West European Environmental Movement.' 1–40 in Matthias Finger and Louis Kriesberg (eds.), *Research in Social Movements, Conflict and Change: The Green Movement Worldwide*. Greenwich, Conn.: JAI Press.

Van Zwanenberg, Patrick. 1997. 'The British National Experience.' 187–221 in Andrew Jamison and Per Østby (eds.), *Public Participation and Sustainable Development: Comparing European Experiences*. Aalborg: Aalborg University Press.

Vig, Norman J. 2000. 'Presidential Leadership and the Environment: From Reagan to Clinton.' 98–120 in Norman J. Vig and Michael E. Kraft (eds.), *Environmental Policy*. 4th edn. Washington, DC: CQ Press.

Vogel, David. 1986. *National Styles of Regulation: Environmental Policy in Great Britain and the United States*. Ithaca, NY: Cornell University Press.

Voisey, Heather, and Tim O'Riordan. 1997. 'Governing Institutions for Sustainable Development: The United Kingdom's National Level Approach.' *Environmental Politics*, 6: 24–53.

Wagner, Peter. 1994. 'Contesting Policies and Redefining the State: Energy Policy-Making and the Anti-Nuclear Movement in West Germany.' 264–95 in Helena Flam (ed.), *States and Anti-Nuclear Movements*. Edinburgh: Edinburgh University Press.

Wainwright, Hilary. 1994. *Arguments for a New Left: Answering the Free-Market Right*. Oxford: Basil Blackwell.

Wall, Derek. 1999. *Earth First! and the Anti-Roads Movement*. London: Routledge.

Walzer, Michael. 1994. 'Multiculturalism and Individualism.' *Dissent*, 41: 185–91.

Wapner, Paul. 1996. *Environmental Activism and World Civic Politics.* Albany, NY: State University of New York Press.

Ward, Hugh, and David Samways. 1992. Environmental Policy. 117–36 in David Marsh and R. A. W. Rhodes (eds.), *Implementing Thatcherite Policies.* Buckingham: Open University Press.

Weale, Albert. 1992. *The New Politics of Pollution.* Manchester: Manchester University Press.

——1997. 'United Kingdom.' 89–108 in Martin Jänicke and Helmut Weidner (eds.), *National Environmental Policies: A Comparative Study of Capacity-Building.* Berlin: Springer.

——2001. 'Can We Democratize Decisions on Risk and the Environment?' *Government and Opposition,* 36: 355–78.

Weber, Edward. 1998. *Pluralism by the Rules: Conflict and Cooperation in Environmental Regulation.* Washington, DC: Georgetown University Press.

Weiger, Hubert. 1987. 'Leistungsvermögen und Leistungsversäumnisse der Naturschutzverbände.' *Jahrbuch für Naturschutz und Landschaftspflege,* 39: 365–84.

Weiland, Sabine. 2001. 'Models of Integrating the Environment into Society: Ecological Modernisation and the Case of Chemicals Control in Britain, Germany, and the US.' Paper presented at Keele University Summer School on Environmental Politics and Policy, 10–21 Sept.

Weinzierl, Hubert. 1993. *Das grüne Gewissen: Selbstverständnis und Strategien des Naturschutzes.* Stuttgart: Weitbrecht.

Welsh, Michael M. 2000. 'Toward a Theory of Discursive Environmental Policy Making: The Case of Public Range Management.' Unpublished Ph.D. dissertation, University of Oregon.

Wildavsky, Aaron. 1995. *But Is It True? A Citizen's Guide to Environmental Health and Safety Issues.* Cambridge, Mass.: Harvard University Press.

Wolfe, Joel. 1991. 'State Power and Ideology in Britain: Mrs. Thatcher's Privatisation Programme.' *Political Studies,* 39: 237–52.

Wolff, Robert Paul, Barrington Moore, Jr., and Herbert Marcuse. 1965. *A Critique of Pure Tolerance.* Boston: Beacon Press.

World Bank. 1998. *Environmental Management and Institutions in OECD Countries: Lessons from Experience.* World Bank Technical Paper No. 391. Washington, DC: World Bank.

Wynne, Brian. 1982. *Rationality and Ritual: The Windscale Inquiry and Nuclear Decisions in Britain.* Preston: British Society for the History of Science.

Yeric, Jerry L. L., and John R. Todd. 1995. *Public Opinion: The Visible Politics.* Itasca, Ill.: Peacock.

Young, Iris Marion. 1992. 'Social Groups in Associative Democracy.' *Politics and Society,* 20: 529–34.

——2000. *Inclusion and Democracy.* Oxford: Oxford University Press.

Young, Stephen C. 2000. 'The United Kingdom: From Political Containment to Integrated Thinking.' 245–72 in William M. Lafferty and James Meadowcroft (eds.), *Implementing Sustainable Development: Strategies and Initiatives in High Consumption Societies.* Oxford: Oxford University Press.

Zeigler, L. Harmon, and Michael A. Baer. 1969. *Lobbying: Interaction and Influence in American State Legislatures.* Belmont, Calif.: Wadsworth.

Zirakzadeh, Cyrus Ernesto. 1997. *Social Movements in Politics: A Comparative Study.* London: Addison Wesley Longman.

Zittel, Thomas. 1996. Marktwirtschaftliche Instrumente in der Umweltpolitik. Opladen: Leske & Budrich.

INDEX

DATE DUE
